Civil Law Studies

Civil Law Studies: An Indian Perspective

Edited by

Anthony D'Souza and Carmo D'Souza

CAMBRIDGE SCHOLARS PUBLISHING

Civil Law Studies: An Indian Perspective, Edited by Anthony D'Souza and Carmo D'Souza

This book first published 2009

Cambridge Scholars Publishing

12 Back Chapman Street, Newcastle upon Tyne, NE6 2XX, UK

British Library Cataloguing in Publication Data
A catalogue record for this book is available from the British Library

ISBN (10): 1-4438-0598-X, ISBN (13): 978-1-4438-0598-8

TABLE OF CONTENTS

PART VI: JUDICIAL CULTURE

PART VII: HISTORY

Appendices

FOREWORD

PROF. (DR.) N.R. MADHAVA MENON

India is a country full of diversities of people, cultures, laws and systems of social organization. As an ancient civilization which has continuously welcomed and assimilated people from all parts of the globe, it reflects their customs, traditions, faiths and beliefs in all its diversity. When India attained the status of a Republic after 300 years of colonial rule, it opted to remain a secular nation, allowing all citizens full and equal freedom to practice the religion of their choice and be governed by their personal laws in relation to marriage, separation, inheritance, succession and related matters. Of course, customs contrary to the guaranteed basic human rights were modified either by the communities themselves, or by state intervention. A Uniform Civil Code is made part of State policy, to be evolved in the course of time when the people concerned are prepared to accept the change.

While the erstwhile French settlements in Pondicherry and elsewhere proclaim their allegiance to the French Civil Code, the former Portuguese settlements in Goa, Daman and Diu are deeply attached with the Portuguese Civil Code. The sizeable section of Muslim citizens, numbering over 150 million, follow the tenets of Islam and practice the dictates of Shariat in family relations. Similarly, the various sects of

significant part of the life of Goan people. The book is a compilation of several articles, some of which are contributed by scholars from Lisbon and elsewhere. The chief editor of the book is Dr. Carmo D'Souza, a senior Faculty member of Salgaocar College. He deserves all appreciation for this wonderful effort in comparative law scholarship, which is yet not popular with legal academies, largely because of inability to access materials in foreign languages.

I have always advocated the establishment of a Centre for Portuguese Law in Salgaocar College, in partnership with Lisbon University and with the patronage of the Portuguese Consulate in Goa and the Government. The Indian legal community can interact with their counterparts in certain South American countries, notably Brazil, if we study the legal systems of Portugal, Spain and other civil law countries. The Government of Goa will be well advised to support this project with a regular grant and liberal scholarships for students and teachers. The Goan Bar Association should also cultivate practice of Portuguese law among the young entrants to the Bar as it governs a sector of Goans within and beyond the Christian community. It is interesting to read from Prof. Carmo's introductory essay how the Civil Law Centre came to be initiated in the Salgaocar College by a chance visit of a Portuguese academic wanting to develop academic links and exchange of ideas on Comparative Law. The Law Faculty of the University of Lisbon nurtured the vision and kept the idea alive. It is now for the management of the Salgaocar College and the authorities in the Goa Government to institutionalise the vision and open the window to the laws of the Continent.

This book offers an overview of the Civil Law System in all its dimensions, particularly in relation to India. The chapter on Family Laws provides a great deal of information on the rich variety of complex sets of existing customs and traditions which must be a fascinating area of study for comparative lawyers. Equally, the chapter on Continental Criminal Law is interesting to those concerned with reforms in criminal justice administration, allowing them to learn from the experiences of those outside the Common Law world.

The proposed Centre should undertake to selectively translate into English important Statutes and Commentaries from Portuguese legal system to promote research among Indian scholars. A collection of all relevant Portuguese laws and books should be assembled and there should be a system to replenish the collection with new legal publications from that country. Facilities for study of Portuguese language should also be arranged. Students should be able to study for a semester in a Portuguese University in the course of their degree, with arrangement for transfer of credits. A Chair in Portuguese Law should be set up, under which leading lawyers, judges and law teachers from Portugal should be invited for short periods to promote research and teaching. I hope, with the publication of this volume, initiatives in this direction will be undertaken to make Salgaocar College a major centre for comparative legal studies. I also hope that another Chair will be endowed in Roman Law, the mother of many European legal systems. It was once a compulsory subject for law students in India.

I offer all my best wishes for this initiative in popularizing Portuguese legal studies and Civil Law Systems among the Indian legal community. Let us hope that very soon we will have a Centre for Comparative Law at Salgaocar College, Goa, providing leadership in comparative law studies and research in India.

ACKNOWLEDGEMENTS

Civil Law Studies: An Indian Perspective is a compilation of articles contributed in response to an appeal made by us to the Faculties of Law at the Universities of Lisbon and Coimbra, as well as various selected scholars from India. The book was conceived when members of the Faculty of Law, University of Lisbon conducted a six-week course in Civil Law, referred to as Lecture Series 2008, at V. M. Salgaocar College of Law, from mid-January to the end of February. Their thought-provoking lectures raised questions as to how a Civil Law Course could benefit Indian academics and students.

We are grateful to all the contributors listed at the end of the book, who have readily sent their articles to this project. We are also grateful to all those who, as part of the publicity for our project, forwarded the e-mail appealing for contributions to their friends and acquaintances. We also thank those who sent us their encouraging messages and advice.

We would like to thank in a special way Prof. (Dr.) N.R. Madhava Menon for the encouraging foreword. This was a difficult task considering the wide range of articles included in the book. He took pains to examine parts of the material before writing his innovative ideas, in spite of his busy schedule. If Comparative Civil Law Studies does gain ground in India it will be due to the vision of this great Indian educator.

Our special thanks to Fundacao Oriente for financial assistance to the present project.

Anthony D'Souza
Carmo D'Souza
Porbavaddo, Calangute, Goa , India
January, 2009.

PART I:

CIVIL LAW

CIVIL LAW STUDIES: AN INDIAN PERSPECTIVE

CARMO D'SOUZA

Introduction

The Civil Law System is based on Roman Law, especially the *Corpus Juris* of Emperor Justinian. This body of law was further developed by medieval scholars and later accepted in various countries of Europe. In some of these countries, it influenced their legislative acts and thus became the positive law of the place. In other countries, Roman Law was processed by legal theorists and thus became accepted in those societies[1].

Section A of the present article advocates a Civil Law Centre based in Goa for the following reasons: (a) Goa's historical past connections with the Civil Law System ensure a better infrastructure for such a centre, (b) The availability of resources in terms of documents, including those of the transition phase, is valuable and useful for comparative research , and (c) The oral experiences of the bench, bar and bureaucracy in Goa who worked under the two systems need to be collected and researched. The second part of the article deals with Civil Law Studies from a pan-Indian perspective, as India seeks to find its rightful place in the community of nations.

A: Advocating Civil Law Studies in Goa

The Portuguese conquered Goa in 1510[2]. In the course of time, along with the Portuguese conquerors, the Civil Law System entered the territory. In the initial period after the Portuguese entry, their rule merely extended to

---

[1] http://en.wikipedia.org/wiki/Civil_law_(legal_system), visited on 25 June 2008 at 11. a.m.

[2] Goa then referred to the Old Conquests, as distinguished from the New Conquests which came under Portuguese control much later.

the territory of the Old Conquests,[3] comprising the areas formerly known as Tiswadi, Bardez and Salcette. Within a few decades, the Portuguese extended their laws and legal institutions, with some reservations, to these conquered territories. However, by and large, Portuguese law, legal institutions and legal culture took root in the Old Conquests. With the addition of the New Conquests in the mid eighteenth century, and especially as a result of changes in diplomacy, concessions were made in favour of the non-Christian population as regarded their customary laws and legal institutions[4]. Later, beginning with the Provisional Judicial Organization of 1836, a uniform judicial structure was envisaged for the Old and New Conquests as regards the administration of justice[5]. By subsequent judicial reforms, in the New Conquests as well as the Old, the Portuguese structures for administration of justice were firmly established. Those reforms eventually did away with all kinds of indigenous institutions for the administration of justice.[6] By the mid nineteenth century, Portuguese laws operated throughout the whole territory of Goa except in the area of Personal Customary Laws for non-Christians residing in the New Conquests[7]. This concession to the inhabitants of the New Conquests was extended to the non-Christian inhabitants of the Old Conquests by the legal provision on Usages and Customs of Gentile Hindus of Goa (1880)[8]. Similar laws existed for the non-Christian communities of Daman and Diu[9]. Thus at the end of the nineteenth century, all the non-Christians of Goa, irrespective of whether they resided in the Old or New Conquests were to be governed in respect of their personal law by their Uses and Customs[10]. This position remained largely unchanged till December 1961, when the Portuguese left Goa. Thus prior to Liberation, the Civil Law System existed in Goa in the substantial and

---

[3] The Island of Goa, to which was soon added Bardez and Salcette. Practically, their hold extended to the Old Conquests. The New Conquests came later, in the mid eighteenth century. Goa is today composed of Old Conquests and New Conquests. The Old Conquests today consist of Talukas of Ilhas, Bardez, Salcette and Marmagoa.

[4] Carmo D'Souza, *Legal System in Goa,* Vol. I, (Goa: Agnelo D'Souza, 1994) pp. 36–43

[5] Ibid, pp. 121–124.

[6] Ibid, pp. 120–126. These areas are also worthy of research.

[7] Carmo D'Souza, *Legal System in Goa*, Vol II, (Goa: Agnelo D'Souza, 1995) pp.203–13

[8] M. .S. Usgaocar, *Family Laws of Goa, Daman and Diu*, Vol I, 3rd ed. (Goa: Vela Associates, 2004) pp. 141–162. See also D'Souza 1994, Vol II, pp.211–13

[9] Usgaocar 2004, pp. 163–193

[10] This step was a reversal to the earlier Portuguese policies.

procedural area except in restricted field of personal laws with respect to the non Christian population of Goa[11]. Civil Law culture also prevailed among the administration, the bar and the bench.

In the post-Liberation period, the prevailing Civil Law System was preserved for a brief term until changes were effected[12]. During this period a unique transition system[13] prevailed with the bar and the bench adjusting to an inevitable switch. Some aspects of the transition period are reflected in the Official Bulletin[14] of the period, which are available for research. However, information regarding Bar and Bench culture, must be collected from oral sources. In a short time, the judges and lawyers trained in Portuguese legal and judicial culture become acquainted with and involved in the Anglo-Indian Common Law culture.

After Liberation, the Portuguese Codes and other laws were replaced by Indian counterparts, especially through the Laws Regulation (1962) and Laws Regulation (1963)[15]. As regards the judiciary, Criminal Courts were introduced by the Goa, Daman and Diu (Separation of judicial and executive functions) Order 1963. It came into force on 1 November 1963[16]. It was necessary to introduce criminal jurisdiction and laws without delay, even before civil courts had been enabled to function. The Regulation of 1963, which came into force on 16 December 1963, instituted the Judicial Commissioners' Court in the place of the *Relacao de Goa*[17]. Later the Legislative Assembly of Goa, Daman and Diu enacted the Goa, Daman and Diu Civil Courts Act, 1965, which introduced the District Court and Civil Courts in place of the earlier ones. It transferred proceedings before the *Comarca* and *Julgado* courts to the newly

---

[11] There existed the laws of Mazanias (Hindu Temples), the law of village communities which contained indigenous element. These areas, with their foundations on traditional customary law but substantially modified with Civil Law concepts, are worthy of further research.

[12] D'Souza 1994, pp.254–257

[13] The system was unique because of the dynamics of the transition, themselves a fascinating subject of study, which depended on a multiplicity of factors: historical, geographical, etc.

[14] Bulletins of the period, sometimes printed bilingually in Portuguese and English, give insight into aspects of Civil and Common Law. It is significant to note differences even in drafting style.

[15] D'Souza 1994, pp. 257–259 and 261–262.

[16] D'Souza 1994 p. 158, especially footnote 14. For Sessions and criminal courts see p. 158.

[17] Ibid, pp. 159–164.

established Civil Courts[18]. With the introduction of new administrative, legislative and judicial institutions, the respective cultures too flowed into those areas. It is interesting to note that many functionaries, lawyers and judges from the old system were absorbed in the new Common Law system and adapted themselves to its legal, judicial and administrative culture. Goa still currently has some personnel among its bureaucrats, bar and bench who are acquainted with both systems; their valuable experiences are a treasure-house for Comparative Law studies, especially in the twenty–first century as Civil Law and Common Law are attempting to find a common ground.

Civil Law Research and Goa

Goa, due to its historical heritage, has a vast potential to become a Civil Law Research Centre. Goa possesses a vast amount of documentation on the subject, much of which is yet to be unearthed and evaluated. It has experience in the Civil Law System which continued till the Portuguese left the Indian shores. In fact, over the last four decades and more, Goa has imbibed Common Law culture as thoroughly as any other part of India. The case law[19] and number of public interest litigations (PIL)[20] emanating from Goa courts are an indicator of this fact. It is desirable also to have comparative study of the legal systems in Goa and Pondichery as they existed under the erstwhile Portuguese and French regimes respectively, as it may provide insights into the dynamics of the Civil Law system in these two small corners of Western and Eastern India. Such research will require the cooperation of scholars from Goa and Pondichery. It will also require the cooperation of Portuguese and French legal scholars as well as certain documentation which is available in Lisbon and perhaps Paris. Setting a Civil Law Centre in Goa with the objective of research would be a valuable contribution to the studies on Legal Systems. This is a need of the modern world, with scholars looking for solutions in Comparative Studies between Civil and Common Law Systems.

---

[18] Ibid, pp. 165–170

[19] There are several dissertations of LL.M. students of Goa University at V. M. Salgaocar Law College analyzing the various case laws emerging from the Courts situated in the territory of Goa.

[20] The PIL is an interesting device created by courts in India which would be a fruitful subject of research for Continental scholars.

Doutor Santos' Vision for Goa

The late Prof. Doutor Antonio Marques dos Santos, on a tourist visit to Goa, shared his vision for cooperation between the University of Lisbon and the Law Colleges in Goa with the faculty of V. M. Salgaocar College of Law. His ideas were further concretized when he later visited Goa as a part of a team of Portuguese experts who had come to address a conference on Civil Law at Hotel Cidade in Goa. On that occasion, he brought with him a substantial collection of books as a gift to V. M. Salgaocar College of Law from the Faculty of Law of the University of Lisbon. Later, when I informed him of my intended presence in Paris for the celebrations of the 500th Anniversary of the Discovery of Sea Route, he insisted that for the sake of strengthening cooperation between Goa and Lisbon, I should fly from Paris to Lisbon. He organized a Conference so that I could address the University of Lisbon on the Evolution of Portuguese Law in Goa[21]. On that occasion he insisted that we should work towards consolidating the vision of cooperation between the two institutions. Later I met him again on my three further trips to Lisbon, but he was disappointed that no further progress had been made. He died with his dream unfulfilled.

It was left to Prof. Doutor Dario Vicente, as head of the Institute of Judicial Cooperation of the Faculty of Law of the University of Lisbon to begin practical efforts towards such initiative. After initial communication, Doutor Dario Vicente dispatched to Goa a team consisting of Prof. Doutor Loureiro Bastos and Prof. Doutor Duarte Pinheiro, to investigate the feasibility of cooperation between Lisbon and Goa, in March 2007. As a consequence of this visit, by the end of August 2007 a Memorandum of Association had been signed between V. M. Salgaocar College of Law and the Faculty of Law of the University of Lisbon. As part of the agreement, the first Civil Law Lecture Series was successfully held at V. M. Salgaocar College of Law from mid-January to the end of February 2007. A team of eminent professors, consisting of Prof. Doutor Ascencao, Prof. Doutor Fausto Quadros, Prof. Doutor Dario Moura Vicente, Dr. Lino Leitao, Prof. Doutor Loureiro Bastos and Prof. Doutor Duarte Pinherio, delived the lectures, on different aspects of Civil Law.

---

[21] *Evolucao do Direito Portuges em Goa*, Revista da Faculdade de Direito da Universidade de Lisboa, Volume XL, No. 1 e 2, Coimbra Editora, 1999

Civil Law Studies: An Indian Perspective

In this globalizing world there is a need to develop Civil Law Studies from India's perspective. The present book has the objective of boosting research in the area of Comparative Studies between the Civil Law System and the Common Law system in India, as the country also has a vast experience of Common Law. Following are the specific objectives of the present publication.

- To foster awareness of the Civil Law System and its intricacies among the bar, bench and academia in India.
- To provide reference material for postgraduate diploma courses on Civil Law which may be planned in the near future in India.
- To promote research in Civil Law Studies in India.
- To promote research into comparative studies between Common Law as prevailing in India and the Civil Law as found in Portugal.
- To highlight the documents, books and material available in Goa relating to the Civil Law System.
- To promote research into the vast practical experience existing amidst the bar and the bench in Goa on the dynamics of both the Civil Law and Common Law Systems.
- To bring about cooperation between legal scholars from Europe and India in the field of Civil Law Studies.
- To motivate participants of the Civil Law courses held in 2008 at V. M. Salgaocar College of Law to contribute articles for journals and publications.

Contents of this Book

The title of this book, *Civil Law Studies: An Indian Perspective*, implies that it has: (a) an eye on India's past Civil Law heritage, especially as experienced in erstwhile Portuguese and French possessions; (b) an eye on the present remnants of Civil Law in those places, varied and modified by the prevalent Common Law culture; (c) an eye on Common Law culture developed in those territories after their integration in the Indian Union; and lastly (d) an eye on the future prospects of developing Civil Law Studies in India, having in mind the country's prospects in the New World Order. Given India has developed a unique Common Law culture under English influence, it may now be important for the country, in the context of harmonization of law in a globalising world, to carry out research on its legal system on the basis of a knowledge of civil law culture.

The book is divided into seven parts with two appendices. The first part, on Civil Law, consists of three articles which discuss the civil law and common law systems and the relation between the two, as well as containing a critical appraisal of their traditions. The second part deals with law in a globalizing world and contains articles by leading academics from Faculties of Law in Lisbon, Coimbra and India, as well as participants in civil law course in Goa. The third part, labelled as "criminal law," raises issues on the existing English inheritance of the adversary criminal justice system in India and looks for solutions to problems faced, if any, in the light of experiences in European countries. The articles have been compiled in the light of the Justice Malimath Committee Report on Administration of Criminal Justice in India, which advocates examination of the inquisitorial aspects of continental law for possible inclusion in India's accusatorial system. The fourth part is devoted to contracts, in two articles critically comparing contracts under the continental and common law systems. The fifth part refers to Family Laws[22], comprising a critical study of Indian Family Law, which, due to its complexities is very useful from a research perspective in understanding systems of family laws worldwide. These articles will provide rich insights into the complexities of family laws of India to scholars worldwide, and motivate comparative research with Western laws. The sixth part, on the legal profession, contains one article which critically reviews the culture which has developed in the legal profession in India, making appropriate suggestions. This article may help researchers to explore on similar lines the legal culture in the Continental System. The last part is devoted to the legal history of Goa, in order to advocate research in that field as an aid to understanding the legal system. The legal history of Goa is fascinating as it experienced the Continental legal system during the Portuguese regime, and was later absorbed into the common law tradition, but not before passing through a transition phase. This transition phase has given unique experiences to those then occupying positions in the judiciary, the bar or the administration.

---

[22] Family law in India as prescribed for Law courses in Goa University also includes the family laws Goa (based on some remnants of laws on family matters such as marriage, divorce etc. dating from the Portuguese period).

Civil Law Study Centres

Cunha Goansalves' landmark contribution to Portuguese jurisprudence, in the form of his voluminous work on the Civil Code, is something for Goa and India to boast about. It is necessary to unearth such treasures. It is also a contemporary need that academics in India produce high-quality doctrinal books exploring the boundaries of jurisprudence and pushing the frontiers of law further with their analysis, especially as the globalizing world faces new problems. Indian scholars cannot depend merely on case law developed with the aid of bar and bench, but must engage in thought-provoking discussion and research. The case law approach is commendable, but it must be also supplemented with doctrinal writings in a process similar to that of Continental Europe. There is in fact a lack of authoritative books produced by academics in India. It is hoped that the present book, with the contributions of some outstanding members of bar, bench and academia, will go a long way to give a boost to high-quality, authoritative, doctrinal publications in India. It is also hoped that the book will provide a boost to Civil Law and Comparative Studies in India. India has developed a high standard of its own jurisprudence post-Independence, based on the common law system As India is preparing to occupy its rightful space in the world community, it is necessary that it be at least well-acquainted with the civil law system, as well as comparative studies between the two systems. Other legal systems too, including the Hindu system, should be of interest to Indian scholars, at least for research purposes. Today India can become an educational destination for the future, and in that case Civil Law Institutes based in Goa, Pondicherry and other parts of India will attract researchers from across the globe. India has many unique legal experiences, as demonstrated by some articles found in this book, which will delight European scholars.

Conclusion

India has inherited the English legal culture, but post-Independence Anglo–Indian jurisprudence has carved a niche for itself. On the other hand, it has a unique continental heritage in the small pockets of Goa and Pondicherry and adjoining territories[23]. This is a treasure house where the Continental system existed and then, through a process of transition, moved into the common law system. This area contains a wealth of research material; much of it in oral form amidst judges, lawyers and

[23] Territories associated with Goa and Pondicherry during the colonial period.

bureaucrats, capable of addressing issues around harmonization of law in a globalizing world. As India prepares to find its rightful place in the global community, it is necessary that its scholars carry out research into civil law systems in order to find solutions to the new global problems. It is of advantage to India to plunge itself into civil law studies and research.

CIVIL LAW CODES: PRESUMPTIONS AND PRETENSIONS

MARIAN PINHEIRO[1]

Legal systems across the globe can be generally divided into two groups, civil law and common law systems. Most countries that have been formerly under British law have adopted the common law system. Many others have come to adopt civil law systems based on Roman law, especially the *corpus juris civilis* of Emperor Justinian. Historically, this was as a result of the domination of Rome over most of Europe, and later European influence over Asian and African countries.

The legal concept of codification dates back to ancient Babylon, where the code of Hammurabi was prevalent. The idea of codification is an offshoot of the conception of the nation-state, wherein the existence of a nation presupposed the existence of a recorded law applicable to that state. Codification, it was believed, brought conductivity to the legal system with the unified recording of the laws. The Napoleonic Code of the 19th century and the German Code of the 20th century are illustrative of this concept of the preeminence of the idea of the nation-state. Codification by itself is not the only defining factor of a civil law system. For example, some of the Scandinavian countries have a large part of their civil law uncodified.

The distinction between civil law and common law goes beyond the mere fact of codification and is rather dependent on the methodological approach taken to courts and statutes. In civil law countries as in common law countries, legislation is seen as a primary source of law. However, in the absence of legislation, courts by default base their judgments on the provisions of the code. To do this, the courts have to reason extensively on the basis of the general principles, often drawing analogies from statutory

---

[1] The writer is the Principal of V.M.Salgaocar College of law, Miramar, Panaji, Goa.

provisions to fill in lacunae and achieve coherence. In the common law system, in addition to the legislation, the courts have recourse to earlier decided cases as a primary source. It is for this reason that the judgments of common law courts are often much longer and contain more elaborate reasoning.

The more interesting distinction is in respect to criminal procedure, wherein the civil law system could be considered as a variant of the inquisitorial system rather than the adversarial system. The concept of presumption of innocence in the common law system has, of course, resulted in a very low percentage of convictions. Justice Malimath in his recommendations for reformation of the Indian criminal justice system to some extent recommended the adoption or incorporation of such a system in the Indian Criminal Procedure Code. He has referred more specifically to the inclusion of the duty of the court to search for truth. Section 311 of the Criminal Procedure Code provides for courts to have the power to summon material witnesses, or examine persons present. Thus the quest for truth is a fundamental duty of every court. Justice Malimath recommends that the judge should take a pro-active role during the trial and give directions to the investigating officers and prosecution agencies in order to unearth the truth.

The obvious distinguishing feature of a civil law system is the presence of a written code of law, a code which is a systematic and comprehensive compilation of legal rules and principles. The code is intended to act as a blueprint of social regulation which attempts to guide individuals through society from birth to death. The role of judges in a civil law system differs considerably from that of a judge in a common law system. When different facts or new considerations arise, common law judges are free to depart from an existing precedent and establish new law. Civil law judges view themselves as administrators of the code, and for them there is only one correct solution to a specific legal problem. Therefore, the judges are not expected to use judicial discretion or to apply their own interpretation to the case. The judges therefore being administrators of the court actively supervise the collection of evidence, examine witnesses in private, cross-examine opposing party witnesses, etc., in their search for truth. This process of truth-finding at times even eliminates the need for a trial. In the common law system, where the law could be derived from custom and precedent, the precedent by itself is law, whereas in the civil law, the judges merely administer law which is created by legislators and supplemented by advice of legal scholars. There is a need to explore and expound the necessity for a systematic study of the civil law system in a country like India where the system is predominantly based on common law. The fundamental issue of judges' role and involvement in the justice delivery system, especially criminal jurisdiction, is worthy of consideration. Considering the failings that exist in the present criminal justice system, such as undue delay in the completion of the adjudicative process, the extremely low rates of convictions, and the tendency of key witnesses to change their statements, there can be no doubt that the criminal justice system needs to be reformed. But whether it should be reformed in such a manner as to adopt the existing practices in civil law systems needs further consideration.

Similarly, in the area of private law, there is of course lack of uniformity as to the personal laws of citizens. Though Article 44 of the Constitution unequivocally recommends adoption of a uniform civil code, being placed in Chapter IV of the Constitution, the enforceability of such a constitutional mandate has remained little more than a distant mirage for India. The apex court, on its part, has been vocal and persuasive to the extent possible to it. The Shah Bano Begum case of 1985 was one earlier illustration wherein, while interpreting the right to maintenance of a wife under Section 125 of the Criminal Procedure Code, the court observed that Article 44 (3) of the Constitution has remained a dead letter. Later, in the Sarla Mudgal case, while dealing with the issue of a Hindu husband embracing Islam for a second marriage, Justice Kuldip Singh was quick to point out that there is an urgent need for a uniform civil code to avoid travesty of law, as happened in this case. The latest of the Supreme Court's interventions to promote a common civil code was in July 2003, when a Christian priest pointed out that Section 118 of the Indian Succession Act is discriminatory against Christians. The three judges deciding the issue unanimously struck down the relevant law as unconstitutional and called for a speedier implementation of Article 44 specifically to promote national integration.

The non-implementation of this hypothetical uniform civil code has been a cause of division between majority and minority communities and of course an opportunity to politicise the issue. The question of a common civil code has caused unbridgeable differences of opinion among the various communities. India, unlike many of its Western counterpart, is multi-cultural, multi-lingual and multi-religious. The task of incorporating the aspirations, views and ideas of all the resident communities may make such a code voluminous.

The only option available may be to enact an optional common civil code which any one, or either of the parties to a marriage, can opt to adopt. The ultimate goal would be, if ever possible, to enact a comprehensive civil code capable of being uniformly applied to all citizens. It is to be noted that even the basic document of the Indian legal system—namely the Constitution of India—has been amended ninety-four times to date, and is likely to be amended many more times in the immediate future.

Legislation of such nature, if made optional in its applicability, should necessarily have incentives for its wide acceptance, or there should be strong and effective disincentives for its non-acceptance. What kind of incentives/disincentives could be incorporated for legislation of this nature? Would such incentives/disincentives be beyond the scope and purpose of the legislation itself? Would it be legally acceptable and justifiable to create incentives in legislation, if created, and how long should such incentives be effective? In addition to these problems, there are certain other fundamental questions as to the quality of justice. Is the civil law system more suited to deliver better quality justice than the common law system? Is not the common law system more akin to social and contextual justice delivery? In a dynamic population, is not socially contextual justice more relevant and suitable than standardized justice? The emergence of the system of PILs to correct public wrongs and malpractice is something that would never have been thought of in a civil law system, where the scope of interpretation is always limited and restricted. Do countries with civil law systems have better-administrated justice; or can it be said that the civil law system is more people/litigant friendly?

There is of course a greater political concern while enacting such unifying legislation. Will such legislation be considered retroactive? The legislature are more likely to imprint their own personal concerns and localized issues upon the system produced. All such influences will certainly dilute and may negate the very idea of uniformity.

Common civil code or no civil code, justice should take precedence. The integrity of a nation should never be at stake. Duties and values need to be stressed in any legal system if it is to sustain itself.

THE CIVIL LAW AND COMMON LAW TRADITIONS: AN APPRAISAL

KIM COUTO[1]

The dominant legal traditions today are the Civil Law system prevalent in most of Europe, Central and South America, on the one hand; and the Common Law tradition, largely found in England and America, on the other. This article is an attempt to compare and contrast these two major systems extant, with their own peculiarities, across the globe today. The two systems being different from each other in various aspects, the result is that the judges within these two systems have their own distinctive approaches. This paper examines some of the major differences existing in the two systems.

There is no virtue so truly great and god-like as justice[2]. Indeed, every human being yearns for justice. The volumes that have been written and spoken about this expression suggest the innate power and richness the concept holds. It is hardly surprising therefore, that the yearning for justice is universal, cutting across barriers of age, race, religion, culture, nationality, language, and economic or even social status.

The concept of justice can best be understood against the background of injustice. An injustice is a tormenting, hurting and unforgettable experience. Whilst injustice brings pain, anguish and despair, justice brings peace, happiness, hope and progress to the society and to the individual in particular. That is why Justice Brennan was so right when he said, "Nothing rankles more in the human heart than a brooding sense of injustice[3]".

---

[1] Lecturer, V.M. Salgaocar College of Law

[2] Joseph Addison. http://www.best-quotes-poems.com/justice-quotes.html.

[3] Justice Brennan of the Supreme Court of the U.S.A., in a speech delivered to the Legal Aid Society of New York.

Conceptualized as giving each man his due, justice has always occupied pride of place in every man's heart. An independent and honorable judiciary therefore becomes the sine qua non for the administration of justice in society. Confronted with the question of how to resolve disputes among its members, many societies preferred designating individuals to resolve disputes in accordance with established norms and customs over a private system of revenge for dispute resolution. These individuals have been usually leaders who are expected to exercise their judgment in a fair and impartial manner. Like the deity in the temple of justice, they hold in their hands a person's life, liberty, property, reputation, marriage, home, and happiness, all of which are sacred and valued. A judge thus hears the pleas and petitions of those before him, resolves their problem, and ensures that justice is done impartially, without fear or favour.

Though judges all over the word perform substantially the same functions, the similarity ends there. Judges in civil law countries are markedly different in background and their outlook differs considerably from their counterparts in the common law systems of the world. Both of these, and the legal system within which they work, assume much significance in distinctly shaping the law in their respective spheres.

The Civil Law System—meaning and origin

The civil law system, often referred to as 'Continental Law', is frequently used to mean a legal system largely drawn from the Roman Law. Distinguishable from the common law of the Anglo-Saxons in England, it is the predominant system of law in Europe, spreading throughout the length and breadth of the continent. The origins of the Civil Law tradition are traceable to the Law of the Twelve Tables which dates from the middle of the 5th century BC. Though not a law code in the modern sense of the word, it contained specific provisions in the form of norms, designed to change the then existing customary law. With the passage of time, the formalism of the law of the State of Rome, or *jus civile*, was diluted by the introduction of more flexible principles in the form of *jus gentium*, largely a creation of the wisdom of the Roman praetors and magistrates. A praetor was not a legislator and did not technically create new law when he issued his edicts. In fact, however, the results of his rulings came to enjoy legal protection and were in effect often the source of new legal rules. It is significant to note that a Praetor's successor was not bound by the edicts of his predecessor. Nonetheless, he did take rules from edicts of his predecessor that had proved to be useful. In this way, the praetoric law supplemented the civil law, moulding and adapting itself to new needs and ultimately being fashioned into the *Corpus juris civilis*, the work of the Emperor Justinian I. This body of law was a remarkable collection and compilation of important laws such as the *Codex Justinianus*, the *Digesta* or *Pandectae*, the *Institutiones*, and the *Novellae*[4].

Honed and perfected by the legal treatises and writings of the great Roman jurists or jurisconsults of the time, this law later on went on to become the 'common law of the civil law systems', or the 'jus commune' in Europe until the 18th century, when Europe was subject to a multiplicity of local customs and laws. In addition, Roman Law was resorted to in the Continent for arriving at a just solution of mercantile disputes, besides influencing the development of the Canon Law and the movement towards early conceptions of international law[5] .

The formal, comprehensive codification of an entire body of law of the type characteristic of modern civil-law systems began primarily in France, with the French Code Civil in 1804 and the German Code of 1896. Only those Roman principles that were embodied in the code came to be applied in the respective countries. Yet, although some of these systems have their own distinct styles, they retain in common their methods of thought and their attitudes to law and its source. Thus an important ingredient in the Civilian tradition is the common inheritance of the Roman law[6] and resultant common legal notions and institutions including similar conceptions of law-making and the interpretation of law.

The Common Law system—meaning and origin

The origin of the common law dates back to England in the early Middle Ages, when local laws gave way to a general law known as the common law. The king's courts became the most important forum for resolving disputes between citizens. Historically, the practice developed with the

---

[4] http://en.wikipedia.org/wiki/Justinian _I. *Codex Justinianus*, a codification of imperial constitutions from the 2nd century onward, was issued on 7 April 529. It was followed by the *Digesta* (or *Pandectae*), a compilation of older legal texts, in 533, and by the *Institutiones*, a textbook explaining the principles of law. The *Novellae*, a collection of new laws issued during Justinian's reign, supplements the *Corpus*.

[5] Carl Stychin and Linda Mulachy, *Legal Methods and Systems*, 3rd ed. (Sweet & Maxwell),p. 429.

[6] Ibid.

judges being sent from the king's central court to hear the various disputes throughout the country. His judges would resolve disputes on an ad hoc basis according to what they interpreted the customs to be. Subsequently, upon their return to London, they would often discuss their cases and the decisions they made with the other judges. These decisions would be recorded and filed.

In time, a rule, known as *stare decisis* (also commonly known as precedent) developed, where a judge would be bound to follow the decision of an earlier judge; if the two cases had similar facts to one another. By this system of precedent, decisions 'stuck' and became ossified, and in this manner, the system of disparate local customs was replaced by an elaborate and consistent system of law that was common throughout the whole country, hence the name, "common law."[7] Thus the common law system is largely a product of gradual historical growth which may be said to have originated from the ancient Roman Law practice of giving judicial recognition to custom. In a sense then, common law was to some extent influenced by the form, though not the substance, of the Roman law.

Source of law

After tracing the meaning, origin and growth of these two major systems of the world, it becomes necessary to delineate the other distinguishing characteristics of these two systems. In countries that have adopted the civil law tradition, Codes or statutes are repositories of the law to which the judge must pay homage. In these countries, the extensive collection and range of the civil, canon, customary and enacted law has given place to Codes. These codes by and large, through general principles, lay down exactly what can and cannot be done. Further, these codes try to cater for every contingency, as far as possible. As the Codes comprise the law, judges turn to the Code to see what it says when there is a problem. As an offshoot, therefore, in these countries, precedent has only a persuasive value and does not form the major source of law.

In contrast, case-law forms the core law in the common law systems of the world. The common law is the result of the creative work of the judges, whose decisions in particular cases have gradually shaped the law. The development of case–law is, so to speak, tentative and casual, the principles crystallizing slowly on a case to case basis. While common-law

---

[7] http://en.wikipedia.org/wiki/common_law

countries have statutes collected into codes to clarify the law in areas where it is unsettled, these codes very often reflect the rules of law enunciated in judicial decisions. Hence, while civil law judges look to the Code provisions to resolve a case, common law judges instinctively reach for casebooks to find the solution to an issue in a case.

A significant point of distinction emerges from the above discussion with respect to the method of reasoning followed in these two systems. The method of reasoning adopted by civil law judges is basically deductive, conclusions about specific situations being arrived at from general principles or rules of law contained in the code itself. This method of reasoning is also responsible for the concise and short judgments of Continental judges.

In common law countries, the process is the reverse. There the judges apply inductive reasoning, deriving general principles or rules of law from precedents and extracting a rule, which is then applied to a particular case. The result, in these circumstances, is that the judgments of these judges are long, with precedents cited, pro and contra.

The role and authority of case-law

According to the theory prevailing in civil law countries, a judicial precedent is not to be regarded as a formal source of law. The doctrine of precedent by which the courts are bound to follow strictly the decisions of the superior courts, though firmly established in common law countries, is not followed within civil law systems. Jurists, in the latter, opine that a judicial decision cannot per se claim any legal authority or binding force, as they do in England. Often referred to as "one of the unsolved problems of comparative jurisprudence," an explanation of this is perhaps to be sought in the circumstance that Continental countries have been more profoundly influenced by the legal notions and institutions of Rome. In the Roman system, decisions were not considered as an authority for the subsequent case. Justinian declared in one of his Constitutions, "No judge or arbitrator is to consider himself bound by juristic opinions which he considers wrong: still less by the decisions of learned prefects or other judges. For if an erroneous decision has been given, it ought not to be allowed to spread and so to corrupt the judgment of other magistrates. '*Non exemplis, sed legibus indicandum est,*' thus means that decisions should be based on laws, not on precedents"[8]. This allows judges more creativity, since they are not bound by the rigid doctrine of *stare decisis*[9]. For this reason, judges may reverse their own opinions or even dissent from a superior court in a new cause, as and when the occasion demands. Though this gives the civilian judges admirable elasticity, the decisions of higher courts nonetheless play a role in view of their persuasive value.[10]

From the discussion above, it becomes clear that the role of case-law in the civil and common law traditions is different in the rendering of decisions by these Courts. Precedent being the primary source of law in common law systems, the doctrine of *stare decisis* comes into operation and binds the common law judges to the decisions of the superior court, unlike their civil law counterparts. It may appear that this approach is superior to that of the civil law judges, as it is argued that the principles frozen into the law codes and their often rigid doctrine frequently impede Continental judges in addressing situations not foreseen. This criticism does not seem to have substance because Continental judges can and will always deal with such problems in the light of principles of natural law and equity.

Statutory interpretation

Indeed, though the codes are comprehensive enough to deal with every possible contingency, judges nonetheless, have to resolve the ambiguities and gaps in the law. Operating within such a framework, the judge's profound knowledge of law, his legal acumen and sound judgment become crucial for effective dispute resolution. As Continental judges are essentially believed to be merely interpreting and applying the law to a case and little more, it is generally suggested that these judges have little opportunity for judicial creativity. Yet in situations where the meaning of a statute is ambiguous, the continental law gives a wider scope for interpretation than its counterpart does. Importantly, the Continental judges, though bound by the written law, interpret and apply the said law extensively and liberally, referring to its spirit and not merely to its literal

---

[8] G.C. Subbarao, *Jurisprudence and Legal Theory*, 9th ed. (Eastern Book Company) p. 99.

[9] Notably the Droit Administratif in France.

[10] See W. Friedmann, *Legal Theory*, 5th ed. (Universal Law Publishing Co.), p. 535.

meaning[11]. In truth therefore, though the Continental judge appears to be bound to slavish obedience to the Code, yet he actually enjoys greater freedom towards the provisions of the Code.

Moreover, the freedom from precedent which he enjoys may be in reality a myth, as there is much greater respect for judicial authority than imagined, as its persuasive value is often considered[12]. The Continental judge thus may not be far from his Anglo-American counterpart in judicial law-making.

As discussed, the common law judge searches for an answer to a question or issue among many potentially applicable judicial precedents. Though apparently playing a more creative role, the truth is that his freedom is curtailed by binding decisions of the superior court and considerations of certainty, consistency and uniformity in the law. His is an arduous task of balancing conflicting needs of stability and certainty with the constructive adaptation of the law to changing social needs. It is only in the absence of any binding precedent that he would have an opportunity of 'creating' the law. Nowadays, with the number of statutes ever increasing, common law judges have increasingly been involved more in the task of statutory interpretation than that of "creating" the law.

The role of jurists and the importance of doctrinal work

A further characteristic of civil systems is the prominence given to doctrinal writings and the opinion of jurists. While not law as such, these serve as useful guides in the interpretation of codes. Jurists, within the civil law system, analyze the basis of the codes, formulate general theories, and extract, enumerate and expound upon the principles of law contained therein. Their treatises and commentaries are, as it were, expositions of the broad legal principles underlying the codes. Thus while the role of jurists in the judicial decision-making process and development of law in common law systems is rather modest, the analytical doctrinal work of these jurists becomes an inherent and important part of the civil law system. Commenting on the different status accorded to jurists in these two systems, John Chipman Gray notes, "If the

[11] See Bodenheimer, *Jurisprudence, The Philosophy and Method of the Law*, revised ed. (Harvard University Press), p. 414.
[12] Friedmann, p. 536.

common law has been wise in attaching great weight to precedents, it has certainly not held out sufficient welcome to jurists"[13].

Approach of the judges

In view of the nature and characteristics each system possesses, the approach and attitude of judges in these two systems is not identical but different. Though they both pursue the objective of justice, they do so in their own distinct styles. Thus while the civil law judge questions how far the facts before him can be fitted into the general principles of the statute, his common law counterpart begins by comparing one set of facts with another set of facts. This difference in approach between the two systems is responsible for creating distinct judicial attitudes, with the civil law judge viewing his role as that of applying the relevant principles rather than creating the law. The common law judge, in contrast, busies himself with the task of finding the law in the goldmine of precedents.

Conclusion

In conclusion, it may be said that the civil law and common law systems of law each have their own distinctive characteristics and features. While these differences have had a bearing and an influence on the development of law in these systems, some of the distinctions have blurred with the passage of time, each system incorporating features from the other, in varying degrees. In essence, the approaches followed in these two systems differ, in as much as while the Continental system of law is scientific in its approach, the common law system is largely empirical.

[13] http://www.au.af.mil/au/awc/awcgate/fjc/civil_law.pdf

PART II:

LAW IN A GLOBALIZING WORLD

THE EUROPEAN CONSTITUTION AND NATIONAL CONSTITUTIONS—A COMPLEMENTARY RELATIONSHIP[1]

FAUSTO DE QUADROS

1. Object of the study

The European Union is at an advanced stage in becoming constitutionalised.

It is true that the European Constitutional Treaty was abandoned after the 'no' vote in the referendum in France. However, the fact is that its content was transferred almost in its entirety to the Treaty of Lisbon, of 2007.

It is also true that the European Constitutional Treaty, despite being entitled "The Treaty establishing a Constitution for Europe," could not be regarded as a formal constitution, in the sense of a national constitution. Indeed, the European Union itself does not yet possess the legal and political characteristics of a state, and the Constitutional Treaty could be nothing other than an *international Treaty*, as in fact it was called, accepted by the Member States and subject to ratification by all of them in order to enter into force.

Nevertheless, although the European Union does not yet have a formal constitution, it has long had a constitution in the material sense. That is, the Treaties establishing it already incorporate a range of basic principles and values which give form to the legal-political skeleton of the Union. They establish an institutional apparatus for the Union, define its powers

---

[1] This text deals with one of the themes discussed by the author within the scope of the module "The European Constitution," of which the author was chair at the Salgaocar College of Law, in Pangim, Goa, in January 2008, within the framework of the postgraduate course offered by the Faculty of Law of the University of Lisbon at that College under the Protocol of Cooperation between the two institutions.

and establish the relationships between these powers and those of the states, with recourse to the principle of subsidiarity. They give the Union a vast array of fundamental rights, above all following the incorporation of the Charter of Fundamental Rights into the Treaty on European Union. They establish a federal-style Economic and Monetary Union, with its own currency (the euro) and its own bank (the European Central Bank). Lastly, they define a vast and diversified system of guarantees in the case of non-compliance with Union law by the Union itself, by its institutions, by the Member States, and by individuals and companies.

Thus, it is legitimate to state that the process of constitutionalising the European Union is gaining speed.

Nevertheless, having reached this point it is important to highlight that it would be wrong to consider that the process of constitutionalising the European Union is taking place at the expense of and via sacrificing the constitutions of the Member States, leading to the disappearance of national constitutions or, at least, to the establishment of a relationship of antinomy or conflict between them and the European constitution. Far from diminishing or destroying national constitutions, the process of European integration enhances their value and establishes a relationship between them and the European constitution not of conflict, but of harmony and complementarity.

Here we will show that this is the case and, in order to do so, four areas will be focused on.

2. The national constitution as an expression of the national identity of the Member States of the European Union

We may begin by recalling that the process of European integration safeguards and protects national identity. Once again we should recall the famous words of Jean Monnet according to which, "Europe will not be achieved without the States and much less against the States". This expression mirrored the thinking of the founders of the Treaties and became, purposely, reflected in them[2]. The bivalency between integration

[2] See Jean Monnet, *Mémoires* (Paris, 1976). See also Walter Hallstein, *Die Europäische Gemeinschaft* (Dusseldorf, 1973), pp. 9 ff., and Fausto de Quadros, *Recordando Jean Monnet* (Lisbon, 1989), pp. 1 ff., *Direito da União Europeia*

and national identity and the dialectic tension between the two define the actual dynamics of the process of integration, inherited from older federal systems.

We may see what the scope of the national identity of each state is within the process of European integration, which the respective national constitutions should respect. National identity encompasses three components. The first of these is the *political* component, the limit of which is, essentially, the power of powers (*Kompetenz–Kompetenz*), that is, the power of the state to define its own political and administrative organisation, yet without the power to use it with the purpose of preventing compliance, by itself or by intra-state bodies, with the commitments that it has assumed pursuant to accession to the Union. Secondly, there is the *legal* component, which signifies that integration respects the specific nature of the national laws, to the point that the principle of subsidiarity imposes the duty to demonstrate the need for community law given the existence of the national laws (Protocol on the application of the principles of subsidiarity and proportionality, annexed to the Treaty of Amsterdam, no. 7). The third component is the *cultural* component, which permits and stimulates the state to preserve its cultural identity (that is, its culture, language, history and traditions)[3].

Although it has always been considered a constitutional principle of European integration, respect for national identity within the process of integration today appears expressly in the wording of the Treaties in Article 6(3) of the EU Treaty now in force. That is to say, *the legal order of the Union itself includes within it the safeguarding of the national identities of the member states.*

As may be imagined, it is the constitution of each state that has the first duty of defining, shaping and preserving the national identity. By this measure, therefore, not only does the European constitution neither exclude nor diminish the national constitution, but it expects the latter's cooperation in building the national identity that the Union seeks to preserve.

(Coimbra, 2004), pp. 29–30, and *Droit de l'Union européenne—Droit constitutionnel et administratif de l'Union européenne* (Brussels, 2008), pp. 16–17.
[3] de Quadros, *Direito*, pp. 85 ff.

3. The Europeanisation of national constitutions

The second area in which it can be seen that the European constitution does not diminish the national constitutions is in the aptly named *Europeanisation of the national constitutions* and, via this, the *Europeanisation of the constitutional laws of the Member States themselves*. The Europeanisation of constitutional laws also brings about, by association, the Europeanisation of the other branches of the law linked to the exercise of the public powers, namely, administrative law, both in general terms and as seen in all its specialities: from the law of administrative organisation to the law of administrative disputes, from financial administrative law to town planning administrative law or environmental administrative law.

The Europeanisation of national constitutions represents an unprecedented phenomenon in the history of international relations between states and is yet another phenomenon typical of federal and pre-federal systems. It is for this reason that in Germany, for example, it has been the subject of an abundant and extremely rich bibliography since the entry into force of the Basic Law of Bonn, of 1949[4]. Europeanisation has occurred in two ways. Firstly, the Member States of the Union have adapted their respective constitutions to the EU treaties, in order to ease their accession to the latter and so that issues of conflict between them do not arise, with these conflicts having to be solved by means of the doctrine of primacy of EU law. Secondly, the simple phenomenon of harmonising the national legal orders with EU law, which is imposed by the intrinsic specific nature of the latter, has forced the member states, progressively, and immediately with regard to first pillar issues, to adapt their national legal systems to EU law. This adaptation begins with the states' respective constitutions. By way of an example, we may take the changes introduced by the Member States to their respective constitutions, whether major or minor, in the area of their respective electoral systems, in order to adapt them to the electoral rights recognised for European citizens within the framework of European citizenship (Article 19(1) and (2), EC, and, for example, Article 15(4) and (5) of the Constitution of the Portuguese Republic, after the 1992 revision); in their respective financial and monetary systems, in order to adapt them to the Economic and Monetary Union, with regards to the states that adopted the euro; in their respective judicial systems, in order,

[4] See, for all, the various studies compiled by von Bogdandy, *Europäisches Verfassungsrecht* (Heidelberga, 2003). Further bibliographical references on the subject can be found in de Quadros, *Direito*, particularly pp. 407 ff.

for example, to adapt them to the "space of freedom, security and justice" created by the third pillar when they abolished extradition within the Union.

The phenomenon of Europeanisation consists of a bi-lateral movement, since not only have the national constitutions become closer to each other and to Union law, in order to allow the Member States to meet the objectives of the Union, in the terms referred to above, but Union law has also absorbed essential contributions from the national constitutions into its own nucleus. This is how we should interpret the absorption, brought about by the Treaty on European Union in the wording given to it by the Treaty of Maastricht, into the *acquis communautaire* of the "*constitutional traditions* common to the Member States" (our italics), in the area of fundamental rights (Article F(2) of the TEU, Article 6(2), after the Treaty of Amsterdam). Moreover, it is also how we should interpret the integration within the Union's Charter of Fundamental Rights, now in the version set out in the Annexes to the Treaty of Lisbon, of those same "constitutional traditions" as sources of fundamental rights that the Charter welcomes. This integration deserves to be particularly emphasised in so far as, from the definition of the highest level of protection of fundamental rights recognised by Article 53 of the Charter, there is nothing in theory to stop that highest level from being, in a concrete case, that supplied "*by the Member States' constitutions*" (our italics), as the final part of that article sets down (in other words, in the concrete case, by the constitution of the Member State in question). We shall return to this subject below.

4. The safeguarding of national constitutions within the doctrine of the primacy of EU law

The third area where we can confirm that the relationship between the European constitution and the national constitutions is not one of conflict is that of the primacy of EU law over national laws.

After a long period at the beginning of integration during which the Community and the Member States found it difficult, not to accept primacy, but rather to define its scope and establish its boundaries, a consensus seems now to have been reached in the relationship between the Union and the Member States concerning the grounds, reach and restrictions of primacy. Expression of this consensus can be found in Article I-6 of the European Constitutional Treaty, completed by Declaration 1 annexed to the Treaty. We may recall that this article of the Treaty was accepted pacifically by the members of the Convention that prepared the Treaty (and we may note that among the members of national parliaments and members of the European Parliament that were part of the Convention were individuals from the far right to the far left and some very well-known names in legal science). Furthermore, this article and the aforementioned declaration were not even discussed at the time of the ratification of the Treaty by the Member States, not even in the two states where the referendum on the Treaty had a negative outcome. Later, the Treaty of Lisbon maintained the same definition of primacy—here too without any kind of protest from the Member States—although encompassing its regime in a declaration annexed to the Treaty (Declaration 17, which, however, is an integral part of the Treaty).

The solution found for primacy, and about which there can be said to be broad consensus, was the result of cooperation between the Court of Justice and the national constitutional courts, especially the German court, closely followed by the Italian court. Besides this, the solution is covered by the national constitutions, since all of them contain "European clauses," some more effectively and in a more correct form from the legal point of view than others. That is, they contain principles which, within the framework of the limitations on sovereignty resulting from European integration and accepted by those clauses, either explicitly or implicitly also accept the primacy of Union law over national law. Albeit in a form which is not particularly adequate, this is the case of the current Article 8(4) of the Portuguese Constitution.

The doctrine of the primacy of Union law,[5] as it results from the conjugation of EU case-law, particularly via the cases *Costa/ENEL*, *Simenthal* and *Factortame*, and German and Italian constitutional case-law, namely via the cases *Solange I*, *Solange II*, *Maastricht*, *Bananenmarktordnung*, *Frontini* and *Granital*, and the cover of the "European clauses" or constitutional provisions of analogous meaning and reach, is today respected by the Member States, including by their courts, with the only exception being the French State Council, and this not on a permanent basis.

Notwithstanding the affirmation of primacy, the principle has, of course, come about and developed not by means of a confrontation between the

[5] For a particularly exhaustive study of primacy, see Craig E. De Burca, *The Evolution of EU Law* (Oxford, 1999), pp. 189–210. See also de Quadros, *Direito*, pp. 398 ff., and *Droit*, pp. 360 ff.

legal orders of the Union and the national laws, but via what we shall call a dialogue between the two. Moreover, in the case of the states, this dialogue, this cooperation, this co-participation in the doctrine of primacy is carried out above all by the national constitutions (and, via them, through the constitutional case-law of the respective states). Even in the area of primacy, therefore, despite the especially delicate and sensitive nature of the issue for the national constitutions, the relationship between EU law and national constitutions is today a relationship of *dialogue* and *cooperation*, rather than one of conflict. The safeguarding in the doctrine of primacy of the highest protection for fundamental rights on the part of the national constitutions (which can lead, in that concrete circumstance, to rejection of the primacy of Union law), resulting precisely from the aforementioned cooperation between the community case-law and the national constitutional case-law, but today set out in the Treaty of Lisbon, in the manner in which it codified the case-law of the community courts (the previously cited Declaration 17, annexed to the Treaty), clearly shows that, on the issue of primacy, the European constitution and the national constitutions *complete each other and are in harmony with each other*, and are not in conflict.

5. The fundamental rights recognised by the national constitutions as *acquis* of EU law

The last area in which it may be seen that the European constitution is not in conflict with the national constitutions, and much less ignores them, is that of the protection and safeguarding of fundamental rights within the legal order of the European Union.

The issue of fundamental rights in the European Union has been gaining ever greater importance within the Union's legal system, as a means of strengthening the Union's democratic, social and humanitarian components[6].

As stated above, the system of protection of fundamental rights in the Union's legal order is, above all, a product of the elaboration given to it by the ECJ in dialogue with the national constitutional courts, particularly the

[6] See the detailed analysis which, for this reason, is given to this issue in de Quadros, *Direito*, pp. 126 ff. and *Droit*, pp. 100 ff. See also in these works the extensive and high quality bibliography on this issue in a number of languages including English.

German and Italian courts. This fact, in itself, demonstrates the penetration of the national constitutions into the area of the fundamental human rights recognised by the Union.

Within the ECJ case-law the judgment which best displays this orientation is, without doubt, that given in 1989 in the *Wachauf* case[7]. In this case the ECJ stated that "fundamental rights form an integral part of the general principles of the law, the observance of which is ensured by the Court. In safeguarding those rights, the Court has to look to the *constitutional traditions common to the Member States*, so that *measures which are incompatible with the fundamental rights recognised by the constitutions of those states may not find acceptance in the Community.* International treaties concerning the protection of human rights on which the Member States have collaborated or to which they have acceded can also supply guidelines to which regard should be had in the context of Community law" (our italics).

The Treaty of the European Union, immediately after the Treaty of Maastricht, progressively welcomed this orientation. Indeed, the current Article 6(2) (article F(1), by the Treaty of Maastricht), codifies the legal theory in the *Wachauf* case, by providing that: "The Union shall respect fundamental rights, as guaranteed by the European Convention for the Protection of Human Rights and Fundamental Freedoms signed in Rome on 4 November 1950 and as they result from the *constitutional traditions common to the Member States*, as general principles of Community law" (our italics).

In other words, the Treaty on European Union accepts, in writing, that the *acquis* of fundamental rights recognised by the Union's legal order encompasses the rights dictated by the "constitutional traditions" of the Member States. Indeed, this was clear in the sense of what had already resulted from the joint effort of the ECJ and the German and Italian constitutional courts in the construction of the doctrine of the relationship between Union law and national laws (particularly the doctrine of primacy), which, in defining the relationship between the sources of law which compose that *acquis*, laid down *the principle of the highest protection*. That is, if the rights supplied by the constitutions of the Member States were more favourable (understood to be: in their content, in their scope, in their procedure or in their effects, in any of their

[7] Ac. 13-7-89, Proc. 5/88, Col. 1989, pp. 2609 ff., point 17.

substantive or adjective aspects) to individuals than any of the other sources indicated in the aforementioned Article 6(2) EU (that is, Community law itself, international law, the European Convention on Human Rights), in this case it would be *the national constitutions that the Union should take into account, in each case, for all purposes.*

The Charter of Fundamental Rights, by finally appearing as a catalogue of fundamental rights for the European Union itself, made an obvious point of consecrating this orientation, in Article 53.

The text of the Charter was integrated, as is known, into the Draft European Constitutional Treaty by the Convention on the Future of Europe and, later, into the text of the European Constitutional Treaty. This having been abandoned, the Charter then passed to the Treaty of Lisbon, although as an annex to that Treaty, yet remaining an integral part of it, pursuant to Article 6(1) of the Treaty on European Union, revised by the Treaty of Lisbon.

The version of the Charter that was included in the Constitutional Treaty and, afterwards, in the Treaty of Lisbon, does not coincide totally with the original text of the Charter, particularly with regard to its horizontal clauses. This also proves to be of interest to us. In the text annexed to the Treaty of Lisbon, the Charter has not one but two articles on the relationship between the Charter and the national constitutions on the subject of fundamental rights: Articles 52(4) and 53.

Article 52(4) did not figure in the version of the Charter proclaimed in Nice in December 2000. It states:

> Article 52
> **Scope and interpretation of rights and principles**
> (...)
> 4. In so far as this Charter recognises fundamental rights as they result from the *constitutional traditions common to the Member States, those rights shall be interpreted in harmony with those traditions.*
> (...) (our italics).

Immediately afterwards, Article 53 provides as follows:

> Article 53
> **Level of Protection**
> Nothing in the Charter shall be interpreted as restricting or adversely affecting human rights and fundamental freedoms as recognised, in their

> respective fields of application, by Union law and international law and by international agreements to which the Union or all Member States are party, including the European Convention for the Protection of Human Rights and Fundamental Freedoms, *and by the Member States' constitutions*. (our italics)

This principle corresponds to the previously cited Article 53 of the 2000 text of the Charter.

The following legal regime results from the combination of these principles:

a) the *acquis* of fundamental rights recognised by the Union's legal order is substantially expanded in the light of the current Article 6(2) of the EU Treaty, since it now encompasses the rights recognised by the Charter itself, and also those conferred by other Union law, by international law (which includes, without exhausting it, the international conventions to which the Union or all Member States are a party, even though immediately afterwards we find a special reference to those conventions—that is, namely, all the declarations, pacts and conventions concluded on fundamental rights within the framework of the United Nations or under its aegis), by the European Convention on Human Rights (which, due to its importance, is distinguished from international law and the international conventions) and by the *constitutions of the Member States*. All of these rights no longer have force as "general principles of Community law", as provided by the current Article 6(2) of the EU Treaty, in relation to the sources cited therein, but as *written* Union law (which is clear from the 5th recital of the Preamble to the Charter);
b) between the Charter and the other mentioned sources that it integrates within the Union's legal order, the Charter adopts the principle of *the highest level of protection*. That is, in relation to each fundamental right, and in each concrete case, the Charter will only be respected if the source which *best protects it* is applied, from among the sources referred to in the transcribed Article 53. It may, therefore, happen that, *by express provision of the Charter*, a fundamental right is regulated within the Union's legal order, *by the national constitution, or by the national constitutions* involved, and not by the Charter, or, at least, that its legal regime will be subject

to an interpretation in line with the national constitution or constitutions, pursuant to articles 53 and 52(4) of the Charter. In such a situation, it is fair to say that, regarding such a sensitive issue for the Union as is that of fundamental rights, the Charter sought for the constitutions of the states to be integrated within the Union's legal order. It would be difficult to find a greater interpenetration or complementarity (call it also friendship and harmony, if you will) between the European constitution and the national constitutions. In the situation we are considering, the national constitutions now become part of the *acquis* of Union law on fundamental rights. In other words, *the national constitutions, on this subject, are integrated within Union law*. Furthermore, this conclusion is in no way harmed by the fact that, given the highly developed nature of the Charter, both in the scope of the rights consecrated, in the content, in the form and the guarantee it provides for them, it would be difficult for it to be surpassed by the constitutions of the 27 Member States with regard to the protection of fundamental rights[8].

6. Conclusion

As we believe to have shown, the appearance of a European constitution (moreover, we repeat, not in the formal sense of the expression) does not lead to the disappearance, the destruction or the lack of a need for the national constitutions. The relationship between the European constitution and the national constitutions is a relationship of dialogue, of complementarity, and in some cases of interpenetration, without prejudice to the *acquis communautaire* or the relationship between them in the case of conflict. However, the first idea considered for this relationship is one of bivalency, in the process of integration, of the state constituting process with the existence of a material European constitution. This bivalency occurs even in the most developed federations, as is accepted in the United States and in Germany and, for this reason, it is not surprising that we find it in the European Union even at a pre-federal stage, although at a stage moving progressively towards a federal model.

In actual fact, this bivalency is nothing new. As we noted in 1984[9], and is

---

[8] We demonstrate in what way in de Quadros, *Direito*, p. 175.

[9] See de Quadros *Direito*, p. 86, and the reference made there.

today noted by all commentators on the Treaties, the process of European integration results precisely from this bivalency, from this dialectic tension, between integration (represented here by the European constitution) and the sovereignty (albeit limited) of the states (represented here by the national constitutions).

For this reason, and returning to the introduction of this study, it is important to be clear that, in the debate on the European constitution, and in the name of legal accuracy, the European constitution calls upon the national constitutions to enrich its own content and, therefore, the *acquis* of the Union's legal order and that, as a result, there is no relationship of reciprocal exclusion between the European constitution and the constitutions of the Member States. The constant dialogue and complementarity that is established between both is one of the reflections of the dialogue between integration and sovereignty, in which the latter is represented by the legitimacy of the states in the process of European integration. Moreover, as has been said, it is this bivalency, this interaction between the two poles—integration and sovereignty of the states—, which makes European integration progress[10].

It should be noted that the conclusion we reach in this study is in no way new with regard to the relationships that are established today between constitutional law and public international law.

In fact, the current state of relations between international law and internal law is heavily dominated by the *principle of harmony of the national constitution with the international law* ("*die Völkerrechtsfreundlichkeit der Verfassung*, in German, given that it was, above all, out of German constitutional law that it was born), or *opening* of the national constitution to international law, or, expressed in an even better form, *duty of conformity* of the national constitution with international law.

This construction was considered above all, although not only, in the sphere of fundamental rights. According to it, the national constitution should welcome the fundamental rights recognised by international law or, at least, should be interpreted and applied in line with international law, of

---

[10] On the subject of this article, see also, Zagrebelsky, *Diritti e Costituzione nell'Unione Europea*, 2nd ed. (Rome, 2004); McCormick, *La sovranità in discussione*, Italian translation (Bologna, 2003); Streinz, Ohler and Herdmann, *Die neue Verfassung für Europa* (Munich, 2005); and Dony and Bribosia, *Commentaire de la Constitution de l'Union européenne* (Brussels, 2005).

course, always on the basis that the international law is more favourable to the fundamental rights of the citizens of the respective state.

The Portuguese Constitution, like many other European constitutions, welcomes this orientation. This has been demonstrated in greater detail in a previous study, to which we direct the reader's attention[11].

---

[11] Fausto de Quadros, *A protecção da propriedade privada pelo Direito Internacional Público* (Coimbra, 1998), pp. 535–552, particularly pp. 535–545 (*with a summary in English*). See today, in the same sense, A. Jyränki, *National Constitutions in the Era of Integration* (The Hague, 1999), and Gomes Canotilho, *Direito Constitucional e Teoria da Constituição*, 5th ed. (Coimbra, 2002), pp. 367–369.

INTERNATIONAL HARMONIZATION AND UNIFICATION OF PRIVATE LAW IN A GLOBALIZED ECONOMY[1]

DÁRIO MOURA VICENTE

Introduction

The growing integration of markets, frequently referred to as globalization, has brought back into the limelight the issues of international harmonization and unification of Private Law[2].

In legal doctrine, a "gradual convergence" of national legal systems (or, at least, of those belonging to the Civil Law and the Common Law legal traditions) has been noted by some authors[3]. The possibility, suggested over four decades ago, of the creation of a "Western Law", which would bring together the systems integrated in those legal traditions, has also once again been put forward[4]. And the formation of a new *Ius Commune*,

---

[1] This text is based on the final lecture of a series on *European Legal Traditions,* given at the V. M. Salgãocar College of Law, Panaji, Goa, between 21 and 25 January, 2008. The author would like to thank Professors Marian Pinheiro and Carmo D'Souza for their kind assistance during these lectures.

[2] See Jürgen Basedow, "The Effects of Globalization on Private International Law", in Jürgen Basedow and Toshiyuki Kono (eds.), *Legal Aspects of Globalization. Conflict of Laws, Internet, Capital Markets and Insolvency in a Global Economy* (The Hague, London and Boston, 2000), pp. 1 ff.; Pedro Alberto de Miguel Asensio, "El Derecho Internacional Privado ante la globalización", *Anuario Español de Derecho Internacional Privado*, t. I, 2001, pp. 37 ff.

[3] See, in this sense, Basil Markesinis, "Learning from Europe and Learning in Europe", in eiusdem, *The Gradual Convergence: Foreign Ideas, Foreign Influences, and English Law on the Eve of the 21st Century*, repr. (Oxford, 2001), pp. 1 ff. (p. 30).

[4] See René David, "Existe-t-il un droit occidental?", in Kurt H. Nadelmann, Arthur T. von Mehren and John N. Hazard (eds.), *XXth Century Comparative and*

suited to the needs of the modern world, is presented by some as an ideal to be pursued[5]. The *universalist concept of law*, which was so deeply influential in Europe up to the beginning of the 19th century, is thus being reborn.

This paper shall discuss the current expressions of that concept. Is there—we ask—a "law of globalization"? In order to answer this question, we shall begin by providing a brief outline of the main contemporary initiatives to harmonize and unify Private Law, both at the worldwide and the regional levels. We shall then consider the reasons that justify them and their limitations. Finally, we shall attempt to determine if and to what extent the coordination of national legal systems through the specific methods of Private International Law is an alternative to the international harmonization and unification of Private Law.

In order to clarify the scope of this paper, we shall first endeavor to define the above-mentioned concepts of harmonization and unification of legal systems.

The *harmonization* of legal systems is the reduction of the differences that separate them with regard to certain subjects, with the aim of ensuring a certain degree of *functional equivalence* between them, but without suppressing the diversity of their rules. Harmonization may be achieved in different ways, as is the case, in the European Union, with Directives, which are binding upon each Member State as to the result to be achieved in the regulation of certain subjects, but leave to the national authorities the choice of the form and methods to achieve that result; and, at the worldwide level, of the Model Laws of the United Nations Commission on International Trade Law (UNCITRAL) and of the International Institute for the Unification of Private Law (UNIDROIT).

The *unification* of legal systems aims at suppressing differences between the legal systems considered. This requires that their legal provisions be identical and that a single court be set up with jurisdiction to decide, on final appeal, the issues raised by their interpretation and integration. Unification may also be achieved through different categories of instruments, *inter alia* international treaties, regulations (in the European Union) and Uniform Acts (in the Organization for the Harmonization of

---

Conflicts Law: Essays in Honor of Hessel E. Yntema (Leiden, 1961), pp. 56 ff.

5 See René David, "The International Unification of Private Law", in *International Encyclopedia of Comparative Law*, vol. II, chapter 5.

Business Law in Africa, or OHADA).

Worldwide harmonization and unification initiatives

I—In modern times, the first expressions of this phenomenon included the unification initiatives which, at the end of the 19th century, addressed intellectual property matters. Two international conventions, which are still in force, introduced a minimum standard of protection for intellectual property rights, today almost universally applicable: the *Paris Convention for the Protection of Industrial Property*, of March 20, 1883, subsequently revised several times; and the *Berne Convention for the Protection of Literary and Artistic Works*, signed on September 9, 1886, also repeatedly revised.

These conventions are still applied today in their member states in order to determine the protection that is to be awarded to copyright and private industrial property rights in international relationships. Thanks to the 1994 Agreement on Trade Related Aspects of Intellectual Property Rights (TRIPS), appended to the agreement that established the World Trade Organization (WTO), which incorporated these conventions, they are now in force in all member states of this international organization.

One must, however, recognize the relatively limited scope of these international instruments: in spite of the enormous progress which they represented, at least in comparison with the preceding situation, a vast number of issues were left unregulated by them, such as the ownership of copyright in the case of works carried out upon request of another person, the exhaustion of that right and the means of enforcing it.

II—In the 1920s, Ernst Rabel, then a professor of law in Berlin, suggested a more ambitious enterprise: the international unification of the rules on sales. Subsequently, a Draft Uniform Law on Sales was prepared, under the aegis of UNIDROIT, and it was published in 1935[6]. The efforts towards the unification of this field of the law, which were interrupted

---

[6] The French and German versions of the Project are available in *Rabels Zeitschrift für ausländisches und internationales Privatrecht* (1935), pp. 8 ff. See also Ernst Rabel, *Das Recht des Warenkaufs. Eine rechtsvergleichende Darstellung*, vol. I, (Berlin and Leipzig, 1936), vol. II, (Berlin, 1957); *id.*, "L'unification du droit de la vente internationale. Ses rapports avec les formulaires ou contrats-types des divers commerces", in *Introduction à l'étude du Droit Comparé: Recueil d'Études en l'honneur d'Édouard Lambert*, vol. II (Paris, 1938), pp. 688 ff.

during the Second World War, were resumed after the end of hostilities. In 1951, at The Hague, a new draft uniform law on this issue was presented. In 1964, also at The Hague, two conventions were adopted containing as annexes, respectively, the Uniform Law on the International Sale of Goods and the Uniform Law on the Formation of Contracts for the International Sale of Goods, which their member states undertook to incorporate into their internal laws[7]. However, these conventions were not welcomed by several states with a relevant stake in international trade, and they obtained only a very small number of ratifications. This is why UNCITRAL, created in 1966 by a Resolution of the General Assembly of the United Nations, listed as one of its priorities the revision of the uniform law on international sales. Eventually, this led to a diplomatic conference, held in Vienna, in 1980, in which the United Nations Convention on Contracts for the International Sale of Goods was adopted. It entered into force on January 1, 1988[8].

In the meantime, other types of contract have attracted attention in international relations. These include financial leasing contracts, which are particularly important as a means of financing the acquisition of equipment by developing countries. The matter was addressed by UNIDROIT, leading to the adoption in Ottawa, in 1988, of the *Convention on International Financial Leasing*, in force since 1995, which unifies the substantive law rules applicable to those contracts[9].

At the same time, attention was also drawn to the legal regime applicable to the so-called factoring contract, which holds an equally important role in international trade as an instrument aimed, inter alia, at facilitating exports by small and medium-sized companies, which usually have little financial capacity and are thus prevented from granting credit to the purchasers of their products or services. This has also been the object of a

[7] Texts available at http://www.unidroit.org.

[8] Text available at http://www.uncitral.org. See, on the Convention, in Portuguese, Maria Ângela Bento Soares and Rui Moura Ramos, *Contratos internacionais: Compra e venda: Cláusulas penais: Arbitragem* (Coimbra, 1986); Dário Moura Vicente, “A Convenção de Viena Sobre a Compra e Venda Internacional de Mercadorias: características gerais e âmbito de aplicação”, in *Estudos de Direito Comercial Internacional* (Coimbra, 2004), pp. 271 ff.; Luís de Lima Pinheiro, *Direito Comercial Internacional* (Coimbra, 2005), pp. 259 ff.

[9] Text available at http://www.unidroit.org. See Rui Pinto Duarte, in *Escritos sobre Leasing e Factoring* (Cascais, 2001), pp. 211 ff.; Sánchez Jiménez, “El contrato de leasing”, in Alfonso Calvo Caravaca et al. (eds.), *Contratos internacionales* (Madrid, 1997), pp. 933 ff.

UNIDROIT Convention: the *Convention on International Factoring*, concluded in Ottawa in 1988, and in force since 1995[10].

III—Another area where the need for unification of the applicable legal provisions has long been recognized is that of international transportation.

It was this recognition that led to the signing of the *International Convention for the Unification of Certain Rules of Law relating to Bills of Lading* (also known as the "*Hague Rules*")[11], on August 25, 1924, on the initiative of the International Maritime Committee. This Convention was revised by the *Visby Protocol* of February 23, 1968, and by the *SDR Protocol*. The same concern led to the adoption of the *United Nations Convention on the Carriage of Goods by Sea*, signed in Hamburg, on March 31, 1978 (the "Hamburg Rules")[12].

In the field of transportation by air, one should consider the *Warsaw Convention for the Unification of Certain Rules Relating to International Carriage by Air*, of October 12, 1929[13], and the *Convention for the Unification of Certain Rules for International Carriage by Air*, signed in Montreal on May 28, 1999[14], which aims at modernizing and consolidating the so-called *Warsaw system*, created by the Warsaw Convention and by the instruments that completed and modified it.

Equally important are the 1956 *Geneva Convention on the Contract for the International Carriage of Goods by Road (CMR)* and the *Convention concerning International Carriage by Rail*, signed at Berne in 1980 (COTIF).

IV—More recently, several international instruments have been concluded relating to payment means and to guarantees: the 1988 *United Nations Convention on International Bills of Exchange and International Promissory Notes*[15]; the 2001 *United Nations Convention on the Assignment of Receivables in International Trade*; and the 2001

---

[10] Text available at http://www.unidroit.org. See Sánchez Jiménez, "El contrato de factoring", in Caravaca, op. cit., pp. 978 ff.; Maria Helena Brito, *O* factoring *internacional e a Convenção do Unidroit* (Lisboa, 1998), pp. 83 ff.; and Duarte, op. cit.

[11] Text available at http://www.comitemaritime.org.

[12] Text available at http://www.uncitral.org.

[13] Text available at http://www.icao.int.

[14] Text available at http://www.icao.int.

[15] Text available at http://www.uncitral.org

UNIDROIT *Convention on International Interests in Mobile Equipment*[16].

Also, the growing use of electronic systems in international trade and the need to clarify certain questions raised as to the validity and effectiveness of these contracts led UNCITRAL to promote the *United Nations Convention on the Use of Electronic Communications in International Contracts*, adopted at New York, in 2005[17].

V—The *Principles of International Commercial Contracts*, first published in 1994 by UNIDROIT, belong to a different category of instruments, aimed at the international harmonization and unification of Private Law[18].

This text includes uniform provisions relating, inter alia, to the formation, validity and interpretation of contracts, the determination of obligations and of rights of third parties, performance and non-performance, as well as the termination of the contract and the assignment of credits[19]. It is, however, a non-binding instrument, aimed at being applied, essentially, when the parties choose it, and not as a source of actual legal provisions.

Some consider it an example of "flexible law" or "soft law"[20], a concept which usually refers to certain instruments regulating economic international relations in a non-binding manner, yet not entirely deprived of effectiveness. This effectiveness would, among other factors, be the result of individuals spontaneously complying with the provisions of such texts, e.g. for fear of being deprived of certain advantages (such as diplomatic protection or the granting of export credits) or because that is required by good faith[21]. It seems doubtful, however, that one may speak

---

[16] Text available at http://www.unidroit.org

[17] Text available at http://www.uncitral.org

[18] See International Institute for the Unification of Private Law, *UNIDROIT Principles of International Commercial Contracts* (Rome, 1994) (new ed. 2004).

[19] See, on this text, Michael Joachim Bonell, *An International Restatement of Contract Law: The UNIDROIT Principles of International Commercial Contracts*, 3rd ed. (Ardsley: New York, 2005).

[20] See Ulrich Drobnig, "Vereinheitlichung von Zivilrecht durch soft law: neuere Erfahrungen und Einsichten", in Jürgen Basedow et al. (eds.), *Aufbruch nach Europa: 75 Jahre Max-Planck-Institut für Privatrecht* (Tübingen, 2001), pp. 745 ff.

[21] See Ignaz Seidl-Hohenveldern, "International Economic 'Soft Law'", in *Collected Courses of the Hague Academy of International Law*, t. 163 (1979-II), pp. 165 ff. (especially pp. 182 ff.); Ulrich Ehricke, "'Soft Law'—Aspekte einer neuen Rechtsquelle", *Neue Juristische Wochenschrift*, 1989, pp. 1906 ff.; António

of law in this respect.

The same could be said of the so-called *Model Laws* adopted by UNCITRAL and UNIDROIT, as well as of the *Legislative Guides* which the latter organization has adopted in recent years, and of the texts adopted by certain non-governmental organizations, such as the International Chamber of Commerce (ICC), which are aimed at codifying the usages of international trade. These include, for example, the so-called *Incoterms*[22], the *Uniform Rules for Contract Guarantees*[23] and the *Uniform Customs and Practice for Documentary Credits*[24], issued by the ICC, which interested parties may adopt, by incorporating them into their contracts.

Regional harmonization and unification initiatives

I—The harmonization and unification of Private Law has also gained great relevance in the context of attempts at regional economic integration[25].

With regard to the European Union, for example, present-day European Law includes a large number of provisions relating to Private Law issues, aimed at harmonizing the laws of the Member States. These include Directives on liability for defective products; on unfair terms in consumer contracts; on the protection of purchasers with regards to timeshare contracts; on the protection of consumers with regards to distance contracts; on the sale of consumer goods and associated guarantees; on electronic commerce; on combating late payment in commercial transactions; on financial collateral arrangements; on distance marketing of consumer financial services; and on unfair business-to-consumer commercial practices in the internal market[26].

Marques dos Santos, *Direito Internacional Privado,* vol. I (Lisboa, 2001), pp. 41 ff.; Paulo Otero, *Legalidade e administração pública: O sentido da vinculação administrativa à juridicidade* (Coimbra, 2003), pp. 172 ff. and 908 ff.

[22] See the UNCITRAL Legislative Guides on Electronic Transfer of Funds (2001) and Insolvency Law (2005).

[23] See *ICC Uniform Rules for Contract Guarantees*, repr. (Paris, 2002).

[24] See *ICC Uniform Customs and Practice for Documentary Credits. 2007 Revision* (Paris, 2007).

[25] See *Worldwide Harmonisation of Private Law and Regional Economic Integration: Acts of the Congress to Celebrate the 75th Anniversary of the Founding of the International Institute for the Unification of Private Law (UNIDROIT),* vol. VIII (2003, nos. 1 and 2) of the *Uniform Law Review.*

[26] Texts available at http://www.europa.eu.

Some see these instruments as the embryo of a new European *Ius Commune*. It should, however, be noted that, while the medieval *Ius Commune which* was in force in Europe was based on the recognition of its superiority over any other source of regulation of social life (i.e. *imperio rationis*), European Union Law is in force because it is adopted by the institutions of the European Union empowered to do so, in pursuit of an ideal of unification of the law of the Member States (*hoc sensu, ratione imperii*)[27].

Be that as it may, it is clear that the European Union *acquis* in Private Law matters has not succeeded in eliminating the differences between national legal systems. As can be seen from the list of European Directives provided above, they cover only specific topics; and they contain, in addition, certain inconsistencies affecting, inter alia, the regime of the pre-contractual duty to provide information, the time-limit for a consumer to rescind a contract and the contractual liability of the supplier of goods or services.

This is one of the main reasons why some authors have endorsed the drafting of a *European Civil Code*, an idea which has been repeatedly advocated by the European Parliament[28]. For this purpose, several preparatory works have been carried out in recent years, including the *Principles of European Contract Law*, published between 1995 and 2003 by the Commission on European Contract Law led by Ole Lando[29]; the draft *European Contract Code*, an initiative of the *Academy of European Private Lawyers*, based in Pavia and coordinated by Giuseppe Gandolfi[30]; and the *Principles of European Tort Law*, published in 2005 by the *European Group on Tort Law*[31].

Generally, all these texts follow the legal technique and the solutions of the Civil Law systems. As was highlighted by Pierre Legrand, they could

---

[27] See Peter Stein, *Roman Law in European History*, repr. (Cambridge, 2004), p. 130.
[28] Texts available in http://www.europarl.europa.eu.
[29] See Ole Lando et al. (eds.), *Principles of European Contract Law, Parts I and II Combined and Revised* (The Hague, London and Boston, 2000); *Part III* (The Hague, London and New York), pp. 538 ff.
[30] See Accademia dei Giusprivatisti Europei, *Code européen des contrats: Avant-projet*, 2nd ed. (Milan, 2004).
[31] See European Group on Tort Law, *Principles of European Tort Law: Text and Commentary* (Vienna and New York, 2005).

only be adopted as the basis of a future European Civil Code at the expense of the Common Law legal tradition[32].

In 1998, a *Study Group on a European Civil Code* was created, under the direction of Professor Christian von Bar, of Osnabrück, with the aim of drafting a codification of patrimonial Civil Law (excluding the rules applicable to immovable property), which should later be incorporated into a European Regulation[33]. Although initially supported by the European Union, this project has since been abandoned, both by the European Commission[34] and by the Council of the European Union[35], in favor of an instrument with a more limited scope: the so-called *Common Frame of Reference*. This aims merely, according to the European Commission's Action Plan with the title *A More Coherent European Contract Law*[36], at establishing "*common principles and terminology in the area of European Contract Law*", being also an "*intermediate step towards improving the quality of the EC* acquis *in the area of contract law*"; it is also stated that, in any case, "*if the common frame of reference is widely accepted as the model in European contract law which best corresponds to the needs of the economic operators, it can be expected also to be taken as a point of reference by national legislatures inside the EU*".

---

[32] See "Against a European Civil Code", *The Modern Law Review* (1997), pp. 44 ff. (55): "[t]he communion assumed to be epitomised by a European Civil Code would in fact represent, beyond the sum of words, the excommunication of the common law way of understanding the world and the relegation to obsolescence of its particular insights".

[33] See Christian von Bar, "Le Groupe d'Études sur un Code Civil Européen", *Revue Internationale de Droit Comparé* (2001), pp. 127 ff.

[34] See the speech by Commissioner Marcos Kyprianou, made on 26 September 2005, in London: "I can indeed categorically state that we are *not* working on a European Civil Code. As early as 2001, in the first consultation round, it was very clear from the responses that this was not the favoured option. So, no Civil Code" (text available at http://ec.europa.eu/consumers/cons_int/safe_shop/fair_bus_pract/cont_law/conference26092005_en.htm).

[35] See the conclusions of the European Council of 28 and 29 November 2005, no. 10: "The Council of the European Union [...] welcomes [...] the Commission's repeated assurance that it does not intend to propose a 'European Civil Code' which would harmonise contract laws of Member States, and that Member States' differing legal traditions will be fully taken into account" (text available at http://www.europa.eu).

[36] In *Official Journal of the European Union,* no. C63, of 15 March 2003, pp. 1 ff.

The draft *Common Frame of Reference* was presented in 2008[37]. It contains principles, definitions and model rules relating to contractual and non-contractual obligations (the latter deriving from damage caused to third parties, from unjustified enrichment and from benevolent intervention in another's affairs). The introduction to this text reveals that its final version will also encompass ownership in movable property. Some of its principles and rules had already been included in the aforementioned *Principles of European Contract Law* drafted by the Commission on European Contract Law. According to its authors, the draft *Common Frame of Reference* does not merely aim at promoting the study of the European Union Member States' Private Law, but also at serving as a possible source of inspiration for national legislators and at helping in the process of improving the existing Community *acquis* and in drafting any future EU legislation in the field of Private Law. It is, thus, a *legislative guide*, with no normative force of its own. However, the said text has also been drawn up with a view to the possible drafting in the future of an *optional legal instrument*, by which parties might choose to govern their mutual rights and obligations, including in consumer transactions.

II—Other continents have also experienced important initiatives to harmonize and unify Private Law. In Africa, OHADA has achieved some success in this field, by adopting several Uniform Acts relating to business law. Such was the case with the Uniform Acts on securities, the carriage of goods by road, the law of commercial companies, the economic interest group and general commercial law (the latter one including a regulation of commercial sale which partly incorporates the Vienna Convention of 1980)[38]. One further Uniform Act, on Contract Law, is currently being prepared on the basis of the *Unidroit Principles*[39].

---

[37] See Christian von Bar et al. (eds.), *Principles, Definitions and Model Rules on EC Private Law: Draft Common Frame of Reference: Interim Outline Edition* (Munich, 2008). On the Common Frame of Reference, see: Christian von Bar, "Working Together Toward a Common Frame of Reference", *Juridica International* (2005), pp. 17 ff.; Nils Jansen, "European Civil Code", in Jan M. Smits (ed.), *Elgar Encyclopedia of Comparative Law,* (Cheltenham and Northampton, 2006), pp. 247 ff. (254 ff.).

[38] Texts available at http://www.ohada.com.

[39] See *Acte Uniforme OHADA Sur le Droit des Contrats: Avant-projet* (2004). On this, see Marcel Fontaine, *Acte Uniforme OHADA sur le Droit des Contrats: Note explicative à l'avant-projet* (available at http://www.unidroit.org); idem, "Le projet d'Acte Uniforme OHADA sur les contrats et les Principes d'Unidroit Relatifs aux

In Latin America, the Andean Community's Commission has also adopted several decisions in the field of Private Law, relating to the transportation of persons and goods, insurance and intellectual property.

Reasons that justify the harmonization and unification of Private Law

a) Legal certainty

We shall now try to determine the reasons that lie behind these initiatives for the harmonization and unification of laws.

In the first place, they are justified by the quest for *legal certainty in international transactions*, which, to a certain extent, is made possible by applying a uniform or at least harmonized set of rules to these transactions[40].

We should, however, bear in mind that harmonization and unification of the formal rules governing international trade, through supranational or international legislation, will often not suffice to eliminate the diversity of rules actually applied by the courts of the countries where those instruments are in force. This becomes quite clear when those rules resort to general clauses and vague concepts (which are frequently the result of arduous compromises arrived at in international fora), as is the case of several provisions of the Vienna Convention of 1980[41], and no international court is given the authority to ensure a uniform interpretation of those rules.

Furthermore, the recent proliferation of international agencies which aim at drafting and adopting instruments to harmonize and unify national laws

---

Contrats du Commerce International", *Uniform Law Review* (2004), pp. 253 ff.; Félix Onana Etoundi, "Les Principes d'Unidroit et la sécurité juridique des transactions commerciales dans l'avant-projet d'Acte uniforme OHADA sur le droit des contrats", *Uniform Law Review* (2005), pp. 683 ff.; and Dário Moura Vicente, "A unificação do Direito dos Contratos em África: seu sentido e limites" (forthcoming in *Boletim da Faculdade de Direito de Bissau*).

[40] See Michael Joachim Bonell, "Comparazione giuridica e unificazione del diritto", in Guido Alpa, Michael Joachim Bonell, Diego Corapi, Luigi Moccia, Vicenzo Zeno-Zencovich and Andrea Zoppini, *Diritto privato comparato: Istituti e problemi*, 5th ed. (Rome and Bari, 2004), pp. 3 ff. (26 ff.).

[41] See, e.g., articles 7, para. 1, and 8, para. 2.

paradoxically makes the attainment of harmony among those laws more difficult.

b) Market integration and the creation of a level playing field for competitors

Two of the most frequently invoked arguments in favor of initiatives to harmonize and unify Private Law are market integration and the inherent need to ensure a level playing field for competing undertakings.

It is, inter alia, stated that disparities in the current contract law, for example, of the Member States of the European Union (e.g. regarding buyers' warranties, liability for defective goods or services, the validity of certain general contractual clauses, etc.), operate as a barrier to free movement of goods and services and lead to inequalities in the playing field for competitors in the single market, and that these inequalities can only be overcome by unifying the rules on those topics. Economic integration would, in sum, require the unification of Private Law[42].

Yet this point of view has not gone unchallenged[43]. Obviously, it cannot

---

[42] See, in this sense, Ole Lando, "European Contract Law", in P. Sarcevic (ed.), *International Contracts and Conflicts of Law* (London, etc., 1990), pp. 1 ff. (6); idem, "Principles of European Contract Law: An Alternative or a Precursor of European Legislation", *Rabels Zeitschrift* (1992), pp. 261 ff. (264); idem, "Does the European Union need a Civil Code?", *Recht der Internationalen Wirtschaft,* (2003), pp. 1 ff.; Ulrich Drobnig, "Ein Vertragsrecht für Europa", in *Festchrift für Ernst Steindorff* (Berlin, 1990), pp. 1140 ff. (1145 ff.); Denis Tallon, "Vers un droit européen du contrat?", in *Mélanges Colomer* (Paris, 1993), pp. 485 ff. (485); Wienfried Tilmann, "Eine Privatrechtskodifikation für die Europäische Gemeinschaft?", in P.C. Müller-Graff (ed.), *Gemeinsames Privatrecht in der Europäischen Gemeinschaft* (Baden-Baden, 1993), pp. 485 ff. (490); Giuseppe Gandolfi, "Verso il tramonto del concetto di 'obbligazione' nella prospettiva di un codice único per l'Europa?", *Rivista di Diritto Civile* (1995, I), pp. 203 ff. (204); Hein Kötz, *Europäisches Vertragsrecht*, vol. I (Tübingen, 1996), p. v; Guido Alpa, "Nouvelles frontières du droit des contrats", *Revue Internationale de Droit Comparé* (1998), pp. 1015 ff. (1020); and Claude Witz, "Rapport de synthèse", in Christophe Jamin and Denis Mazeaud (eds.), *L'harmonisation du droit des contrats en Europe* (Paris, 2001), pp. 161 ff. (167 ff.). See also Arthur Hartkamp et al. (eds.), *Towards a European Civil Code*, 3rd. ed. (Nijmegen, 2004).

[43] This doubt is expressed in Arthur S. Hartkamp, "Modernisation and Harmonisation of Contract Law: Objectives, Methods and Scope", *Uniform Law Review* (2003), pp. 81 ff. (pp. 82 ff.); and Jan Smits, "Convergence of Private Law

be disputed that Private Law regimes have a significant impact on the economic conditions for undertakings acting in an integrated market. It is also undeniable that, in a single market, some harmonization of those regimes is necessary. This harmonization should be carried out through the adoption of *functionally equivalent* rules, capable of overcoming market failures, by imposing e.g. a certain level of information to consumers before and upon entering into a contract, so as to counter the asymmetries of information which frequently occur in such contracts.

However, as long as the rules on conflicts of laws are applied equally in each country to local citizens and to foreigners, the diversity of the substantive law in force in states belonging to an economically integrated market does not necessarily imply a distortion of the conditions to which competitors are subject. In fact, those rules usually allow the interested parties to choose, within certain limits, the law to be applied to the international contracts that they enter into. Thus, in international situations, the contracting parties may exclude the Private Law regimes which are less favorable to their interests, and they may agree which law will determine their contractual obligations and, consequently, the risks inherent in their economic activity.

On the other hand, as stated in several opinions of the European Court of Justice[44] and, more recently, in EU legislation[45] (even in issues of Private Law[46]), mutual recognition of legal situations validly created under the rules in force in the different Member States of a single market, relating to the exercise of certain economic activities, which may be deemed as functionally equivalent, makes it possible for one country's products and services, lawfully manufactured and traded in its territory, to be introduced into other countries, without having to conform to local legislation and, thus, without losing their competitive advantages[47].

---

in Europe: Towards a New *Ius Commune*?", in Esin Örücü and David Nelken (eds.), *Comparative Law: A Handbook* (Oxford and Portland, Oregon, 2007), pp. 219 ff. (221 ff., 236).

[44] See, e.g., the ruling of the European Court of Justice of 20 February 1979, *Rewe-Zentral AG c. Bundesmonopolverwaltung für Branntwein* (*Cassis de Dijon*), available at http://www.curia.eu.

[45] See, e.g., article 16, para. 1, of Directive 2006/123/EC, on the provision of services in the internal market.

[46] See article 3, para. 2, of Directive 2000/31/EC, on e-commerce. On this rule, see Dário Moura Vicente, *Problemática internacional da sociedade da informação* (Coimbra, 2005), pp. 203 ff.

[47] See Heinz-Peter Mansel, "Anerkennung als Grundprinzip des Europäischen

When applied to commercial companies, such recognition further allows companies incorporated in one country, in accordance with local laws, to carry out their activities in other countries without having to adjust to the requirements of these countries' laws, e.g. concerning the minimum capital to be provided by the partners, the powers of the respective bodies or the liability of their managers towards third parties[48].

Finally, the fact that some countries with a single internal market have different local legal systems which are in force in different parts of the respective territories (such as Canada, Spain, the United States of America and the United Kingdom), and which do not affect the normal functioning of the market, lends support to the idea that diversity of laws among different countries does not necessarily hamper the free movement of goods and services across borders and the equal standing of competitors.

Probably, linguistic diversity, barriers to long-distance communication, and bureaucratic formalities imposed by some countries on the entry of persons, goods, services and capital, have a greater impact as non-tariff barriers to cross-border trade.

c) Reduction of transaction costs

Furthermore, it is often argued that diversity of national laws increases certain transaction costs, such as information costs, which only harmonization or unification of laws could reduce or eliminate[49].

Rechtsraums. Zur Herausbildung eines europäischen Annerkennungs-Kollisionsrechts: Anerkennung statt Verweisung als neues Strukturprinzip des Europäischen internationalen Privatrechts?", *Rabels Zeitschrift für ausländisches und internationales Privatrecht* (2006), pp. 651 ff.; Mathias Audit, "Régulation du marché intérieur et libre circulation des lois", *Clunet* (2006), pp. 1333 ff.; Alfonso-Luis Calvo Caravaca and Javier Carrascosa González, *Derecho Internacional Privado*, vol. I, 8th ed. (Granada, 2007), pp. 322 ff.

48 See the ruling of the European Court of Justice of 9 March 1999, *Centros Ltd. contra Ehvervs- og Selskabsstyrelsen*, available at http://www.curia.eu, and Dário Moura Vicente, "Liberdade de estabelecimento, lei pessoal e reconhecimento das sociedades comerciais", in *Estudos em memória do Professor Doutor António Marques dos Santos*, vol. I (Coimbra, 2005), pp. 135 ff.

49 See Ugo Mattei, "A transaction costs approach to the European Code", *European Review of Private Law* (1997), pp. 537 ff.; Gerhard Wagner, "The Virtues of Diversity in European Contract Law", in Jan Smits (ed.), *The Need for a European Contract Law: Empirical and Legal Perspectives* (Groningen, 2005), pp. 3 ff.; Helmut Wagner, "Economic Analysis of Cross-Border Legal Uncertainty:

Indeed, it is said, undertakings wishing to export their products or services have higher costs as a result of the information which they must obtain concerning the legal regimes of the countries of destination of those products and services, in order to assess their potential liabilities; and consumers also incur those costs whenever they wish to challenge the defective nature of the products or services they acquired from undertakings established in a different country. Such costs would also derive from undertakings not being able to use the same types of contracts (and possibly not even the same company structure) in all countries where they offer their products or services.

In so far as they are usually passed on to those who acquire these undertakings' products or services, these costs imply higher prices and are, therefore, a burden on cross-border trade, nullifying the scale economies made possible by such trade and the inherent opportunities for economic growth. Also, when assessing the risk involved in international business transactions so as to grant credit thereto, financial institutions will normally take into account the legal uncertainty that results from the diversity of the applicable laws, which can thus also render such transactions more costly.

The importance of these issues need not be emphasised. It is, however, important to note that, rather than determining the existence of transaction costs associated with the diversity of national legal systems (which, in any case, are far from having been precisely calculated), it is more important to know whether these costs outweigh the benefits which can be derived from that diversity.

On the other hand, it should be noted that conflict-of-laws rules which, in the absence of a choice of the applicable law by the parties, determine the application of the law of the party that owes the characteristic performance—usually the exporter of the products or services in question—or of the law of the country of origin of the services or goods in question[50] (*home country rule*[51]), effectively reduce, to the benefit of that

---

The Example of the European Union", in ibid., pp. 27 ff.

[50] See article 4, para. 2, of the Rome Convention on Contractual Obligations. See also Hans-Bernd Schäfer and Katrin Lantermann, "Choice of Law from an Economic Perspective", in Jürgen Basedow and Toshiyuki Kono (eds.), *An Economic Analysis of Private International Law* (Tubinga, 2006), pp. 87 ff. (98 ff.).

subject, the costs and risks inherent in the application of a foreign law.

Limits to which harmonization and unification of Private Law are subject

a) Preservation of legal pluralism

One may also ask to what limits, if any, harmonization and unification of Private Law are subject.

In this regard, one must admit that the unification of national laws basically runs counter to the preservation of *legal pluralism* at the international level. Such preservation is desirable, even in a time of economic globalization, for three main reasons.

Firstly, this is because each people's national identity includes its *cultural identity* (which is constitutionally safeguarded in Portugal[52] and other countries[53]), and this comprises its legal identity.

Plurality of laws is, indeed, inherent to the diversity of cultures—i.e., to the diversity of customs and institutions which make up a community's social inheritance—and to the different valuation of the same issues by different local legal systems[54]. This is true even in legal areas which are sometimes deemed to be axiologically neutral or empty of cultural significance, such as contracts. Consider, for example, how national legal systems value differently the need to comply with certain pre-contractual duties and the defects of one's will which affect the decision to contract. Such differences reflect the diverse permeability of national communities to values such as individual freedom and solidarity. Consider also the

---

[51] See article 3, para. 1, of the e-commerce Directive, mentioned above.

[52] See Jorge Miranda, "Notas sobre cultura, Constituição e direitos culturais", *O Direito*, pp. 751 ff. (762).

[53] See Peter Häberle, *Verfassungslehre als Kulturwissenschaft,* 2nd. ed. (Berlin, 1998), pp. 10 ff.

[54] See Hugh Collins, "European Private Law and the Cultural Identity of States", *European Review of Private Law* (1995), pp. 353 ff.; Pierre Legrand, "Le primat de la culture", in Pascal Vareilles-Sommières, *Le droit privé européen* (Paris, 1998), pp. 1 ff. (10 ff.); idem, *Droit Comparé*, 2nd ed. (Paris, 2006); António Menezes Cordeiro, *Tratado de Direito Civil português*, I, *Parte geral*, vol. I, 3rd. ed. (Coimbra, 2005), p. 45; Alfonso-Luis Calvo Caravaca and Javier Carrascosa González, *Derecho Internacional Privado*, cit., p. 50.

different value awarded by national legal systems to verbal contracts, mirroring the diverse social relevance given to mutual trust between contracting parties.

As recognized in the *UNESCO Convention on the Protection and Promotion of the Diversity of Cultural Expressions*, adopted in 2005, cultural diversity is a *common heritage of humanity*, which must be preserved—even in politically and economically integrated areas such as those that exist in Europe, Africa, America and Asia.

Secondly, it should be borne in mind that legal pluralism guarantees the law's suitability to the real needs of the respective society and to the ethical-legal sentiment of those to whom it is addressed. Its preservation is, thus, necessary for the law's effectiveness: in order for the law to be a living reality, it must reflect the *soul* of the society it aims at regulating; otherwise, society will reject it.

Thirdly, it must be noted that competition between different models of legal regulation for the same social issues (i.e. regulatory competition) is desirable in itself, since it favors the adjustment of law to society's necessities and the correction of possible legislative errors, being therefore an element of progress[55]. In fact, this is just one of the many possible

---

[55] See Dário Moura Vicente, *Da responsabilidade pré-contratual em Direito Internacional Privado* (Coimbra, 2001), p. 357, and "Ofertas públicas de aquisição internacionais", in Alfonso-Luis Calvo Caravaca and Javier Carrascosa González (eds.), *Estudios sobre contratación internacional* (Madrid, 2006), pp. 373 ff. (reprinted in *Direito dos Valores Mobiliários,* vol. VII (Coimbra, 2007), pp. 465 ff.). See further on this subject: Hein Kötz, "Rechtsvereinheitlichung—Nutzen, Kosten, Methoden, Ziele", *Rabels Zeitschrift* (1986), pp. 1 ff.; Claus Canaris, "Theorienrezeption und Theorienstruktur", in *Wege zum japanischen Recht: Festschrift für Zentaro Kitagawa* (Berlin, 1992), pp. 59 ff. (93 ff.); Norbert Reich, "Competition between legal orders: a new paradigm of EC law?", *Common Market Law Review* (1992), pp. 861 ff.; Anthony Ogus, "Competition Between National Legal Systems: A Contribution of Economic Analysis to Comparative Law", *The International and Comparative Law Quarterly* (1999), pp. 405 ff.; idem, "The Economic Approach: Competition between Legal Systems", in Esin Örücü and David Nelken (eds.), *Comparative Law: A Handbook* (Oxford and Portland, Oregon, 2007), pp. 153 ff.; Paul B. Stephan, "The Futility of Unification and Harmonization in International Commercial Law", *Virginia Journal of International Law* (1999), pp. 788 ff.; Rodolfo Sacco, "La diversità nel diritto (a proposito dei problemi di unificazione)", *Rivista di Diritto Civile* (2000), pp. 15 ff. (21 ff.); Horatia Muir Watt, "The Challenge of Market Integration for European

expressions of the value of competition as a discovery procedure, as highlighted by Friedrich A. Hayek[56]. In this sense, it could be said that the diversity of national laws is a *source of efficiency*[57]. Unification of national laws, on the other hand, restricts competition between alternative solutions and implies certain costs (inherent, e.g., to the adjustment of non-unified law, to the training of jurists, to the translation of legal texts, etc.), which may exceed any economic benefit that could be derived from it.

In sum, there is an intrinsic value to plurality and diversity of laws[58]. It is in this light that one should understand the inclusion of the *principle of subsidiarity* in the European Community Treaty, under which the Community's legislative intervention, in areas which do not fall within its exclusive competence, should take place "only if and in so far as the objectives of the proposed action cannot be sufficiently achieved by the Member States and can therefore, by reason of the scale or effects of the proposed action, be better achieved by the Community"[59]. One must thus recognize that this Treaty does not grant the Community legislator a general competence to regulate the internal market[60] and that,

---

Conflicts Theory", in Arthur Hartkamp et al (eds.), *Towards a European Civil Code*, 3rd. ed. (Nijmegen, 2004), pp. 191 ff. (197 ff.); idem, "Concurrence d'ordres juridiques et conflits de lois de droit privé", *in* AAVV, *Le droit international privé: esprit et méthodes: Mélanges en l'honneur de Paul Lagarde* (Paris, 2005), pp. 615 ff.; Mathias Audit, "Régulation du marché intérieur et libre circulation des lois", *Clunet* (2006), pp. 1333 ff.; Jonathan Mance, "Is Europe Aiming to Civilise the Common Law?", *European Business Law Review* (2007), pp. 77 ff.; Luís de Lima Pinheiro, "Concorrência entre sistemas jurídicos na União Europeia e Direito Internacional Privado", *O Direito* (2007), pp. 255 ff.; Jan Smits, "Convergence of Private Law in Europe: Towards a New *Ius Commune*?", cit., pp. 234 ff.

56 See *Law, Legislation and Liberty*, vol. III (London, 1993), *The Political Order of a Free People,* pp. 67 ff.; "Competition as a Discovery Procedure", *The Quarterly Journal of Austrian Economics* (2002), pp. 9 ff.

57 See the speech by the then British Lord Chancellor, on 26 September 2005, (available at http://www.europa.eu). He stated: "blanket harmonization across the EU of contract law, or any other sphere of law, will not work. A single law imposed across the whole of the EU, whether by regulation or directive, is not an efficient and effective way to resolve problems in civil law and justice".

58 See Erik Jayme, "Zum Jahrtausendwechsel: Das Kollisionsrecht zwischen Postmoderne und Futurismus", *IPRax* (2000), pp. 165 ff. (168).

59 See art. 5 of the Treaty. On this provision, see Fausto de Quadros, *O princípio da subsidiariedade no direito comunitário após o Tratado da União Europeia* (Coimbra, 1995); Margarida Salema d'Oliveira Martins, *O princípio da subsidiariedade em perspectiva jurídico-política* (Coimbra, 2003).

60 See the ruling of the European Court of Justice of 5 October 2000, *Federal*

consequently, some room must be left to the Private Law regimes of each Member State, even in legal relations connected to two or more of those states.

b) Axiological and ideological differences

The very viability of complete unification of Private Law has been questioned. In fact, as is widely recognized, many of the differences between the laws of several countries in this field do not merely derive from legal technique, but are instead the result of meta-legal factors, including axiological and ideological ones, which a legislator is incapable of eliminating.

This is particularly clear, for example, with regard to pre-contractual liability[61]. The principle of good faith in contractual dealings, as well as the duties derived from it in several European laws, and, generally, the underlying *solidarism* in the Law of Obligations, have so far not been introduced into Common Law systems. Consequently, current English case-law does not allow for liability on the basis of an arbitrary break in contractual negotiations. Even in francophone legal systems it is not as broadly accepted as in, e.g., Portugal and Germany. But even if all national legal systems accepted this principle, it would certainly not have the same significance or impact in all of them[62].
The difficulties encountered by international initiatives for the unification of Private Law are also demonstrated, with regard to contracts, by the above mentioned Convention on Contracts for the International Sale of Goods, which took over half a century to be finalized, and still could not fully unify the rules on the relationships it envisaged.

Republic of Germany vs. The European Parliament and The Council of the European Union, available at http://www.curia.eu, which annulled Directive 98/43/EC, of 6 July 1998, on the harmonization of national laws on the advertising of tobacco products.

61 See, on this, Dário Moura Vicente, *Da responsabilidade pré-contratual em Direito Internacional Privado*, cit., pp. 239 ff.; idem, "Precontractual Liability in Private International Law: a Portuguese Perspective", *Rabels Zeitschrift für Ausländisches und Internationales Privatrecht* (2003), pp. 699 ff.

62 See Dário Moura Vicente, "A Convenção de Viena Sobre a Compra e Venda Internacional de Mercadorias: características gerais e âmbito de aplicação", in *Direito Internacional Privado. Ensaios*, vol. II (Coimbra, 2005), pp. 39 ff.

c) Procedural matters

It is equally noteworthy that, in the absence of a single international system of courts, the disparities between national laws would probably resurface through the interpretation of uniform law by national courts, especially when this contains general clauses or vague concepts with no tradition in those legal systems (such as the concept of good faith in English law).

One should also not overlook the inevitable impact of the differences between national procedural laws on the substantive solution of disputes submitted to courts. Mechanisms such as class actions, pre-trial discovery and juries, as well as the diverse distribution of tasks between judges and lawyers, are largely responsible for different solutions arrived at by American and European courts when addressing the same fundamental issues. From this perspective also, the uniformity of solutions envisaged by some international initiatives for the unification of Private Law proves elusive.

Coordination of national laws as an alternative

In conclusion, economic globalization does not require, nor does it necessarily lead to, complete unification of Private Law; instead, it highlights the importance—we would say, in many cases, the inevitability—of legal pluralism[63].

One of the greatest resulting challenges is, therefore, the need to find a desirable balance between *unity* and *diversity* of national laws. Certainly, we must eliminate unnecessary barriers to the circulation of persons and goods and to foreign investment; but national laws should not lose their individuality in that process.

And how should we ensure the *unity in diversity* (or *ordered pluralism*, as it is called by Mireille Delmas-Marty[64]) thus required?

---

[63] See Werner Menski, *Comparative Law in a Global Context*, 2nd. ed. (Cambridge, 2006), pp. 3 ff.; Duncan Fairgrieve and Horatia Muir Watt, *Common Law et tradition civiliste* (Paris, 2006), pp. 57 ff.; H. Patrick Glenn, *Legal Traditions of the World*, 3rd. ed. (Oxford, 2007), pp. 344 ff.

[64] See *Critique de l'intégration normative* (Paris, 2004), p. 19; *Les forces imaginantes du droit,* vol. II, *Le pluralisme ordonné* (Paris, 2006).

In order to do so, we must resort to Private International Law, since that objective implies a regulation of international trade which ensures both the coexistence of different national legal traditions and the fluidity of cross-border trade, which is possible only through the *coordination* of the national legal systems by rules of spatial conflicts of law, not through its unification.

One does not question that certain advantages can be derived from legislative unification in some areas, especially those of an economic nature. Yet unification should, in our opinion, be considered as a measure of *last resort*. Frequently, the creation and functioning of a single market can be assured by minimal harmonization, together with the parties' freedom to choose the law applicable to international contracts and the mutual recognition of legal situations validly created under those laws.

Where this coordination is in itself insufficient to comply with the requirements of international trade, harmonization and unification of national laws should, as far as possible, allow the interested parties to choose whether or not to subject themselves to the instruments in question, as has been the case in recent years with UNCITRAL and UNIDROIT instruments in several areas. This would allow uniform law to prevail thanks to its own merits.

GLOBALIZATION: THE NEED FOR CONVERGENCE AND BETTER KNOWLEDGE OF LEGAL SYSTEMS

MANUEL PORTO

1. Introduction

It makes sense to write about the coming developments of the world economies in an India-focussed book mainly concerned with legal problems.

We can discuss to what extent we will have a "flat world" (in the so well known characterisation of Friedman, 2005) in the 21st century; but it is certain that the openness of economies will continue, with all kinds of movements: of commodities, of services, of people and of capital[1].
And it is particularly relevant to have this evolution in mind in a paper to be published in a book under the heading "Civil Law Studies: An Indian Perspective," as the subcontinent is an extremely important example of the benefits of globalisation: probably the best example in the world of the benefits of global trade in services.

2. The new map of the world

It is now clear that we will have in the 21st century a new or renewed map of the world.

1.1. There are no accurate numbers, but it is sure that until the 15th century Asian countries, particularly China and India, were among the

[1] Perhaps with a much greater role for the regional blocs, with rising transport costs due to the increasing price of energy (see, with recent contributions, Limão and Venables, 2007, Rubin and Tal, 2008, and Krugman, 2008; cf. Rodrigues, 2008).

most developed countries of the world, with advanced cultural standard[2] and strong and diversified economies, not only producing primary products but manufacturing at the highest quality being achieved at the time (in, for example, ceramics and textiles).

It was of course the knowledge of these circumstances and of the quality of these products (not only spices, and in no case raw materials) which attracted the interest of the Europeans, intending to reach India (and shortly thereafter China) either by the east (as Vasco da Gama did) or by the west (as Cristóvão Colombo attempted, thinking that the American landmass was part of India).

1.2. An important change occurred with the discoveries beginning with the Portuguese navigators and followed by explorers from other European countries.

In the centuries up to this point, communications between continents were dangerous and expensive, therefore scarce. For this reason, the improvement in communications by sea was the point of departure for globalisation[3].

A better knowledge of navigation gave to the Europeans the opportunity to reach all the other continents in much better conditions. But it remains difficult to explain how Europeans could retain supremacy all over the world for four centuries: over territories that were not only much more populated but also richer than Europe[4].

In particular, we should remember that in 1820, China still had 28.7% of global GDP and India 13.4% (so the two together 42.1%), when (in terms of the later territories of these countries) France had 5.5 %, the Soviet

---

[2] Recent descriptions of this situation can be seen in Sen 2005 and in Baru 2006, also showing the interrelationship and the good relations that existed for centuries between India and China.

[3] The contribution of Portugal to the openness of the world economy is well expressed in the titles (and contents) of two books: Charles Vindt, *Globalisation, from Vasco da Gama to Bill Gates* (1999) and Martin Page, *The First Global Village: How Portugal Changed the World* (2002). Vasco da Gama became famous precisely for reaching India, in 1498.

[4] Even having in mind the usual arguments of better technology, in particular in navigation, or better weapons; which of course could be imitated, without difficulty, by so advanced Asian countries.

Union also 5.5 %, the United Kingdom 5 %, Japan 3.1%, Germany 2.4%, Spain 1.9%, the United States 1.8%, Indonesia 1.6% and Pakistan 1.0% (see Maddison, 1995, annexe C, and Wei, 2006, pp.55–6). The effects of the industrial revolution, with its origin in England in the 18th century, cannot explain the already existing dominance of Europe, nor the dominance which prevailed in the two following centuries.

1.3. In the 20th century there was already a bi-polar or a tri-polar world.

This century was especially relevant to this situation, since its early decades saw the emergence of the United States of America (USA) as both a political and an economic world power.

In the political arena, after the Second World War, there was a bi-polar world, with the "cold war" between capitalism and communism: the capitalist "bloc" led by the United States and the communist "bloc" by the Soviet Union.

This was a situation which disappeared with the failure of communism, near the end of the century. And the fall of communism was indeed to a great extent due to the economic incapacity of that system, at least after a certain degree of development.

In the economic arena, disputing the world markets, we have recently had a tri-polar world, the so called "triade", composed of the United States, the European Union (an increasingly integrated economic space) and Japan.
It is a picture well illustrated by map 1.

Map 1: Countries´ GDPs (absolute values)

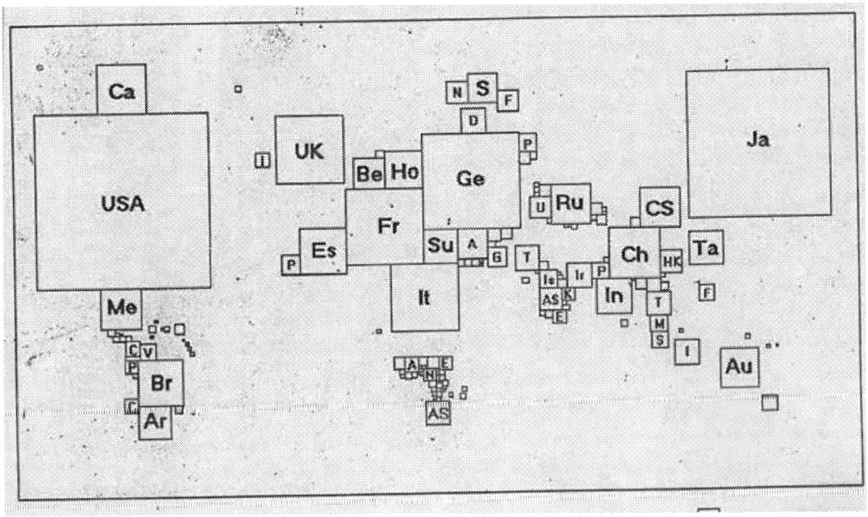

Source: *L´Etat du Monde 96*
Scale: 100 billion US dollars

It is, however, certain that in the 21st century we will have a new or renewed map of the world: a map in which the "triade" will remain, but in which, together with new members, we will have again China and India as world powers.

This probable evolution can be seen in figure 1:

Figure 1: Countries' GDPs (percentages)

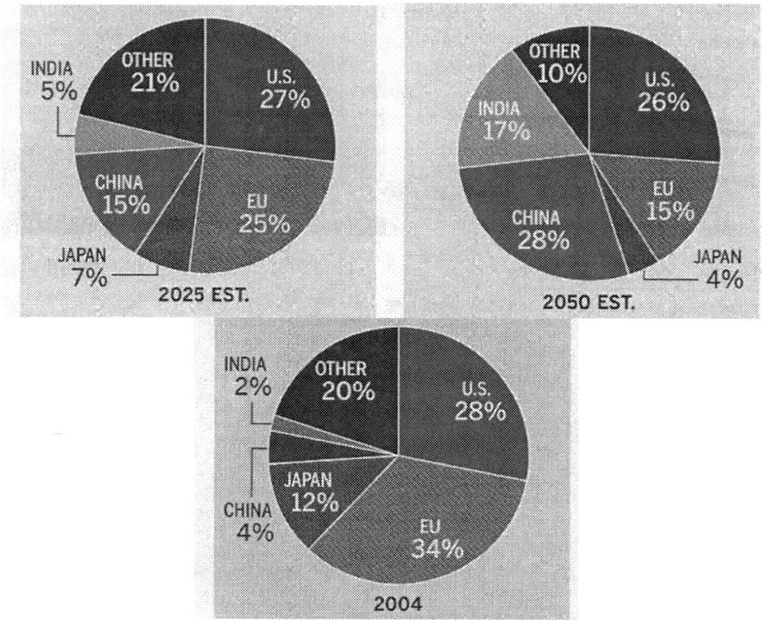

Source: *Business Week,* 22–29 August 2005, p.38

In 2004 China and India, which, as pointed out, in 1820 still produced 42% of world economic output, had fallen to producing 6% (China contributing 4% and India with 2%).
It is, however, predicted that by 2025 they will account for 20%, but both still behind the US, with 27 %, and the EU, with 25%.[5]

The picture predicted for 2050 is quite different again, China being then expected to produce 28% of world output, India 17% (so, the two

[5] The much better forecasts for the USA than for the EU depend on the better performance of that country in the last few years, before 2007. The situation has, however, changed quite recently, with the US economy growing 1.5% in 2008, where the Euro zone (the area where the euro is used as the single currency) grew 1.6%, it being predicted that in 2009 both will grow by 1.2 % (*Economist* of 30th August–5th September 2008, p.85).

countries together will account for 45% of the total![6]), the USA 26%[7], the EU 15% and Japan 4%.

With this evolution, in particular the steady increase of the GDPs of China and of India[8], already more than 10 years from its beginning, the map of GDPs, map 1, will become closer to the map of populations (map 2):

It is of course not certain that the growth forecasts will be fulfilled. In particular, difficulties may perhaps arise (though we hope not) in the growth processes of China and India[9]. Moreover, an important role should be expected also from the two other BRIC´s, Brazil and Russia[10], the first one with a rate of growth of 4.6% foreseen for 2008 (see, again, figure 1 in

---

[6] In the words of an Indian author (Baru 2006, pp. 26–7), "in the pre-colonial world, India, China and Europe were the three poles of equal power. European colonisation weakened India and China. The history of the 20th century has been the history of recovering this process. In the 21st century India and China will regain their place in a new 'multipolar,' or 'poli-centric' world in which the United States will continue to be the pre-eminent power but will have to accommodate the aspirations of many other nations, including India"(see also Frank 1998, pp.126–7 and Fernandes 2005, pp. 204–5).

Anticipating some features of the 21st century see also, for example, Dicken 2003, or, more recently and also considering non-economic circumstances, Gnesotto and Grevi 2007–8.

[7] With pessimistic views on the evolution of the USA (mainly in the political sphere), being more optimistic about the prospects of the European Union, see Kupchan 2002, Rifkin 2005, Schnabel 2005, and Leonard 2005, speaking in terms of a "European invisible hand", or McCormick 2007, writing of a "European civil power". The US has, however, in different fields good arguments to respond to the challenges of the 21st century.

Of course, we should expect that with the improvement of European competitive conditions (see Porto 2007a and 2007b), by 2050 the EU will be well above the percentage shown in figure 1.

[8] In the Appendix, in figure 1, are reproduced the IMF forecasts for 2008, with China growing 10% and India 8.4% (Angola having the highest rate of economic growth in the world, with 27.4%).

[9] Among a growing literature on the economies and on other conditions in these two countries reference can be made, on China, to Gu 2001, Lenoine 2006, Hutton 2007–8 or Leonard 2008; and on India to Das 2002, Acharya 2003, Boillot 2006, Luce 2006 or Kandar 2007.

[10] Goldman Sachs, after having distinguished the BRICs, in a 2008 report distinguishes *The Next Eleven*. But it is certain that other countries will also emerge economically in the multipolar world of 21st century, both larger and smaller.

the Appendix: with a rich agriculture, enormous mineral resources and quite developed manufacturing in some sectors, for example aircraft production) and Russia with a foreseen rate of growth of 6.5% in 2008 (loc cit.: with enormous energy resources and the largest territory of the world, between Europe and Asia).

Map 2: World population

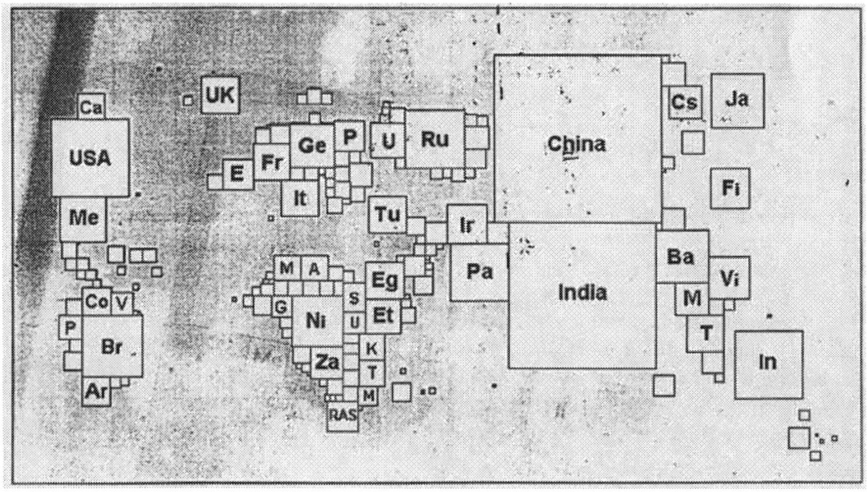

The role that small countries can play, in Europe and in the other continents, should, however, be mentioned at this point. The first cases of great success in Asia were the so-called Asian Tigers, countries of small size and population. But the European case (including non-EU countries) is also significant, with the success of smaller countries, some of them with the highest GDP per capita (six small countries have the highest GDP per capita of the EU-27, pushing Germany into seventh position) and with some of the biggest firms of the world: knowing from the beginning that they could not depend on the national market or even on the European market, they have always followed outward-looking policies (see Dumoulin and Duchenne, eds., 2002, including a paper of Porto, and the references made here; and also Porto, 2004(9), pp. 175–6).

3. With the convergence of economies, an increasing role for intra-industry trade (IIT), for trade of intermediate goods (inputs) and for trade of services

The traditional pattern of international trade, in particular between countries of different degrees of development, was trade of different finished goods, the entire chain of production being in the same country (or only raw materials being imported). Most textbooks on international economics reproduce the famous example of Ricardo (1817), England exporting textiles to Portugal and Portugal exporting wine to England.

The convergence of countries, with their development, an easier access to technological improvements, a general improvement in education of the people (albeit with important differences between countries) and of course also better transport and communications, has led in recent decades to a new pattern of competitive advantage and trade.

Now many less developed countries are no longer specialized only in the export of raw materials and primary products; in several cases they have also developed diversified manufacturing products (in some cases, leaving the category of less developed countries altogether).

With this development, we see an increasing number of countries exporting and importing products in the same sectors.

The evolution of IIT in Europe clearly showed this pattern of convergence. In the 60s (of the 20th century) the degree of IIT was already high in the more industrialized countries, but very low in Greece, Portugal and Spain. However, since then a sharp increase has occurred in these countries, with the convergence of the economies[11].

Looking at trade between the European Union and third countries, the expected results are found, with high levels of IIT with high-income countries and low levels of IIT with low-income countries (high-intermediate and low-intermediate being in between)[12]. Today, we also

---

[11] See Brilhart and Elliot 1999, pp.107–9, and Porto and Costa 1999, on the Portuguese case.

[12] These differences, represented in a figure, can be seen in Belessiotis *et al.* 2006, pp. 38–9, with data from the European Commission, 2005.

have an evolution towards higher levels of IIT with some countries previously having lower incomes.

In many cases IIT, or trade in general, is trade in intermediate goods (inputs), firms buying them wherever they are offered on better terms (outsourcing). The increase in the percentage of intermediate goods in international trade was high between 1995 and 1999, but, curiously, not between this year and 2002[13].

Finally, another feature in recent patterns of international trade, with special relevance to India, is the increase in trade of services, justifying the creation of the GATS (General Agreement on Trade in Services), with the Uruguay Round.

This is a development which should be expected. The services sector now accounts for over 70% of GDP in the more advanced economies and 50% in developing countries. However, for the time being, only 10% of services are traded, compared with 50% for manufacturing. With new extremely favourably conditions (in particular with new technologies) which will be discussed later, there is indeed "a clear potential for continued rapid expansion" (Belessiotis et al., 2006, p. 42): an estimated annual increase of 30% between 2003 and 2008, according to McKinsey & Company (2005, pp.17–8).

Also with services, in an increasing number of cases it is not trade of finished goods (services) which is involved, but trade of services which constitute inputs for different activities, for the supply of other services (e.*g*. travelling or banking services) or for manufacturing[14].

Finally, in the provision of services we can also see a clear convergence between economies, with thus far less developed countries providing

---

[13] See again Belessiotis et al., op. cit., p.38.

[14] India has the world's largest role in the outsourcing of services, with 12.2% of the total, followed by Ireland (a good example for other European countries, even with high wages) with 8.6 % (see McKinsey & Company, 2005, p. 13).

Interesting examples from India can be seen in Friedman 2005–6, with the particular specialization of Bangalore; and a similar evolution can be seen in China, currently providing 3.4% of the total, with Dallian, for example, having a special role in outsourcing for Japanese firms.

The possibility is increasing that important services (inputs) for public administration are also supplied by outsourcing (McKinsey, op. cit., p.55).

services of increasingly high quality. They are no longer just the less specialized services provided in the call centers; increasingly, there is more participation, for example in more requiring back offices, in programming (*e.g.* for offices of taxation in the USA), in medical diagnosis, in engineering and architectural projecting or in activities of scientific and technological research (R & D).

Comparing India with China, the following figure (figure 2) shows that the success of India is mainly based on the exports of services, *e.g.* by outsourcing , while China is performing much better in manufacturing:

Figure 2: India v. China

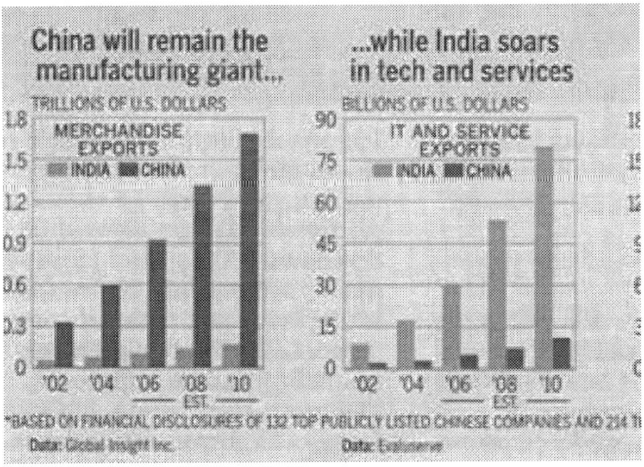

Source: *Business Week* of 22–29 August 2005, p.34

4. A foreseeable greater openness of economies, despite difficulties in the WTO negotiations

Even with the acknowledgement of the better arguments in favour of free trade and of free economy, according to theory and experience[15], we should always expect that in periods of difficulty protectionist temptations arise again[16].

It is interesting to see today a clear change of attitude in more developed countries relative to free trade in manufacturing and in services. Traditionally they have been protectionist for agricultural products, three main examples being the "triade": the European Union, with the Common Agricultural Policy, the United States, with enormous public subsidies (of course now—though not during the Uruguay Round—also contested by many less developed countries) and Japan, with extremely strong protectionist measures. Already, in manufacturing and in the provision of services the industrialized countries were generally in favour of free trade. A clear change of attitude can be noticed today, with delocalisations to and outsourcing from less developed countries[17]. But both in Europe and in the United States the institutions and most economists continue to promote free trade, of course together with the required measures for the restructuring of sectors, the promotion of competition and compensation for the people, sectors and regions harmed by globalisation.

Among an extensive and expanding literature in favour of globalisation (e.g. bearing in mind the movements toward delocalisation and outsourcing)

---

[15] The results of thorough researches made by institutions of the greatest prestige, such as the OECD, the World Bank and the National Bureau of Economic Research (see the references in Porto, 2001(4), pp.32–6),were quite clear, as well as the conclusions of well-known economists, such as Sachs and Werner (1995), Frankel and Romer (1999), Wang, Liu and Wei (2004) and Santos-Paulino (2005).

[16] This is clearly an area in which, according to the theory of "public choice" ("economic theory of politics"), well organized groups (including trade unions and associations of entrepreneurs, lobbying together, with a common interest in the protection of their sectors), are able to organize themselves and lobby with success. This is not the case with the main beneficiaries of free trade, the consumers (see the references in Porto, 2001(9), pp. 165–73).

[17] On the change of attitude of the people relative to delocalisation and outsourcing see Belessiotis et al.2006, p.13, pointing out as well (p.40) other factors leading to a great extent to the present levels of unemployment (see again Porto, 2007a and 2007b).

Up to now the European movement of delocalisation has been primarily to the previously communist countries of Central and Eastern Europe.

special reference may be made to Bhagwati 2004 and Bhagwati, Panagariya and Srinivasan 2004; on and arising doubts, to Samuelson 2004[18] or to Stiglitz 2002[19].
In any case, it is clear that the movement of openness will go on, despite delays and difficulties in the negotiations of the World Trade Organization.

Of course, each country or bloc (in the case of the EU, necessarily with a common position, being a customs union) will always try to have the highest gains and the lowest losses, even if these are only short-term losses, in many cases trying to postpone the effects. But the overall gains of trade finally lead the countries to accept the negotiations.

In particular, realistically, no-one can expect that other countries accept their protectionist measures without retaliation. Some protectionist defenders seem to have a "dream" of no reaction: their home countries would establish or increase barriers, while the others, "friendly", would remain with fully open borders.

This is something which Europe should have particularly in mind, having usually a surplus in the balance of trade (which is not the case of the United States, with a large deficit)[20]. In 2006 the Euro zone had a trade

---

[18] The doubts of Samuelson were dispelled by Bhagwati, Panagarya and Srinivasan (2004; see also for example Fontagné 2005, pp. 12–4, and Monteagudo 2005, pp.10–1).

Bhagwati was among the first contributors to the theory of domestic divergences (see Bhagwati and Ramaswamo 1963, and Bhagwati 1971); and it is interesting to see the role of Indian economists (of course together with many others), most of them up to now professors in the leading universities of the United States, in defending free trade views since long before the opening-up of the economy of their country of origin.

[19] Stiglitz became perhaps the most quoted critical author, with his book from 2002 (*Globalization and its Discontents*). But he seems to have a more positive view in his more recent book (2005, with Charlton), in a position reflected also in the title of the book (*Fair Trade for All: How Trade can Promote Development*), in which the previous book is not mentioned.

[20] Not only in commodities but also in services Europe is the main world actor, with surpluses, as the biggest exporter, with 27.7% of the total, and the biggest importer, with 25.0% of the total, in the world (the USA having 20.2% of global trade in services). And, in the words of Amiti and Wei (2005) "trade in services, like trade in goods, is a two-way street".

The European Union remains also by far the largest destination of foreign direct investment, as shown in the following table (see also fig.2 in the Appendix).

surplus of 1.5 billion euros, with 113 billion euros of exports and 111.5 billion euros of imports.

Of course, a general retaliation of the other countries of the world would in the end have more costs than benefits for the Europeans[21].

It should finally be stressed that a revival of protectionism would perhaps be possible for commodities, with limitations (even prohibitions) at the borders of countries. This is however a possibility not available for many services, in their immateriality, with new technologies of communication,

---

Table (with percentages) :

Région	1986 1990	1991 1992	1993 1998	1999 2000	2001 2004	2005 2006
Developed countries	82.41	66.50	60.92	78.25	68.98	64.30
European Union	36.26	45.29	31.73	46.90	45.38	41.77
Japan	0.20	1.22	0.33	0.85	1.05	-0.17
United States	34.60	12.68	21.78	24.14	13.63	12.28
NAFTA	39.96	19.14	28.81	29.04	18.30	18.35
Developing countries	17.44	21.27	35.50	19.57	27.53	30.79
Latin America and Caraiben	5.03	11.73.	12.39	8.28	8.98	7.07
Mercosul	1.44	3.10	4.37	3.90	2.82	2.05
Asia-Pacific	10.60	17.39	21.33	10.47	16.10	20.82
Africa	1.82	2.16	1.77	0.82	2.44	2.90
Central Europe	0.15	2.23	3.58	2.18	5.47	3.41
Less developed countries	0.40	0.60	0.65	0.38	1.20	0.74

Source: Mouhoud (2008, p.23).

With 41.77% of the total, the European Union has more than twice the inward investment of the enormous and growing space which is in the second position, the Asia-Pacific area; while the NAFTA has 18.35% and the USA 12.28%, not much more than a quarter.

[21] Public opinion is however concerned by the great and increasing deficit of the European Union (and other countries and areas) with China. All efforts should therefore be made to force this country to follow "the rules of the game", where they are not being followed, and to increase European competitiveness (see Schambaugh et al., eds., 2008).

On the challenges of China and India on another continent, Latin America, see Lederman, Olarreaga and Peery ed. (2008). And on the environmental problems caused by the growth of China see World Bank (2008).

without difficulties and very low costs of transmission: services being provided instantaneously in any point of the world.

Having in mind the lessons of history, it can be said that to a great extent the loss of power by China and India in the last four or five centuries was due to their inward-looking policies: with implications in various areas. And it is clear that their actual success is due to the opening-up of their economies (beginning with Deng Xiao Peng in China and Manmohan Singh in India).

With the right policies, the steady economic growth of the biggest (i.e. most populous) countries of the world is particularly welcome: firstly, because only in this way are quick improvements of the living conditions of hundreds of million of people made possible[22]; and secondly, it is a unique occasion opening up opportunities for European entrepreneurs.
If Europe follows their bad previous example with protectionism and avoiding globalization (nowadays delocalization and outsourcing), in the third millennium we will probably have in Europe the evolution (involution) of China and India in the second half of the second millennium.

In the sixties Gunnar Myrdal wrote a very influential book with the significant title *Asian Drama* (1968). If Europe does not follow the right strategy, strengthening its competitiveness with open borders (without protectionism), within a few years somebody will write a book on the *European Drama.*

It would be suicide, bad for Europe and for the other countries of the world, who rightly expect from Europe a space of cooperation[23] and of opportunities[24], to continue disputing markets all over the world.

---

[22] It is reported that in the time of Mao Zedong 30 million people died of starvation in China. On the Indian case see for example Sen 1991.
[23] Europe is by far the biggest contributor to aiding less developed countries. Besides the contribution of the EU budget and of the European Development Fund (EDF), only European countries having contributions over the minimum suggested by the United Nations: 0.7 percent of national GDP (see figure 3, in the Appendix, with a picture which is not improving with time).
[24] In particular African countries can not have, outside Europe, meaningful markets for their exports (see Porto, 2001(9), p. 514).

5. The need of a convergence and a better knowledge of legal systems

With the acknowledgement of the impossibility and in any case of the disadvantages of protectionist policies, the main path to follow is to increase the conditions of competitiveness of both countries and regional blocs[25].

But special attention is being given, as well, to a much better knowledge of legal systems, probably leading in some cases to significant convergences.

Firstly, this knowledge is required for business, for example for trade or for the delocalization of firms or branches of firms. Only through this is it possible to have a good understanding of the opportunities: seeing whether they are worthwhile or not, and if so exploiting them to the maximum extent.

Secondly, it is required to see to what extent legal conditions are perhaps a burden for domestic firms; creating the possibility of competing with more favourable legal systems.

This can be the case with administrative law, if one country has a more bureaucratic and complicated system; with commercial law, if in one country it is more difficult to form or to develop the activity of a firm; with tax law, if the other countries have lower rates or more tax exemptions; with environmental law, if there are big differences in the requirements made; etc.

Nowadays, much-discussed issues include labour laws and environmental laws, in particular the more "protectionist" European social model and our higher environmental concerns being compared with much less demanding systems.

---

[25] These acknowledgements are well reflected in the policies of the European Union (see for example once more Porto, 2007a and 2007b, in particular the references made; with the worries on world competitiveness reflected in the priorities of the Financial Perspectives for 2007–2013: see Porto, 2006).

We should not expect a total or even close convergence of legal systems: in many cases cultural or other national conditions do justify different laws.

A good knowledge of other systems is in any case required to make sensible changes to the national systems (or, in this case, the EU legal framework).

6. An increasing role for the world institutions

With globalization, of course, an increasing number of issues arise between countries or entrepreneurs of different blocs.

World institutions should therefore be increasingly committed to promote fair global competition. Only through them can unfair competition, stemming from differences between legal systems, be avoided.

Among them, a special role should be expected from the World Trade Organization, where in fact in recent years attention being given to new areas, for example foreign investment, intellectual property and taxation (an area in which the role of the OECD has been also very important).
And even where specialized world organizations exist, as is the case with the International Labour Organization and environmental organizations, we should expect from the more demanding system of the World Trade Organization the full accomplishment of the "rules of the game"[26].

[26] On this institution see the recent books of Mota (2005) and Cunha (2008).

Appendix

Fig. 1: Expected GDP growth in 2008

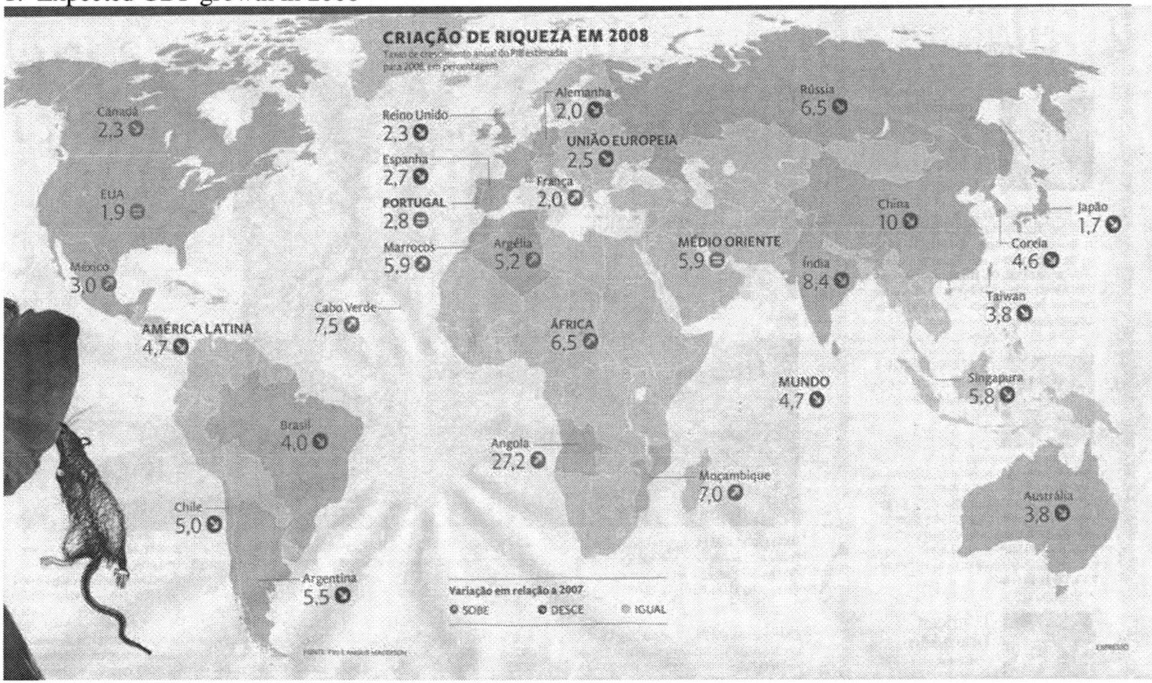

Source: International Monetary Fund (IMF)

Fig.2: Foreign Direct Investment

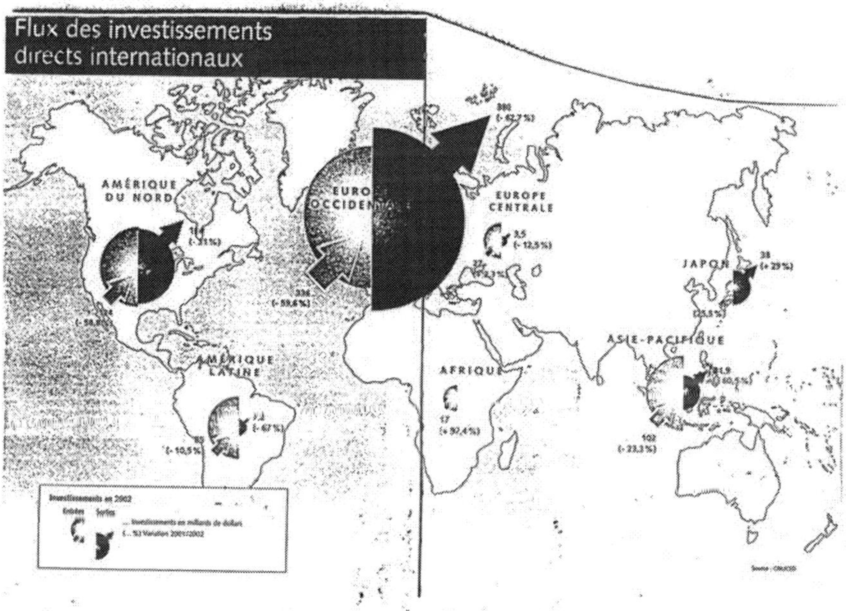

Fig. 3: European Donations to other Countries

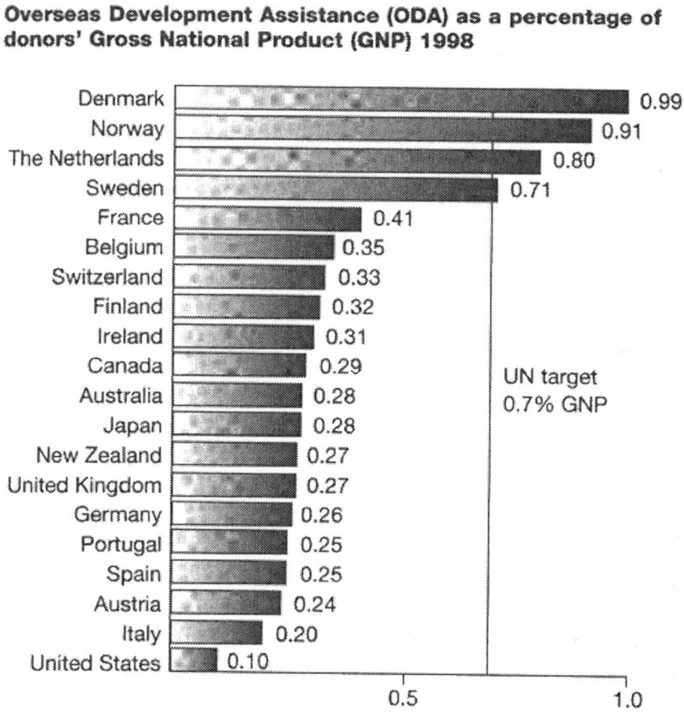

Source: Black 2002, p. 31)

References

Acharya, Shanka, *India´s Economy: Some Issues and Answers*, (New Delhi: Academic Foundation, 2003)

Amiti, M. and Wei, S., "Fear of Service Outsourcing: Is it justified?", in *Economic Policy*, April 2005 (London: CEPR)

Baru, Sanjaya, *Strategic Consequences of India´s Economic Performance*, (New Delhi: Academic Foundation, 2006)

Belessiotis, Tassos, Levin, Mattias and Veugelers, Reinhilde (coords.), *EU Competitiveness and Industrial Location*, (Brussels: European Commission, Bureau of European Policy Advisers, 2006)

Bhagwati, Jagdish N., "The Generalized Theory of Distortions and Welfare", in Jagdish N. Bhagwati, Ronald W. Jones, Robert A.

Mundell and Jeroslav Vaneck (eds.), *Trade, Balance of Payments and Growth: Papers in International Economics in Honor of Charles P. Kindleberger*, (Amsterdam and London: North-Holland Publishing Company, 1971), pp. 69-90

—, *In Defense of Globalization*, (New York: Oxford University Press, 2004)

Bhagwati, Jagdish N., Panagariya, Arvinds and Srinivasan, T.N., "The Muddles over Outsourcing", in *Journal of Economic Perspectives*, vol. 18, pp. 93–114

Bhagwat, Jagdish N. and Ramaswami, V.K., "Domestic Distortions, Tariffs and the Theory of Optimum Subsidy", in *The Journal of Political Economy,* vol. 71 (1963), pp. 44–50

Black, Maggie, *The Nonsense Guide to International Development*, (Oxford: New International Publications, 2002)

Boillot, Jean-Joseph, *L'Économie de l'Inde*, (Paris: Repères, La Découverte, 2006)

Brulhart, Marius and Hine, Robert C. (eds.), *Intra-Industry Trade and Adjustment: The European Experience*, (London: Macmillan, and New York: St.Martin's Press, 1999)

Cunha, Luis Pedro, *O Sistema Comercial Multilateral e os Espaços de Integração Regional*, (Coimbra: Coimbra Editora, 2008)

Das, Gurcharan, *India Unbound. From Independence to the Global Information Age*, (New Delhi: Penguin, 2002)

Dicken, Peter, *Global Schif: Reshaping the Global Map in the 21st Century*, 4th ed., (London: Sage, 2003)

Dumoulin, Michel and Duchenne, Genevieve, *Les Petits États et la Construction Européenne*, (Brussles: PIE–Peter Lang, 2002)

European Commission, *EU Sectoral Competitiveness Indicators*, (Brussels, 2005)

Fernandes, José Pedro Teixeira, *Elementos de Economia Política Internacional*, (Coimbra: Almedina, 2005)

Fontagné, Lionel, *Faut-il Avoir Peur des Délocalisations ?,* in *En Temps Réel*, Cahier 21 (2005)

Frank, Andre Gunder, *ReOrient: Global Economy in the Asian Age*, (Berkeley: University of California Press, 1998)

Frankel, Jeffrey A. and Romer, David, "Does Trade Cause Growth?", in *The American Economic Review*, vol. 89 (1999), pp.379–99

Friedman, Thomas L., *The World is Flat: A Brief History of the Twenty-First Century*, (New York: Farrar, Straus and Giroux, 2005) (Portuguese ed., Lisboa: Actual Editora, 2006)

Gnesotto, Nicole e Grevi, Giovanni, *Le Monde en 2025*, (Paris: Robert Laffont, 2007/8) (tr. into Portuguese as *O Mundo em 2025 segundo os especialistas da União Europeia* (Lisboa: Bizâncio, 2008)

Gu, Zhibin, *Made in China: O Maior Palco da Globalização no Século XXI*, (V.N. Famalicão: Centro Atlântico, 2005)

Hutton, Will, *The Writing on the Wall: The West in the 21st Century*, (London: Abacus, 2007/8)

Jin, Jang C., *On the Relationship Between Openness and Growth in China: Evidence from Provincial Time Series Data*, in *The World Economy*, vol. 27 (2004), pp. 1571–82

Kandar, Mira, *Planet India: The turbulent Rise of the world´s largest democracy*, (London: Pocket Books, 2007)

Krugman, Paul, "The World Gets Bigger", in the *New York Times* of 15.01.2008

Kupchan, Charles A., *The End of the American Era: US Foreign Policy and the Geopolitics of the Twenty-First Century*, (New York: Vintage, 2002)

Lederman, Daniel, Olarreaga, Marcelo and Perry, Guilhermo (eds.), *China and India's Challenge to Latin America: Opportunity or Threat?* (Washington: World Bank, 2008)

Lemoine, Françoise *L´Économie de la Chine*, (Paris: Repères, La Découverte, 2006)

Leonard, Mark, *Why Europe will run the 21st Century*, (London and New York: Fourth Estate, 2005)

—. *What does China Think?*, (London and New York: Fourth Estate, 2008)

Limão, Nuno and Venables, Anthony J., *Infrastructure, Geographical Disadvantage, Transport Costs and Trade* (mimeo, 2007)

Luce, Eduard, *In Spite of the Gods: The Strange Rise of Modern India*, (London: Brown, 2006)

Maddison, Angus, *Monitoring the World Economy: 1820–1992*, (Paris: OECD, 1995)

McCormick, *The European Superpower*, (Basingstoke and New York: Palgrave Macmillan, 2007)

McKinsey & Company, *The Emerging Global Labour Market*, (June, San Francisco, McKinsey Global Institute, June 2005)

Monteagudo, Josefina, *A Brief Review of the Literature on Offshoring*, (Brussels: Directorate General for Enterprise and Industry, European Commission, February 2005)

Mota, Pedro Infante, *O Sistema GATT / OMC: Introdução Histórica e Princípios Fundamentais,* (Coimbra: Almedina, 2005)

Mouhoud, El Mouhoub, *Mondialisation et Délocalisation des Entreprises*, (Paris: Repères, La Découverte, 2008)

Myrdal, Gunnar, *Asian Drama: An Inquiry into the Poverty of Nations*, (New York: Pantheon, 1968)

Page, Martin, *The First Global Village: How Portugal Changed the World*, (Lisboa: Notícias, 2002)

Porto, Manuel, *Teoria da Integração e Políticas Comunitárias*, 3rd ed., (Coimbra, 2001; 4th ed. Of 2009) (English ed., Macau: Institute of European Studies, 2004, and Chinese ed., Macau: University of Macau, 2004)

—. "The Role of Small States in the European Union", in Dumoulin and Duchenne (eds.) 2002, pp.159–79

—. *Economia: Um Texto Introdutório*, 2nd ed., (Coimbra: Almedina, 3rd ed., 2009)

—. *O Orçamento Comunitário: As Perspectivas Financeiras para 2007-2013*, (Coimbra: Almedina, 2006)

—. "Deslocalizações e Fornecimentos Externos ('outsourcing'): Algo de Novo para a Teoria e para as Políticas Económicas?", in *Nos 20 Anos do Código das Sociedades Comerciais: Homenagem aos Profs. Doutores A. Ferrer Correia, Orlando de Carvalho e Vasco Lobo Xavier*, (Coimbra: Coimbra Editora, 2007), pp.397–429

—. "The New Map of the World", in *Temas de Integração*, n 24, 2nd semester (2007), pp. 9–36

Porto, Manuel and Costa, Fernanda, "Portugal", in Brulhart and Hine (eds.) 1999., pp.239–51

Ricardo, David, *The Principles of Political Economy and Taxation* (1817) (Portuguese ed., Lisboa: Fundação Calouste Gulbenkian, 1965)

Rifkin, Jeremy, *The European Dream: How Europe´s Vision of the Future is Quietly Eclipsing the American Dream*, (Cambridge (UK): Polity, 2005)

Rodrigues, Jorge Nascimento, "Deslocalização posta em causa com o choque petrolífero", in *Expresso* of 15.08.2008

Rubin, Jeff and Tal, Benjamin, "Will Soaring Transport Costs Reverse Globalization?", in *StrategEco*, May 2008, pp. 4–7

Samuelson, Paul A., "Where Ricardo and Mill Rebut and Confirm Arguments of Mainstream Economists Supporting Globalization, in *Journal of Economic Perspectives*, vol. 18 (2004), pp. 135–46

Santos-Paulino, Amelia, "Trade Liberalisation and Economic Performance: Theory and Evidence for Developing Countries", in *The World Economy*, vol. 28 (2005), pp.783–821

Shambaugh, David, Sandsschneider, Eberhard and Hong,Zhou (eds.), *China-Europe Relations: Perceptions, Policies and Prospects*, (London and New York: Routledge, 2008)

Schnabel, Rockwell A., *The Next Superpower? The Rise of Europe and its Challenge to the United States*, (Lanham: Rowman & Littlefield, 2005)

Sen, Amartya, *Development as Freedom*, (New York: Anckor Books, 1991) (Port. ed.: Gradiva)

—. *The Argumentative India: Writings on Indian History, Culture and Identity*, (London: Penguin, 2005)

Stiglitz, Joseph E., *Globalization and its Discontents,* (New York: W.W.Norton & Company, 2002)

Stiglitz, Joseph E. and Charlton, Andrew, *Fair Trade for All: How Trade Can Promote Development*, (Oxford: Oxford University Press, 2005)

Vindt, Gerard, *A Globalização: De Vasco da Gama a Bill Gates*, (Lisboa: Temas e Debates, 1999)

Wang, Chengang, Liu, Xiaming and Wei, Yingqi, "Impact of Openness on Growth in Different Country Groups", in *The World Economy*, vol. 27 (2004), pp. 567–95

Wei, Dan, *Globalização e Interesses Nacionais*, (Coimbra: Almedina, 2006)

World Bank, *The Cost of Pollution in China: Estimates of Economic and Physical Damage*, (Washington: 2008)

PUTTING SUSTAINABLE DEVELOPMENT INTO PRACTICE IN EUROPE: THE RIGHT TO THE ENVIRONMENT AND THE ROLE OF SCIENTIFIC INSTRUMENTS

ALEXANDRA ARAGÃO[1]

1. The evolution of environmental law

European environmental law has seen great changes in the last three decades. In the late seventies, the right to environmental law relied only on vague legal proclamations of a right to a safe, decent or healthy environment. The environment was protected by using the classical reactive instruments to punish the most serious environmental offences to personal rights.

But soon environmental law developed its own legal instruments, more adapted to the holistic nature of the environment, and to the preventative nature of the protection required. Just a few examples of the new tools developed with success in the European Union to respond to the most recent environmental challenges are: environmental impact assessment in 1985[2], environmental labelling in 1992[3], eco-management and environmental audits in 1993[4] and environmental permits in 1996[5]. These instruments

---

[1] Professor at the Faculty of Law of the University of Coimbra (https://woc.uc.pt/fduc/person/ppgeral.do?idpessoa=130).

[2] Council Directive 97/11/EC of 3 March 1997 amends the Directive 85/337/EEC on the assessment of the effects of certain public and private projects on the environment.

[3] The revised Community Eco-label Award Scheme was approved by Regulation (EC) No 1980/2000 of the European Parliament and of the Council of 17 July 2000.

[4] Currently it is Regulation (EC) No 761/2001 of the European parliament and of the council of 19 March 2001 which allows voluntary participation by organisations in a Community eco-management and audit scheme (EMAS).

proved to be more effective in the prosecution of a broader objective: a wider environmental protection, balanced with economic development and social cohesion, or, to say it all in two words: sustainable development.

The new trend for the evolution of European Environmental Law consists of the legal assimilation of new scientific developments, creating a new category of lawyers which some authors call "scientific lawyers"[6].

The need for modernization of environmental law is imposed firstly by the fundamental principles of environmental law which, in EU law, have a constitutional nature. This is located specifically in the precaution principle, included in the European Treaties in 1992 by the Maastricht Treaty.

In fact, the incorporation of scientific concepts in environmental law is more important in fields where risk and uncertainty dominate. Fields such as chemicals, genetically modified organisms, electrical smog, or industrial hazards, are ruled by the precaution principle and decisions about them are very often based on presumptions of risk alone.

Therefore, every environmental protection measure based on the precaution principle is temporary and should be submitted to periodical revision according to the evolution of scientific knowledge, demanding a rapid incorporation of new scientific instruments into environmental laws.

Also, according to the European Commission, "analyses of scientific evolution"[7] are inherent to the precaution principle.

Complementarily, since the institution of the European Environmental Policy, by the Single European Act, in 1986, this European policy must be

---

[5]Now regulated by Directive 2008/1/EC of the European Parliament and of the Council of 15 January 2008, concerning integrated pollution prevention and control.

[6] José Esteve Prado uses the expression when talking about the "ecological shift of the law", in: *Técnica, riesgo y Derecho: Tratamiento del riesgo tecnológico en el Derecho ambiental*, (Barcelona: Ariel Derecho, 1999). Other authors, such as Tiago Antuness assume a critical position on the "contamination of the Law by the Technic", although recognizing that both science and law are important to economic progress. (*O Ambiente entre o Direito e a Técnica*, (Lisboa: Associação Académica da Faculdade de Direito de Lisboa, 2003).

[7] Communication from the Commission on the precautionary principle, COM(2000)1final, Brussels, 2.2.2000, page 19.

based on scientific and technical realism[8], reinforcing the need to take scientific data into consideration.

The most elucidative example is Council Directive 76/769/EEC of 27 July 1976 on the harmonisation of the laws, regulations and administrative provisions of the Member States relating to restrictions on the marketing and use of certain dangerous substances and preparations. This directive approves rules on the placing of dangerous substances and preparations on the market, with the purpose of protecting the public and the environment from all polluting and toxic or ecotoxic substances and preparations, and it has been amended 48 times in 32 years.

Also, in the Resolution of 7 October 1997 on the drafting, implementation and enforcement of Community environmental law (97/C 321/01), the Council "stresses that environmental protection has, in fact, to take into account, *inter alia*, the environmental media (air, water, soil) and living organisms (human, flora and fauna) as well as their inter-relationships, constantly changing environmental situations, the developing state of scientific knowledge and the close relation of environmental protection with complex and developing technology".

In some European environmental legal acts, scientific concepts are already side by side with legal concepts. This is true in the case of water law, nature conservation law and waste law.

In water law[9] we find the concepts of "ecological flow", "river basin" and "river basin district".

In nature conservation law[10], there are the concepts of biogeographical region, natural habitat and ecological corridor.

In waste law[11], concepts like dangerous waste, energetic recovery, material recovery, critical point, integrated management, and so on are referred to.

---

[8] Article 174, no.2: "In preparing its policy on the environment, the Community shall take account...available scientific and technical data (…)" (previously article 130R no.2).

[9] Directive 2000/60/EC of the European Parliament and of the Council, establishing a framework for Community action in the field of water policy.

[10] Council Directive *92/43/EEC* of 21 May 1992, on the conservation of natural habitats and of wild fauna and flora.

2. Ecological modernization of law: some examples

There are several consensual scientific concepts likely to be used for environmental purposes. We will briefly explain the meaning and context in which these concepts can be used.

Ecological footprint

The *ecological footprint* is used to measure the area of productive soil employed directly or indirectly for some activities (for instance, meat production). This concept was first developed by William Rees and Mathis Wackernagel[12] and is used to calculate the level of individual consumption—an individual's ecological footprint[13]—or aggregate consumption—the ecological footprint of a family, region or country. Assessments of the consumption habits of Canada (William Rees) and the Netherlands (Ton Buitenkamp and Teo Wams) led to the conclusion that the ecological footprints of both of these countries are superior to their territories[14], reflecting the unsustainable public and private consumption in these countries. Some authors estimate that 16 square kilometres is the area of productive soil available per person in the world, which is about one-third of the territory of the countries studied.[15].

Ecological rucksack

The *ecological rucksack* represents in a simple way the weight of the materials used in manufacturing a certain product. This concept can be applied to products or to services, and it expresses the quantity, in kilograms, of natural resources displaced by the production, maintaining

---

[11] *Directive 2006/12/EC of the European Parliament and of the Council* of 5 April 2006, on waste.

[12] *Our Ecological Footprint: measuring human impact on the Earth*, (Gabriola Island, B.C.: New Society Publishers, 1996).

[13] Many NGOs developed software to measure individuals' ecological footprints. See for instance, Leadership for Environment and Development (LEAD), http://www.lead.org/leadnet/footprint/intro.htm.

[14] The results are mentioned by Ernst Ulrich von Weizsäcker, Amory Lovins and Hunter Lovins in *Factor 4—Factor Four: Doubling Wealth, Halving Resource Use: A Report to the Club of Rome*, (Earthscan, 1998).

[15] Matias Wackernagel, *How big is our ecological footprint? Using the concept of appropriated carrying capacity for measuring sustainability* (University of British Columbia, *http://www.iisd.ca).*

and using a certain good. For instance a journal weighing less than half a kilogram has an ecological rucksack of over 10 kilograms; a golden ring weighing 10 grams has a three tons ecological rucksack..

Created by Friedrich Schmidt-Bleek, this concept is already present in some documents published by the European Environmental Agency[16], but not yet in laws.

Material input per unit service

The *material input per unit service* or *MIPs* is a resource productivity indicator, which measures the quantity of natural resources used, over its lifetime, for the production of a unit of a certain service. The material intensity of a good symbolises its "ecological price" in relation with its economic utility. According to the creator of the concept, Friedrich Schmidt-Bleek, measures like goods sharing, reuse or recycling are the most adequate ways to promote an increased productivity of natural resources.

Carbon intensity

The *carbon intensity* index is a measure of energy efficiency, also applicable to both products and services. This ecological indicator is based on the emissions of carbon dioxide resulting from the use of fossil fuel necessary for the production of a certain good. In spite of ignoring impacts like soil degradation, water contamination, noise pollution, etc., in favour of atmospheric impacts, this is, nevertheless, an interesting analytical tool[17]. As a matter of fact, the relevance of carbon intensity as a sustainability criterion is undeniable, in the first place considering the relative importance of the use of fossil fuels for energy generation—three-quarters of carbon emissions of human origin are caused by the burning of hydrocarbons—and, in the second place, considering the immense climatic influence of carbon emissions on the global scale.

---

[16] Joachim H. Spangenberg et al, (eds.), *Material Flow-based indicators in environmental reporting*, (Stockholm: EEA, 1998); Stephan Moll and David Gee, *Making sustainability accountable: eco-efficiency, resource productivity and innovation*, (Stockholm: EEA, 1999).

[17] The calculation of individual carbon emissions can be carried through the ICLEI–Local Governments for Sustainability portal (http://www3.iclei.org/co2/co2calc.htm).

Life cycle analysis

Life cycle analysis or *LCA* is a detailed examination of the environmental impacts of a product during its entire life cycle.

This tool provides a global and quantified vision of the impacts of the production process, from the moment the raw materials are extracted, transformed, distributed, consumed, reused, recycled, and thrown away. It allows a comparison between products based on the use of raw materials, on energy consumption, on pollution emissions or on waste production.

The life cycle analysis is a two step process.

The first step is called *life cycle inventory* and consists of the collection of data on all the impacts to be considered. One of the biggest difficulties in this phase is the selection of the relevant impacts. The collection of data on impacts cannot go on indefinitely[18], which implies a good methodology in the establishment of the limits.

The second step is called *life cycle assessment* and consists of data interpretation. Here, the major difficulties are the huge differences in the productive processes, in the materials used, or in the functions performed, which may impair the comparability of the data and prevent the drawing of credible conclusions as to the relative impacts of the goods or processes analysed.

3. Conclusion

Finally, we will briefly sketch some possible applications for these scientific concepts.

In a contest to recruit civil servants, in case of equal competence, why not select the candidates according to their individual **ecological footprint**?

To promote a fair distribution of public financing among municipalities, why not take into account the municipal or regional **ecological footprint**?

---

[18] In the life cycle analysis of a table the data to be collected are: the impacts of tree cutting, of wood transportation and processing, and of paint production. But should we also consider the impacts of the extraction of the stone, which was used to produce the cement, which was used to build the installation for the factory that produces the tools to cut the trees, that will be used to manufacture the table?

In public procurement contracts, is it not reasonable to request from the supplier the submission of the necessary data for the calculation of the **ecological rucksack** of the goods to be supplied?

Why not make consumption taxes rates dependent on the **ecological rucksack** of the goods? In this case, products having a light rucksack could benefit from a reduced VAT rate.

Why not dematerialize public services, rendering the service with less **material intensity**? Digital access to the official journal instead of the printed version should be mandatory.

When granting public subsidies or loans, why not consider the **material input per unit service** as an ecological criterion to select among the applicants?

Carbon intensity could also be a factor to take into consideration when analysing a request for an industrial authorisation or a construction permit.

In concessions of public land for the exploitation of public domain resources (namely extraction of geological materials), a life cycle analysis would allow the establishment of working restrictions more in accordance with the environmental impacts of the activity.

In sum, a coherent and efficient environmental policy requires a comprehensive approach, using methods and tools that are reliable and objective, if we want to achieve comparable and accountable results. In a word: sustainable development, with a high level of environmental protection, requires a stronger integration between scientific and legal instruments.

References

AAVV, Managing a material world, (Kluwer Academic Publishers, 1998).

Antunes, Tiago, *O Ambiente entre o Direito e a Técnica*, (Lisboa: Associação Académica da Faculdade de Direito de Lisboa, 2003)

—. *O ambiente entre o direito e a técnica*, (Lisboa: AAFDL, 2003)

Aragão, Alexandra, *Direito Comunitário do Ambiente*, (Cadernos CEDOUA, Almedina, 2002).

Esteve Pardo, José, *Técnica, riesgo y derecho: tratamiento del riesgo tecnológico en el derecho ambiental*, (Barcelona : Editorial Ariel, 1999).

Gomes, Carla Amado, "Dar o duvidoso pelo (in) certo? Reflexões sobre o 'princípio da precaução'", in *Revista Jurídica do Urbanismo e do Ambiente*, nº15-16 (2001).

Guyomard, Jacques, *L'Intégration de l'Environnement dans les politiques Intra-Communautaires*, (Rennes: Éditions Apogée, 1995).

Hohmann, Harald *Precautionary legal duties and principles of modern international environmental law*, International Environmental Law & Policy Series, (London: Graham & Trotman-Martinus Nijoff, 1994).

Incertitude juridique, incertitude scientifique, Actes du Séminaire de l'Institut Fédératif Environnement et Eau, (Limoges : Presses Universitaires de Limoges, 2001).

Kiss, Alexandre, *L'écologie et la loi: le statut juridique de l'environnement*, (Paris: Éditions l'Harmattan, 1989).

von Kloepfer, Michael, *Zur Rechtsumbildung durch Umweltschutz*, (Heidelberg: C.F. Müller, 1989).

—. *Zur Rechsumbildung durch Umweltschutz*, (Heidelberg: C.F. Müller, 1990).

Kohout, Franz, *Vorsorge als Prinzip der Umweltpolitik: eine Analyse rechtlicher Instrumente der Umweltpolitik*, (München : Tilsner, 1995).

Larmuseau, Isabelle, "The precautionary principle introduced in Belgian Jurisprudence: the need for consistency", in *European Environmental Law Review*, February 2000.

Lash, Scott, Szerszynski, Bronislaw and Wynne, Brian, *Risk, environment and modernity: towards a new ecology*, (London : Sage Publications, 1998).

Marburger, Peter; Reinhardt, Michael and Schröder, Meinhard, *Die Bewältigung von Langseitrisiken im Umwelt- und Technikrecht*, (Berlin: Erich Schmidt Verlag, 1998).

Martins, Ana Gouveia e Freitas, *O Princípio da Precaução no Direito do Ambiente*, (Lisboa: Associação Académica da Faculdade de Direito de Lisboa, 2002).

Medeiros, Carlos Alberto Baptista, "Padrões técnicos e direito do ambiente" in *Scientia Ivridica* 42 (1993).

de Munagorri, Rafael Encinas, "Expertise scientifique et principe de précaution", in *Revue Juridique de l'Environnement*. N. Esp. (2000).

Muñoz Machado, Andrés, and Pavón, Julián, "Perspectiva tecnológica", in *El Análisis Interdisciplinar de la Problemática Ambiental vol II.* (Madrid: Fundación Universidad-Empresa, 1997).

Murswiek, Dietrich, *Die staatliche Verantwortung fuer die Risiken der Technik*, (Berlin: Duncker und Humblot, 1985).

O'Riordan, Timothy; and Cameron, James, *Interpreting the precautionary principle*, (London: Earthscan Publications, 1994).

Ost, François, and Gutwirth, Serge, *Quel avenir pour le droit de l'environnement?: actes du colloque organisé par le CEDRE et le CIRT*, (Bruxelles: Facultés Universitaires Saint-Louis, 1996).

Petersen, Frank, *Schutz und Vorsorge*, (Berlin: Duncker und Humblot, 1993).

Robinson, Nicholas A, "Legal systems, decision making, and the science of earth's systems : procedural missing links", in *Ecology Law Quarterly* Vol. 27, No. 4 (2001).

Serrano Moreno, José Luís, *Ecología y Derecho: Principios de Derecho Ambiental y Ecologia Jurídica*, (Granada, 1992).

Trouwborst, Arie, *Evolution and status of the precautionary principle in international law*, (The Hague: Kluwer Law International, 2002).

Wolf, Lord, "Environmental risk: the responsibilities of the law and science :the Environmental Law Foundation Professor David Hall Lecture", in *Environmental Law and Management*. Vol. 13, No. 3 (2001).

THE INTERNATIONAL CRIMINAL COURT: THE ZEITGEIST

OJASVITA SRIVASTAVA

Age of Human Rights

Thanks to television and radio, today millions of people worldwide have learned of the atrocities suffered by other human beings, and have become outraged at what they have seen and heard. While the crimes committed are not necessarily new, widespread respect for human rights is. Slowly, but steadily, the international community has developed conditions in which the long-guarded notion of national sovereignty has yielded to a higher order of international justice.

Samantha Power, Harvard professor and author of *Problem from Hell—America and the Age of Genocide*, visited Darfur, western Sudan, in the summer of 2005. She asked many people where they would go if they could escape the violence that oppressed them daily. The common answer was "The Hague". Power said they had heard it was home to a court and they "wanted to go testify".

People are beginning to realise that there are courts outside their own countries—international courts—where the culture of impunity may finally be stemmed and where those guilty of abuses may be punished. The dream of "The Hague" for brutalised Darfurians is emblematic of this change.

Cesare Romano, of the New York-based Center on International Cooperation, echoes the views of many observers who claim that international criminal justice is "one of the most significant changes in the international architecture that has taken place in the post-Cold War era".

Evolution of Internationalised Justice

The aftermath of the First World War saw several failed attempts to create an international judicial body to try suspects for major crimes against humanity. It was not until 1922 that the Permanent Court of International Justice, sometimes called the World Court, was established by the League of Nations. It was replaced in 1946 by the International Court of Justice (ICJ) when the United Nations was founded. It only handled cases between states and cases could not be brought by individuals or non-governmental groups, nor could individuals or groups be tried.

An ambitious international treaty was developed in 1928 as the Kellogg-Briand Pact, also known as the 'Pact of Paris'. This pact provided for the "renunciation of war as an instrument of national policy". The Pact was signed by 62 nations, among them Germany. This paved the way for the conviction of those found guilty of starting World War Two (WW2) at the 'Nuremberg Trials'.

Up until recent years, Tokyo and Nuremburg served as the most powerful examples of, and most symbolic inspiration for, international justice. The Chief Prosecutor of the Nuremburg trials, Robert Jackson, described them thus: "Four great nations, stung with injury, stay the hand of vengeance and subject their captive enemies to the judgment of the law…one of the most important tributes that Power has ever paid to Reason".

The Cold War period that followed, and which lasted until 1990, spawned a number of conventions and commitments for a peaceful world, but as one critic has suggested, "the road to hell is paved with good conventions."

While prosecutions for human rights violations were left to the national courts to hear, in practice, such crimes went unpunished during this period. In particular, large-scale violations of human rights took place throughout colonial Africa, Spain, apartheid South Africa, Stalinist Russia, China under Mao and the Gang of Four, during the Korea and Vietnam wars and in Central and Latin America.[1]

But the drive to prosecute and avert impunity for international crimes picked up speed at the end of the Cold War. Jurist and human rights writer Geoffrey Robertson writes: "After a half-century of ineffectual treaties and

---

[1] *Justice Unfettered? Internationalizing Justice in the Human Rights Era*, (Integrated Regional Information Networks, 2006).

diplomatic thumb-twiddling, there came this end-of-century stampede to put global justice systems in place: an international court, a 'prosecute or extradite' regime for torturers, a precedent for intervening in the internal affairs of sovereign states out of humanitarian necessity."

General Pinochet was arrested in London; Serb and Croat generals, and concentration-camp commandos, were arrested by NATO forces in the Balkans; and in Arusha, Tanzania, the former prime minister of Rwanda was convicted of genocide. Even Libya finally handed over the two suspects implicated in the bombing of a Pan American jumbo jet over the Scottish town of Lockerbie.

For Robertson, this movement may have owed something to: "A sickness at the atrocities of the twentieth century and a wish to do better in the twenty-first. But it did seem to foreshadow a millennial shift, from appeasement to justice, as a dominant factor in diplomatic relations."

The International Criminal Tribunal for the Former Yugoslavia (ICTY) was established while the conflict still raged. Those indicted ranged from soldiers to generals and police commanders, as well as prime ministers. The International Criminal Tribunal for Rwanda (ICTR), based in Arusha, Tanzania, is another ad hoc international court operating under the auspices of the United Nations. Jean Kambanda, the interim prime minister, pleaded guilty to and was convicted of genocide. Another important court illustrating recent progress towards international justice is the Special Court for Sierra Leone.

According to Cesare Romano: "These internationalised criminal bodies are an expression of the international community's concerns but, at the same time, they are part of the reconstruction enterprise of a new judicial system in countries where the entire administration had been destroyed by civil wars (Kosovo, East Timor), or they facilitate acceptance of accountability to justice of former national rulers (Cambodia and, in some respects, Sierra Leone), in view of a purely national process of reconciliation."

The International Criminal Court (ICC)

The ICC was established in 2002 as a permanent tribunal to prosecute individuals for genocide, crimes against humanity and war crimes, as defined by several international agreements, most prominently the Rome Statute of the International Criminal Court of 1998 (the "Statute").

The Statute became a binding treaty after it received its 60th ratification, which was deposited at a ceremony at United Nations Headquarters on 11 April 2002. The ICC legally came into existence on 1 July 2002, and can only prosecute crimes that occurred after this date.

With this institution, major perpetrators of terror and violence have their nemesis. A system and a court have been specifically created to deal with the individuals who wreak havoc, holding them individually responsible. However, with more than 100 countries refusing to sign or ratify the Rome Statute to date, there remain many places for indictees to hide.

The ICC and its Jurisdiction

The ICC derives jurisdiction over a particular case in three ways according to Article 13 of the Rome Statute. These are if the Security Council refers a case to the ICC by passing a resolution in respect of the same; if the victim state itself refers the case to the ICC for the trial of the accused; or if the ICC Prosecutor *suo motu* starts investigation in a particular case.

The accused persons in turn can question the jurisdiction of the court and admissibility of a case under Article 19(2)(a) and 19(6) of the Rome Statute. The Court can, however, determine a case inadmissible in accordance with the provisions of Article 17 of the Rome statute.

By virtue of Article 17(1)(a) of the Rome Statute, the ICC can determine a case inadmissible if the case is being investigated or prosecuted by a State which has jurisdiction over it, *unless* the State is unwilling or unable genuinely to carry out the investigation or prosecution.

The *travaux préparatories* of the Rome Statute show that the phrase 'principles of due process recognised by international law' in article 17(2) of the Rome Statute to determine 'unwillingness' was added to restrict ICC discretion.[2]

[2] UN Diplomatic Conference of Plenipotentiaries on the Establishment of an ICC, Committee of the Whole, 42nd Meeting, A/CONF 183/C1/L76, add 1-14 (July 17, 1998). Available at www.un.org/icc/journal/717joue.htm .

The criteria to determine 'inability,' as enunciated in article 17(3), are factual questions.[3] Article 17(3) does not include possible defects in the quality of the national legal or, more specifically, judicial systems as a ground that might authorise the ICC to conclude that it could take jurisdiction.[4] To counter the war crimes and crimes against humanity that occurred in Darfur, the UN Security Council adopted Resolution 1593, after determining that the Sudanese legal system was 'unable' and the Sudanese government was 'unwilling' to try the crimes concerned.[5]

The most straight forward scenario is where no state has initiated any investigation (the inaction scenario). In such a scenario, none of the articles 17 (1) (a) to 17 (1) (d) of the Rome Statute are satisfied and there is no impediment to admissibility.[6]

Refuting the idea of ICC conflicting with Sovereignty

The edifice of the International Criminal Court stands on the bedrock of 'complementarity'. Acceptance of the principle of complementarity was fundamental to states' willingness to accept the ICC. The principle of complementarity is recognised in many regional conventions, particularly in Europe.[7] The principle is also voluntarily recognized by the English courts.[8] The ICC is to be activated only when no credible domestic alternative exists.[9] It is therefore called the court of last resort.

---

[3] John T.Holmes, "The Principle of Complementarity", in Roy S. Lee (ed.), *The International Criminal Court: The Making of the Rome Statute* (1999), pp. 41, 49.

[4] Mahnoush H. Arsanjani and W. MIchael Reisman, "The Law in Action of the International Criminal Court", *AJIL* 99 No. 1 (2005), pp. 385, 391.

[5] Security Council Resolution 1593 (2005), 31.03.2005, para 2.

[6] ICC, Office of the Prosecutor, Informal Expert Paper: The Principle of Complementarity in Practice (2003) Part III(a)(I), paras 17-18. Available at http://www.icc-cpi.int .

[7] *European Convention on Transfer of Proceedings in Criminal Matters*, 1972, ETS No. 73, *Convention between Member States of European Communities on Double Jeopardy*, Cm 438 (1987), *Convention Applying the Schengen Agreement* of 14.06.1985 between governments of the States of Bernelux Economic Union, the Federal Republic of Germany and French Republic on the gradual abolition of checks at their common borders, 1990, (1991) 30 *ILM* 84 and the *Council framework decision on the European Arrest Warrant*, 18.07.2002, OJ L 190.

[8] *R* v. *Thomas*, [1984] 3 ALL ER 34.

[9] S. Brown, "Primacy or Complementarity: Reconciling the jurisdiction of national courts and international criminal tribunals", *Yale J Int'nl L.* 23 (1988), pp. 383,

Many make the criticism that any UN action would inevitably result in another tool in the hands of the five permanent members of the Security Council and become another instrument of abuse, just like Chapter VII of the UN Charter. David Rieff calls it, "a *de facto* colonial office to US power"; cleaning up after American invasions and "used like a piece of fancy Kleenex...as usual".[10] The widespread perception is that the Security Council may misuse its power to initiate ICC action by passing a Resolution directing the Court to initiate proceedings against an unfriendly legitimate government.

But the Rome Statute in itself incorporates safeguards against such a scenario. These safeguards are twofold. Firstly, the Prosecutor is not obliged to initiate proceedings against any person unless he is himself satisfied of the criminality of the alleged humanitarian law violations after conducting due enquiry into the matter, and is thus not bound by Security Council resolutions. Therefore, only giving the power to pass a resolution directing the ICC to initiate proceedings against anyone cannot be looked upon as an instrument of abuse by the Security Council as the Resolution in itself is neither binding on the working of the ICC nor penalising the accused.

Secondly, even if the Prosecutor of the ICC starts investigation and files a charge sheet, the accused can challenge the jurisdiction of the Court and, by virtue of Article 119 of the Rome Statute, the ICC has the *compétence de la compétence*, i.e. it has the power to decide its own jurisdiction. Such a challenge to jurisdiction includes 'challenging the jurisdiction flowing out of an illegal or uncalled-for UN Security Council resolution'.

Several precedents have been set in this regard. Notable among these are those of *Dusko Tadic* and Lockerbie. In *Dusko Tadic*, the legality of Security Council resolutions was put to review before the ICTY Appeals Chamber. The question before the court was whether, by exercising the 'incidental' jurisdiction, it could examine the legality of its establishment by the Security Council, solely for the purpose of ascertaining its own 'primary' jurisdiction over the case before it. The court went on to review

---

424, 426-7, 433; Patricia A. McKeon, "An International Criminal Court: Balancing the Principle of Sovereignty against the demands for International Justice", *St. John's J. Legal Comment* 12 (1997), pp. 535, 555.

[10] Tony Judt, "The New World Order", ***New York Review of Books,*** July 14, 2005.

the validity of Resolution 827, which established the Tribunal, and in doing so it discussed the limits of the powers of the Council.[11]

A Security Council resolution can further be tested on the touchstones of propriety and procedure in passing of the resolution, both of which go to check any unwarranted resolution. If the UN Security Council passes a resolution with ulterior motives to achieve an ill design of influencing the sovereignty of a nation, its *raison d'être* of that resolution can be questioned before the ICC.

Albrecht Randelzhofer opines that[12] Article 2(4) of the UN Charter, prohibits the use of force in the international relations of states, i.e., not with regard to their internal situations, which according to Article 2(7), belong to states' domestic jurisdiction. For example, a civil war is not in itself a breach of international peace,[13] and no resolution can be passed by the UN Security Council initiating action on such grounds.

The Council's authority exclusively depends on its acceptance by the member states. This acceptance will not be enhanced if the Council claims for itself a place above the Charter. On the contrary, an authority that negates its legal foundations negates itself.[14]

Further, Article 39 of the UN Charter, is 'the single most important provision of the Charter',[15] it is the key to the broad powers of the Security Council under Chapter VII of the UN Charter.[16] Without a determination that a given situation poses either a threat to international peace or constitutes a breach of international peace or an act of aggression, the Council cannot pass a resolution taking enforcement action under Chapter VII and directing a case to the ICC. This is borne out by both the

---

[11] *Tadic* (02.10.1995), Case No. IT-94-1-A72, (1996) 35 ILM 32 at para 20.

[12] Randelzhofer on Article 2(4) MN 29 in Bruno Simma, *The Charter of the United Nations: A Commentary*, 2nd ed. (Oxford: Oxford University Press, 2002).

[13] UN Doc. S/PV 392 (Dec. 24, 1948), pp. 7-12 (esp. p. 10); RPII p. 344, paras 31-4.

[14] Koskennieimi, "The Police in the Temple—Order, Justice and the UN: A Dialectical View", *EJIL* 6 (1995), pp. 325, 327: 'Authority is a normative and not a factual category'.

[15] US Secretary of State, Report to the President on the Results of the San Francisco Conference (1945), pp. 90-91.

[16] Berld Martenczuk, "The Security Council, the International Court and Judicial Review: What Lessons from Lockerbie", *EJIL* 10 no. 3 (1999), pp. 517, 534.

authoritative commentaries on the Charter and the practice of the Security Council itself.[17]

For example, in view of the war crimes and crimes against humanity that had occurred in Darfur, the International Commission of Inquiry submitted a report to the UN Secretary-General on 25/01/2005, and recommended that the Security Council refer the Darfur situation to the ICC.[18]

Moreover, when the Security Council reaches a decision which is *ultra vires*, in the sense that a procedural requirement contained in the Charter is clearly violated or ignored, then the normal legal consequence would be that such a decision would be void and without legal effect upon Member States.[19] For example, if the Security Council failed to conduct any investigations under Article 34 of the UN Charter to determine whether there existed any threat to peace, breach of peace, or act of aggression, such a resolution would be rendered *ultra vires* the UN Charter.

Above all, the ICC is designed to complement existing national judicial systems; however, it can exercise its jurisdiction if national courts are unwilling or unable to investigate or prosecute such crimes, leaving the primary responsibility to exercise jurisdiction over alleged criminals to individual states.

The Chief Prosecutor of the court, Luis Moreno-Ocampo, is realistic about the situation and has said: "It is only my job to do one or two cases, to make my contribution and then leave. The countries themselves continue the work. This doesn't mean our work is only symbolic. The ICC is just

---

[17] L. M. Goodrich and E. HAmbro, *The United Nations and the Maintenance of International Peace and Security* (1955), pp. 346–347; O. Schachter, I*nternational Law in Theory and Practice* (1991), p. 392, and T. D. Gill, "The Second Gulf Crisis and the Relation Between Collective Security and Collective Defense", *Grotiana* (New Series) 10 (1989, published in 1991), pp. 47, 58. The Council rarely invokes specific articles in carrying out its functions, choosing rather to refer to Chapter VII in general terms. However, a determination that a threat to or breach of the peace exists has to date preceded any enforcement action the Council has taken.

[18] Security Council Resolution 1593 of 31.02.2005, para 2.

[19] D.M. Walker, *Oxford Companion to Law* (Oxford: 1980), p. 1246. The doctrine of *ultra vires* and the consequences of such acts as being void recognized in numerous legal systems and can be considered to be a general principle of law. V. Gowlland Debbas, "The International Court and the Security Council", *AJIL* 88 (1994), pp. 643, 672.

part of the solution not the whole solution. But we have practical issues and have to try to maximise the impact by gathering the leaders. To stop organised crime you have to stop the leaders."

The "Peace of Westphalia" of 1648 saw the end of the outright authority of the Pope or the Holy Roman Empire, and ushered in a state system that has been in use ever since. The "Westphalian Model" means that individual states need not recognise any superior authority beyond their own sovereignty. Before the 'globalisation' of criminal courts, it was the job of national courts to prosecute human rights offenders. Governments and politicians may remain resistant to any erosion of the "Westphalian Model" and state sovereignty, but support for international justice is gathering momentum and looks set to continue.

To conclude, in today's international society, a growing number of states agree that the worst human rights abuses should be punished at an international level. As the former UN Secretary-General, Javier Perez de Cuellar, put it in 1991: "We are clearly witnessing what is probably an irresistible shift in public attitudes towards the belief that the defence of the oppressed in the name of morality should prevail over frontiers and legal documents."

Towards universal jurisdiction

Prosecuting perpetrators is a key element of the increasingly active sphere of activity known as "transitional justice", where societies emerging from repressive rule or armed conflict seek to address past abuses through different mechanisms that which include the ICC as well as the many truth commissions. In such situations, upholding the inviolability of sovereignty at the cost of ignoring large-scale human rights violations is neither sensible nor reasonable.

On the eve of the first ICC arrest (Thomas Lubanga in early 2006 from the DRC), investigations Prosecutor Ocampo re-emphasised his personal commitment to the success of universal jurisdiction: "We need to have this idea of world justice. If we have global communication and global business, we also need global justice. Ultimately I am optimistic." To date, however, the ICC is the only palpable evidence of concrete change.

In 1993, Belgium passed an extraordinary War Crimes Law that embodied universal jurisdiction. They argued that certain crimes pose so serious a threat to the international community that any single state should be able to prosecute an individual responsible for it. It allowed anyone to bring war crimes charges in Belgian courts, which is exactly what several people did, resulting in an explosion of impossible depositions often involving serving world leaders.

By 2003, the scope of the 'Belgian Law' was restricted by its own government after considerable criticism from outside Belgium. But its existence and aspirations were emblematic of the current zeitgeist where activists, in some cases states, agree that forms of universal jurisdiction are now required and appropriate. Its failure is indicative that the world is not ready for the inherent degree of loss of sovereignty *to another equal sovereign power* that such a law expressed. But the ICC cannot be equated with this example or rebutted on these grounds, as it is formed out of the mutual consent and the will of nations that have ratified the Rome Statute and thus derives sanctity from the fact that it has been accepted and incorporated by its member nations to exercise a universal jurisdiction, though to a limited extent.

Sacrificing Sovereignty for Security?

The embryonic value which now animates much of this discussion is "sovereignty as responsibility," first articulated by Francis M. Deng in 1993 and quickly adopted by the UN Secretary-General, which holds that sovereignty not only protects a state from unwarranted outside interference but also obliges the state to respect the basic rights and interests of its members. But where a sovereign power fails to take action in a scenario of flagrant human rights violations, the UN has often resorted to humanitarian intervention under Chapter VII of the UN Charter.

Without delving into the propriety of humanitarian interventions themselves, let us analyse the rationale of the ICC in situations of humanitarian intervention or in the absence of a humanitarian intervention, and the contribution of the ICC in both situations in deterring egregious human rights violations.

In the absence of a Humanitarian Intervention

Humanitarian interventions have been vehemently opposed by many. The gravest problem while dealing with humanitarian interventions is that as soon as we accept that an attack by a powerful nation against a weak one is legitimate, we open the door to any number of acts of conquest masquerading as humanitarian action. As Chomsky points out, Japan claimed that it was invading Manchuria to rescue it from "Chinese bandits"; Mussolini attacked Abyssinia to "liberate slaves"; Hitler said he was protecting the peoples he invaded from ethnic conflict. It is hard to think of any colonial adventure for which the salvation of the bodies or souls of the natives was not advanced as justification. Faced with this dreadful choice, a sort of moral numbness takes over. To accept that force can sometimes be a just means of relieving the suffering of an oppressed people is to hand a ready-made excuse to every powerful nation that fancies an empire. To deny it is to tell some of the world's most persecuted peoples that they must be left to rot.[20]

Nevertheless, in situations where an intervention needs to be avoided, the other option is criminal prosecution. There is no guarantee that prosecution would stop human rights abuse, and one might have justified omitting it had large-scale slaughter been underway. This is so because an indictment, of course, is not the same as arrest, trial, and punishment. A mere piece of paper will not stop mass slaughter. But as a long-term approach, justice holds some promise. The experiences of former Yugoslav President Slobodan Milosevic and former Liberian President Charles Taylor suggest that an international indictment profoundly discredits even a ruthless, dictatorial leader. The enormous stigma tends to undermine support for the leader, both at home and abroad, often in unexpected ways.

So far the international legal authority for action has also been ambiguous. Although there is now a consensus that nations have a moral obligation to stop genocide, international law has not historically been very clear earlier. The 1948 *U.N. Convention on the Prevention and Punishment of Genocide*, despite its name, was largely concerned with defining genocide and creating rules for prosecuting perpetrators rather than preventing or stopping genocide before or as it occurred. Article 8 granted states the right to appeal to the U.N. for help, but it gave states no right to take military steps outside the U.N. framework unless it was in self-defense. [21]

---

[20] George Monbiot, "A Charter to Intervene: Human Rights Interventions Can Only Be Divorced from Imperialism with New UN Rules", *Guardian*, March 23, 2004.

[21] Paul F. Diehl, "Once Again Nations Agree Genocide Must Be Stopped. Can They Find the Mechanism to Do It?", *Washington Post*, May 15, 2005. Paul F. Diehl is Henning Larsen Professor of Political Science at the University of Illinois

But after the coming into force of the Rome Statute and the ICC, the state of affairs points to a better future where crimes such as genocide, crimes against humanity and war crimes can be prosecuted and punished and, maybe, even stopped in the process. Therefore, recourse to the ICC is the best option in the absence of a humanitarian intervention.

In Case of a Humanitarian Intervention

Let us picture a small, comparatively weak, nation, governed by someone who commits any number of atrocious crimes to stay in power. Let us assume that the citizens are incapable of overthrowing him by themselves. Let us assume, too, that all non-violent means have been exhausted, that the dictator shows every sign of living for another 30 years and has children to succeed him. What, if anything, should the people of more powerful nations call on their governments to do?

Some members of the anti-war movement would say "nothing more", and would put forward the following arguments to support that position: First is that any force with the power to intervene will have interests which extend beyond the liberation of the oppressed. It will use the intervention to further those interests. This was demonstrably the case in Iraq. As Noam Chomsky says: "One choice, always, is to follow the Hippocratic principle, 'First, do no harm.' If you can think of no way to adhere to that elementary principle, then do nothing." As it is impossible to send in an army and do no harm, or to exercise power in another nation without affecting the balance of power elsewhere, this surely means that it is always better to do nothing. Is hypocrisy always worse than cynicism? Chomsky would appear to say yes. But a flawed power intervening in a flawed manner in the Congo is better than no-one intervening at all.[22]

The second argument against intervention is that it will only ever be exercised against the weak. As David Rieff points out, it is impossible to conceive of force used against Russia on behalf of the Chechens, or against China on behalf of the Tibetans. Humanitarian action will always be a matter of *victors' justice*. But there are surely circumstances in which victors' justice is better than no justice at all.

---

and director of the Correlates of War project, which collects data on international conflicts.

[22] George Monbiot, "A Charter to Intervene: Human Rights Interventions Can Only Be Divorced from Imperialism with New UN Rules", *Guardian*, March 23, 2004.

"Genocide, whether imminent or ongoing, is practically always, if not by definition, a threat to the peace", Kofi Annan said in an address to the Stockholm International Forum on preventing genocide. "It must be dealt with as such—by strong and united political action and, in extreme cases, by military action".

He further added, "… we now understand that the issue is not one of a right to intervention, but rather of a responsibility—in the first instance, a responsibility of all states to protect their own populations, but ultimately a responsibility of the whole human race, to protect our fellow human beings from extreme abuse wherever and whenever it occurs," he declared.

But the intervention alone does not guarantee justice and peace. A trial of the perpetrators involved in the violations of human rights not only restores the faith, of the people of the victim nation, in the international community but also serves as a deterrent to future violations. It also goes a long way towards establishing international peace and security. The most effective and proficient trials can undoubtedly take place only in the ICC. This is so because of two major reasons. Firstly, the ICC cannot be marred with the label of victor's justice, and a fair trial where the accused has the right to defend himself can take place in accordance with the well-established principles of legal procedure under the Rome statute. The ratification of the Rome statute by all member nations demonstrates their faith in the procedure of the ICC.

Secondly, the ICC does not function under the auspices of the UN and has an independent functioning. The judges of the ICC are appointed from among the member nations. They have a fixed tenure and remuneration which ensures transparency. The accused also has the right to a counsel of his choice. Thus it ensures a fair trial.

All this goes to show that even in the case of a humanitarian intervention, the role played by ICC is indispensable.

The Hope called ICC

The so-called Third World countries symbolize humanity's immemorial pain. Its institutions may be summed up in the staccato style of Micawber. Votes doubled, expectations multiplied, income stationary, result misery. The case of the Third World countries is so strong that it almost argues itself. It is an instance of what can be called 'res ipsa loquitur'—the thing speaks for itself. The absolute gap between rich countries and poor countries widens every year.[23] In such conditions, human rights abuses, almost always, take place in these countries. To such countries the ICC is the guardian angel that guarantees protection and a respectable future.

Moreover, the ICC is valuable in and of itself. A permanent tribunal of this kind should exist for principled reasons alone, despite the limitations it will face and questions of whether it will actually deter future violence. For Samantha Power[24], the deterrent effect remains important, albeit unquantifiable. She cites other effects the court may have: "Perhaps its greatest impact will be to expedite the development of domestic legal enforcement tools in countries where atrocities actually happen. Where proud statesmen don't want to turn over their thugs and want to do it at home for a range of reasons. So the threat of the ICC, the spectre of Louis Moreno Ocampo, might make countries go ahead and prosecute their bad guys themselves."

Historically, the willingness of nations to yield some sovereignty to give space to justice represents a huge change. Despite major forces resisting theses changes, Samantha Power put it this way: "A shift has occurred. Is it a sufficient shift? Hardly. Is it the beginning, potentially, of a movement towards accountability and enforcement? I think it is, unquestionably."[25]

---

[23] Nani A. Palkivala, *We, the Nation, the lost decades,* (16th reprint) (UBSPD, 2000).

[24] Harvard professor and author of *Problem from Hell—America and the Age of Genocide*.

[25] *Justice Unfettered? Internationalizing Justice in the Human Rights Era* (Integrated Regional Information Networks, July 2006).

THE CHARTER OF FUNDAMENTAL RIGHTS—A PERSPECTIVE

BABUGOUDA SHIVANAGOUDA PATIL AND JATIN NAIK

Introduction

The main global concern of the last century has been the protection of human rights. This concern has been addressed through various attempts made by the international community. In this regard, the European Union adopted a federal setup. The main aim of the federal setup is to protect human rights.

India too has a similar setup, but a quasi-federal one. Though the form of governance differs, the political, economical and cultural challenges faced are similar. In such federal forms of government, the protection of individual rights and identities become a priority. The existence of a state which joins a union depends upon its ability to protect its own identity, individuality and culture.

In addition to this, the people of Europe, endowed a legal status to the federation. It is an important requirement to achieve the ends of a just and equitable society, and also a fundamental principle of democratic rule[1]. A just and equitable society would be created by providing 'equality' and 'liberty'; as well as by providing protection to all the recognized human rights. This article undertakes a study of the concept and jurisprudence behind the Charter of Fundamental Rights of the European Union, 2000, providing protection to all human rights. The study also extends to understanding the importance of the Charter in the light of the Constitution of India.

---

[1] See Introduction, Charter of Fundamental Rights of European Union (2000/C 364/01). *Official Journal of European Communities* 18.12.2000

The Charter

The Charter of Fundamental Rights adopted by the European Union is based on the concept of Dignity, Solidarity, Justice, Equality, and Freedoms. These concepts are also a foundation for the very core of the universal concept of Human Rights.

Though the Charter itself is a replica of the Universal Declaration of Human Rights, commendable efforts have been made by the "Drafting Committee" to categorize this complex superstructure of the fundamental concepts of human rights into watertight compartments. Similarly, the Universal Declaration of Human Rights has also inspired the incorporation of the fundamental rights into the Constitution of India. The approach of the Constituent Assembly of India was to place the entire body of fundamental rights within one part of the Constitution[2]. The Indian Judiciary, in its capacity as watchdog of the Constitution of India,[3] has time and again affirmed the relationship between them[4]. Further, it has created 'Core Fundamental Rights'[5] and 'Buffer Fundamental Rights'. This is the striking difference between the approaches in these two democratic setups.

The Charter of Fundamental Rights has acted as an instrument to bring the entire European Union together on the issue of protection of human rights. The treaties of the federations had silently recognized fundamental rights. For instance, the Preambles of several treaties have mentioned that the purpose or objective behind the incorporation of the treaty is peaceful existence of all communities in Europe, which can be interpreted as "Right to Life".[6] The recent growth of international law in the area of human rights suggests that human rights violations cannot be solely internal affairs. The international community holds the right to interfere and exert

---

[2] The Fundamental Rights are contained in the Part III of the Constitution of India, from Art 12 to 32.

[3] See Kameshwar Prasad v. State of Bihar (AIR 1962 SC 1166), L.Chandrakumar v. Union of India

[4] In R.C. Cooper v. Union of India (AIR 1970 SC 564), the court established a relationship between Art 19 and 31; in Maneka Gandhi v. Union of India, (AIR 1978 SC 597) the court established a relationship between Art 19 and 21.

[5] I.R. Coelho v. State of Tamil Nadu; Maneka Gandhi v. Union of India, (AIR 1978 SC 597), declared Art 14, 19 21 as the core Fundamental Rights under Part III of the Constitution of India

[6] See Preamble supra 1.

international pressure to ensure the curtailing of excesses of the State[7]. This act of the European Union was therefore in conformity with the present trend of international law.

However, since the establishment of the European Union a trend came into existence, which has developed over passage of time into a practice. When the main purpose of the treaties between members of the Union is for the satisfaction of economic or political purposes, the idea of evoking or rather of creating any rights which would be uniform and fundamental for a member or a non-member throughout the Union was questionable. But the sanctity to the Charter of Fundamental Rights can be assumed as it is on similar lines to the European Convention of Human Rights; which is in conformity with the European Parliament. It is submitted that, even though the Union was formed for economic and political purpose, the success and longevity of the union depends on its utility. The first world [8] in the Union benefited by the sure flow of labour, and the second world [9] in the Union benefited due to job opportunity and better labour standards. The Union also ensures a proper democratic setup, which is parliamentary in form. All these add to the need for protection of fundamental human rights. The survival of the Union depends upon its ability to protect the economic interests of each state and thus indirectly upon establishing fair government. The European Union passed the Charter with the primary purpose of protecting the universal values of human dignity, such as equality and solidarity. It places a citizen at the core of the activities of the State.

The Charter and Individuality of States

The Charter though prescribes sustainable growth in achieving the common aspects and goals, it also mentions and creates a right for the citizens and member states of the Union to preserve their own identity and their customs, which are not against public order and morality and moreover, not against the principles laid down in the Charter.[10]

---

[7] The violence against the Christian community at Khandamal, India, in 2008 was condemned by France. Violence against the Muslim community during the Godhra incident at Gujarat, India, in 2002, provoked a sharp response from the international Community.

[8] States such as the United Kingdom, Germany, France, etc.

[9] States such as the Balkans,the Caucasus, Turkey, Georgia, etc.

[10] Supra No 6

The Charter also provides for a fundamental right for every state to organize its public association at national, regional and local levels. It seeks to promote balanced and sustainable development and ensures free movement of persons, goods, services and capital, and the freedom of establishment. In order to achieve this, it suggests strengthening the protection of fundamental rights in the light of changes in society, social progress, and scientific and technological developments.

The Charter and the Concept of Dignity

The concept of human dignity has not been elaborated in the Charter. Nevertheless, the concept itself is beyond definition. It is one of the few concepts, which is better described than defined. Yet it is understood, with the aid of the Preamble, which relates to the core of human values. Article 1 of the Charter denotes that human dignity is inviolable and must be respected and protected. This protection, however, can be overruled in the public interest.

The Chapter relating to Human Dignity also deals with the concept of "Right to Life". Article 2, in its first part, stipulates that the right to life is not extended to every one, which means that the Charter distinguishes between a citizen and a non-citizen of the European Union.[11] Under the Indian Constitution, the right to life is extended to every person. It is therefore submitted that the approach of the Indian Constitution is much wider than that of the Charter of Fundamental Rights.

The second part of Article 2 condemns the death penalty or execution for any sort of crime. Furthermore, with reference to the "right to integrity" of persona, the Charter of Fundamental Rights provides that, "every person has a right to respect for his or her physical and mental integrity". Hence, it dictates that any selection of fetuses should be strongly condemned.[12] The above-mentioned right is not recognized under the Indian Constitution. In particular, the debate as to the abolition of death penalty has been long ongoing. Due to advent of new socio-psychological problems such as terrorism, the tenor of the debate has tilted in favor of the continuation of the death penalty. Therefore, its abolition seems unlikely to be achieved in near future. The Indian legal system has

[11] Article 1 and proviso to Supra No 1
[12] See, Article 3 (2) ibid

abolished the selection of fetuses long back.[13] However, the implementation of this has left much to be desired. The dwindling ratio of women to men is an indicator to prove the failure of the right in practice.[14]

In the field of medicine, the Charter makes strict observance of procedural law as laid down by the legislature or any subsequent treaty mandatory, when it concerns to amputation or any sort of surgery.[15] It is interesting to note that the Charter, which governs some of the most developed nations both economically and scientifically, prohibits human cloning and considers it violative of the integrity of the human body.

The Charter and the Concept of Freedoms

The Charter of Fundamental Rights dedicates a separate chapter to Freedoms. For instance, Article 6 of the Charter enumerates the "right to liberty and security" of persons. Furthermore, the Charter also protects personal data pertaining to one's self or to one's good. It further says that such data, if it needs to be processed, must be treated with absolute confidentiality. The "Right to Freedom" also guarantees a right to marriage and the building of a family.[16]

The right to freedom also includes freedom of conscience and religion. The Charter, under Article 10, protects the right of a person to practice his own religion, but the right to conscientious objection is recognized, in accordance with national laws governing the exercise of this right.

The concept of freedom has been further extended to make freedom of 'expression' and 'information' as fundamental rights[17]. In a democratic setup, the right to voice one's own opinion on issues of public importance is essential. However, to voice one's opinion one must be able to corroborate one's opinion with facts and information, which can only be done if the right to information is recognized. This important requirement of the democracy has been achieved under the provisos of this Charter.

---

[13] The Pre-Natal Diagnostic Techniques (Regulation And Prevention Of Misuse) Act, 1994 (act no. 57 of 1994) abolished the sex determination of fetuses.

[14] http://www.capitalmarket.com/Macro/EconomySurvey/EcoSur2002/es2001-02/chapt2002/tab95.pdf shows that the male: female ratio in India is 1000:933, and in State of Haryana it is lowly placed at 1000:861

[15] Supra No 1

[16] Article 8, Chapter I of the Charter on Dignity.

[17] See, Article 12, ibid

Another important political right which is an integral part of democracy is freedom of 'assembly' and of 'association'. The Charter enables any citizen to assemble and agitate against the Government or even against a private person. This freedom comes with a duty for such agitation to be peaceful.[18] The Charter of Human Rights has addressed most of the direct requirements of the democracy. However the Charter is under duty to address the indirect requirements also. One such indirect requirement is addressed under Article 13.

Humans differentiate themselves from animals based on their intelligence. Intelligence is a virtue which grows with more usage. Darwin's theory of use and disuse is apt for the intelligence of the human being. In relation to this, the freedom of the arts and sciences becomes a necessity for existence of the human being as a civilized, social and intelligent animal. At the same time, one might examine further and state that this particular freedom, which is enshrined in Article 13 of the Charter, is unusually far-reaching, as it steps beyond human rights of a physical nature and makes an attempt to protect art and science by stipulating an absence of constraints on their growth.

In continuation of the above object, the right to education also plays a major role in creating value additions to humans' labor, skill and salability. Another significant aspect of the right to education is that the parents of the pupil themselves be able to verify and monitor that the education which is provided is in accordance with their religious principles. If the case is otherwise, they have the right to move their child to another institution or seek redress from the institution.[19]

The freedom which protects the economic or financial aspect of human beings is freedom to choose an occupation and right to engage in work. Under the Charter, every person has the right to engage himself in any business of his choice. Even a person who comes with a permit to work from another country has the right to enjoy the same freedom as the workers or employees of the same country.[20] The freedom prescribed is a second level of freedom, which the countries of the rest of the world have to follow. At present, globalization means free movement of capital. However, the objection against the globalization is that it is an attempt to

[18] Article 12, Supra No 1
[19] Article 14, ibid
[20] Article 15, ibid

create neo-colonization. The proponents of globalization have always faced this objection. The only way to overcome it is to convince 'third-world' countries of their fair intentions. This can be achieved if the rest of the world follows the footsteps of the European Union and creates free movement of labour. This freedom involves a restriction that every worker should obtain a 'permit to work'. Even though, the right work has come with a restriction which affects persons' right to work, nevertheless, this is an appreciable effort towards the formation of a "global village".

The other freedom is again directed to protect the economic interests of the individual. This interest is protected by ensuring the freedom to conduct business and professions and the right to hold property. As far as freedom of business is concerned, it is permitted in accordance with community and recognized national laws.[21]

The Charter also confers the right to property. The Constitution of India provides for a constitutional right to property. Historically this was part of fundamental rights, but later this fundamental right created a hindrance in the implementation of the socialistic ideologies of the State. To overcome it, only the right to business and profession continued as a fundamental right and the right to property was reduced to its present status of a constitutional right.

However, the wording of the Charter of Fundamental Rights of the European Union, though it provides for the right to property, it also put restrictions in place. It clearly denotes that "everyone" means anyone, whether a resident, a national or a foreign citizen, has a right to occupy, buy or bequeath property. It further states that the right to property may be regulated and may be seized by the sovereign State in view of the public interest for compensation.[22]

Another right is the right to asylum and protection in the event of extradition, removal or expulsion. This is a right created to protect people against political vengeance. The right to asylum is guaranteed with due respect for the rules of the Geneva Convention relating to the status of refugees, and in accordance with the Treaty establishing the European Community.

---

[21] Article 16, Supra No 1.
[22] Article 17, ibid.

The Charter and the Principle of Equality

Though the Charter makes an impressive distinction between the basic human rights enshrined within it, it fails to define its core terms. For instance, the chapter on Equality (Article 20 to Article 26), a very significant pre-condition is stipulated for a just and democratic society: i.e., equality before the law.[23] Further, the Charter also makes it mandatory that cultural, religious and linguistic diversity should be necessarily preserved.

The Charter calls for equality among genders in the society and rejects the categorization of any particular gender as a weaker sex. On the other hand, the Charter does not deem a legislation to be void on the grounds of it being beneficial or for the protection of one particular gender. Another significant aspect associated with the Charter is its consideration for children's rights and the rights of the elderly towards maintenance and care as fundamental rights, rather than a "statutory right".[24]

The Indian Constitution calls for a similar provision. The concept of equality before the law includes classification and, most importantly, absence of arbitrariness. Under this concept of equality, the legislature enjoys sufficient freedom to provide special protection to minorities, socially and economically disadvantaged groups, gender equality and children. The major difference lies in recognition of the rights of the elderly. India has never recognized the importance of acknowledging and enforcing the rights of the elderly. Now, after substantial passage of time, the rights of senior citizens are recognized as a statutory right[25]. This can never be equivalent to the fundamental rights recognized under the Charter.

The Concept of Solidarity

The concept of solidarity is very closely linked with the concepts of labor welfare and worker rights. According to the Charter, workers or their representatives must at appropriate levels be guaranteed information and consultation regarding the relevant laws and practices. The Charter further advocates the right of workers to engage in collective bargaining and the

---

[23] Art. 20, Supra No 1.
[24] Art. 21, ibid.
[25] Maintenance and Welfare of Parents and Senior Citizens Act, 2007 (Act No. 56 of 2007).

formation of trade organizations in accordance with National law or Community law.[26] The Charter not only provides for free placement services for citizens but also protects every citizen from any kind of unjustified dismissal in accordance with Community and National laws.

The Charter further imposes a positive liability on the employer to provide the employee with a safe and convenient working environment. By recognizing the concept of human rights and an all round development of community, it very rightly imposes a ban on child labor. The minimum age of admission to employment may not be lower than the minimum school-leaving age, without prejudice to such rules as may be more favorable to children. The Charter, not only grants recognition to the needs of an individual citizen or non-citizen but also grants sanctions for the needs of the family. The Indian legislature exhibits contradictions regarding a ban on child labor. The law in India provides for a ban on child labor in hazardous industries only, but with regard to other industries it attempts merely to regulate child labor[27]. What is the need of the hour is stringent action as taken under the European Union Charter, by way of a complete ban on child labor.

Furthermore, the Charter also recognizes a need for providing "Social Assistance and Social Security" for the members of Unions and the individuals, in accordance with the provisions laid down in Community or National law for housing and other requisites, so that they do not face destitution.[28]

The Charter also recognizes the need for health care facilities, and puts the burden on the nation to provide the same and hence makes it a fundamental right. The chapter on Solidarity provides for the right of access to services of general economic interest and the rights of consumer protection and environmental protection as fundamental rights.

These rights regarding labor, consumers and persons in need of social assistance or security suggests that the Charter is an advanced document as compared to part III of the Indian Constitution. These rights are recognized under the Indian legal system, but only as statutory rights. Rights regarding social assistance are unenforceable rights. The fulfillment of the obligation directly relates to the financial capability of the State.

---

[26] See the chapter on Solidarity, Supra No 1.

[27] The Child Labour (Prohibition and Regulation) Act, 1986 (act No. 61 of 1986).

[28] Article 34, under the chapter heading of Solidarity, chapter IV, Supra No 27 .

This creates an incomplete obligation because of which the State will enact legislation and pass the burden on to the private sector. Passing of the buck and avoiding of responsibility results in violation of human rights. This is possible because of the unenforceability of rights mentioned under the Indian Constitution.

The Concept of Citizen's Rights

The Charter of Fundamental Rights provides for the right to vote and right of candidature in parliamentary elections as a fundamental right. The voting per se happens by means of secret ballot, as the right to confidentiality is embodied in Art.39. The Charter in itself is very far-reaching, as it makes it a fundamental right for every citizen to seek good administration. Though the wording of article 41 on first reading may confuse a reader, a careful reading of the provision shows that it denotes nothing but the existence of pure "natural justice", where fairness and impartiality are concerned. In addition, the Charter further makes provisions of immunity for consuls and ambassadors of any member state. It also provides for the freedom to access any document under the consideration of European Parliament. Citizens, under the Charter, whether 'legal' or 'natural,' have a "right to petition" in the European Parliament against any unjust action which may be brought by the government. The Charter also provides under the heading of Citizens' Rights freedom of movement to any place within the European Union.

The Concept of Justice under the Charter

The ultimate objective of law is justice, and to seek justice there needs to be the right to achieve justice. Article 47 of the Charter makes fair trial a fundamental right, and allows the taking of effective redress against unjust actions of a private person or the state itself. It also makes Court's Proceedings open to everyone, unless there is a law which bars other persons from being present during the hearing of the same. The Charter also provides, under Article 48, a presumption of innocence until proven guilty. One shall not be liable to be tried or punished of an offence another time for which he or she has already been finally acquitted or convicted within the Union in accordance with law.

The General Provisions of the Charter

Chapter VII, Articles 51 to 56 of the Charter deals with the scope of the general provisions of the Charter. The provisions enshrined in this Charter are addressed to the institutions and bodies of the Union with due regard for the principle of subsidiary. These principles are applicable to the Member States only when they are implementing Union law. This restriction is required to make the Charter acceptable to all the member states. This cannot be treated as limiting the implementation or effectiveness of the Charter as law, being a living organism, evolves and develops gradually, and becomes more effective. Keeping this in mind, the first step of putting most of legal or statutory rights in the category of fundamental rights is an appreciable step. History teaches that international law grew in stages. Human rights are here to stay and the restriction on them is a temporary phenomenon which will die down by passage of time. This being an initial stage, such restrictions can be treated as necessary for initial acceptance and can be overlooked at the later stage.

The authorities shall therefore respect the rights, observe the principles, and promote the application thereof in accordance with their respective powers. Any limitation on the exercise of the rights and freedoms under the Charter is allowed only if provided for by law.[29] Subject to the principle of proportionality, limitations may be placed only if they are necessary and genuinely meet objectives of proportionality and general interest recognized by the Union, or the need to protect the rights and freedoms of others.

Conclusion

Part III of the Constitution of India, with judicial interpretation, creativity and acclimatization, has kept pace with changes in the society. However the study reveals that the Charter on Fundamental Rights, though being a recent document, has mutated considerably as compared to Part III.This Charter also provides for new methods that can be adopted to achieve the goal of protection of human rights. Such regional, multilateral treaties help to reduce conflict between neighbors, develop cooperation, reduce geo-political conflict in the region and encourage globalization. This sure forward step of the European Union will definitely protect and propagate a civilization which everyone will be proud of.

---

[29] Chapter VII, Supra 1.

PART III:

CRIMINAL LAW

THE CRIMINAL JUSTICE SYSTEM: A CORNERSTONE OF GOOD GOVERNANCE

VISHWANATH MARAIAH
AND SHURPALI SHRUTI ARVIND

I- Introduction

The object of criminal law is to protect the right to personal liberty of individuals against the invasion of it by others.[1] It aims to protect the weak from the strong, the law-abiding from the lawless, and the peaceful from the violent. To achieve this, the State has laid down certain rules of conduct, sanctions for their violation, special machinery to enforce these sanctions and procedure to protect the system in its entirety. The State intervenes for the protection of citizens' rights when selfishness, greed and intolerance reach intolerable levels leading to deprivation of life, liberty and property of the citizens.

The criminal justice system is the system of practices and organizations which are used by national and local governments, directed at maintaining social control, to deter and control crime and punish with criminal penalties those who violate laws. The primary agencies charged with these responsibilities are: law enforcement bodies (police and prosecutors), courts, defense attorneys, and local jails and prisons, which administer the procedure for arrest, bringing charges against violators, adjudication, and punishment for those found guilty. While processing the accused through the criminal justice system, the government keeps itself within the framework of the law that protects individual rights. The pursuit of criminal justice is, like all forms of "justice," "fairness" or "process," essentially the pursuit of an ideal. The criminal justice system, in general, has to ensure, promote and enhance the philosophy of equity and fair-play amongst its interdependent sub-systems for quick, just and fair delivery of justice to people at large. Throughout history, criminal justice has taken

---

[1] Committee on Reforms of the Criminal Justice System, Vol. 1, March 2003, para. 1.4, p.5.

many different forms which often reflect the cultural background of society.

II—Society, Crime and Law

Man is a social being; thus, living apart from society is impossible for him. Born, bred and educated in society, it is in the interests of the society that his activities should be for its good. From primitive times to the present day, man has lived in associations, in groups—never in isolation, which signifies that life has always involved interaction between individuals at various levels. Everywhere, some human beings always fall outside the pattern of permitted conduct. Weakness, anger, greed, jealousy and other forms of human aberrations surface everywhere, and even human sanctions have not been successful against the irrational, the misguided, the impulsive, and the ill-conditioned. There is no society that is not confronted with the problem of criminality. Crime is eternal—as eternal as society. As far as we know, human fallibility has manifested itself in all different forms of human organization. For reasons too subtle and too complex to understand, the ordinary pressures and expectations that pattern an individual's conduct into conformity break down under certain circumstances. They have always done so; they always will. No satisfactory policies have yet been discovered to ensure satisfaction of all needs, of all human beings, at all times;[2] it does not follow that the law does not regulate the behaviour (satisfactorily) of the people in the society. Social institutions were created to regulate the social relations of men, and facilitate the relations between men and society. One of the most important and essential social institutions, the State, is entrusted with the duty of protecting man and his property and also conferring certain rights and privileges, along with certain duties which are to be observed by him. To ensure the same, the State has to look to, guide and protect, in every possible manner, the welfare of its individuals, by healthy laws and by devising and promoting ideal economic and social conditions to enable its individuals to display their creative instinct and to live a higher, fuller and truer life.

[2] Frank Tannenbaum, 'Foreword' to *New Horizons in Criminology,* 1st ed., (Englewood Cliffs: N.J.Prentice-Halls, inc., 1943), p.6.

III—Criminal Law—Past and Present

The concept of crime is essentially concerned with the conduct of individuals in society. As man by nature is social, his interests are best protected as a member of society. Every individual possesses certain rights and privileges which he expects others to respect; on the other hand he also has certain duties towards his fellow men.[3] With the evolution of mankind from primitive stages to that of a social welfare state, the administration of criminal law has assumed great importance. As long as the human beings were "God-fearing" and believed that their actions were being watched by the "Almighty", the need for the administration of criminal justice was not felt. However, with the passage of time and people becoming more materialistic, section of the society consisting of misguided and discontented human beings lost faith in the "Almighty" and scorned divine intervention, to control these misguided persons who indulged in criminal activities, paved way for the administration of criminal justice system. In addition, the activities to be termed as "criminal activities" have also undergone change with the passage of time. What was regarded as not destructive fifty years ago has become the greatest evil of the day in view of changed circumstances, new researches, new thinking and a modern way of life.[4]

Historically, the concept of crime has always been changing with variations in social conditions during the evolutionary stages of human society. The first civilizations generally did not distinguish between civil and criminal law.[5] In ancient Greece and Rome, for the most part, crime was viewed as a private matter. Other duties associated with modern policing, such as investigating crimes, were left to the citizens themselves. The Roman Empire had a reasonably effective law-enforcement system until the decline of the empire.[6] Self-preservation was the first instinct of crime, and people followed "A tooth for a tooth, an eye for an eye, and a

---

[3] M.A. Samad, "Traditional and Modern Approach to Criminal Law", in K.D. Gaur (ed.), *Criminal Law, Criminology and Criminal Administration*, 1st ed., (New Delhi: Deep & Deep Publications, 1992), p.5

[4] 155th Law Commission of India Report, p.1.

[5] The Sumerians (who produced the first written codes of law) and the Code of Hammurabi, which formed the core of Babylonian law, did not separate penal and civil laws.

[6] For details see http://en.wikipedia.org/wiki/History_of_criminal_justice.

life for life", which marked a distinct step towards criminal justice.[7] During the middle ages, payment to the victim, known as "wergild", was another common punishment, even for violent crimes. The early Anglo-Saxon laws contained minute details of compensation (bot) which was payable for different wrongs with a view to help the person wronged in seeking redress.[8] However, if 'bot' was refused, the law had no other means to enforce its payment. In that event, it was for the victim or his kindred to prosecute a 'blood-feud' against the wrongdoer and law could help him only by declaring the wrongdoer as an 'outlaw' who could be chased and killed by anyone like a wild beast. During the 17th century, the English common law system was prevalent in England, colonial America, France and Holland, which was based on the history of decisions that the judges had made, instead of lawmaking codes or laws. The victim of the crime was responsible for instigating the prosecution and financing it. It was these fundamental principles that remained with the colonists and were used selectively to create a new and unique criminal justice system. Religion, especially in the colonial period, exerted a strong influence on law-making process.[9]

A dispassionate observer who looks at India with detachment and penetration would be struck by two mutually contradictory features: diversity and unity at the same time. The endless variety is striking, often incongruous. Costume, speech, the physical appearance of the people, customs, standards of living, food, climate, and geographical features all offer the greatest possible differences.[10] As a country India looks a new world in its own. It will be a difficult task to bring in every aspect into words. In ancient India, conduct was influenced by concepts of 'Dharma,' or rules of right conduct, as outlined in the various manuals explaining the Vedic scriptures such as 'Puranas' and 'Smritis,' and the King derived his powers from 'Dharma,' which he was expected to uphold. The Mauryan dynasty, during the 4th century B.C., had a rigorous penal system which prescribed mutilation as well as the death penalty for even trivial offenses. The Dharmashastra code was drawn by Manu (2nd-3rd century A.D), an important Hindu jurist. The code recognized assault and other bodily

---

[7] Balbir Sahai Sinha, *Principles of Criminal Law*, 2nd ed., (Lucknow: Eastern book Company, 1974), p.1.

[8] Radcliffe and Cross, *The English Legal System* (1954), p.6.

[9] Supra n.2.

[10] D. D. Kosambi 'The Culture and Civilisation of Ancient India in Historical Outline',
http://gyanpedia.in/Portals/0/Toys%20from%20Trash/Resources/books/cultddk.pdf

injuries and property offenses such as theft and robbery. During the rule of the Gupta dynasty (4th to 6th century A.D.), the judicial hierarchy was formed. The judiciary was comprised of the guild, the folk-assembly or the council and the king himself.[11] During the Moghul reign, Muslim criminal law was enforced, which classified all offenses on the basis of the penalty which each merited.[12] Later, when the British arrived in India in the 17th century, they considered the Muslim criminal law to be irrational and draconian, and brought about several reforms through a series of regulations which modified or expanded the definitions of some offenses, introduced new offenses and altered penalties to make them more logical and reasonable. The Indian Penal Code 1860 (I.P.C.), the Criminal Procedure Code 1973 (Cr.P.C.) (earlier Act of 1861), with the Indian Evidence Act, 1872,(IEA) which drew inspiration from English criminal law, form the essence of Indian criminal law today, along with a large number of special and local laws to address various other anti-social activities.

Law should not sit limply while those who defy it go free and those who seek its protection lose hope; [13] it can be observed that the criminal justice system has evolved since ancient times, with new forms of punishment, added rights for offenders and victims, and policing reforms, which have reflected changing customs, political ideals, and economic conditions.

Criminal law, is defined as " A body of specific rules regarding human conduct which has been promulgated by authority, which apply uniformly to all members of the classes to which the rule refer, and which are enforced by punishments administered by the state',[14] thus, it has four important characteristics:

a. ***Politicality:*** it is regarded almost universally as a necessary element in criminal law. The rules of a trade union, the church, or the family are not regarded as criminal law, nor are violations of these rules regarded as crimes. Only violations of rules enacted by the state are crimes.

---

[11] K.D.Gaur, "Crime and Criminal law", in K.D. Gaur (ed.), *Criminal Law, Criminology and Criminal Administration*, 1st ed., (New Delhi: Deep & Deep Publications, 1992), p.7

[12] P.S. Atchuthen Pillai, *Criminal Law*, 4th ed., (Trivandrum: Rajan Brothers, 1977), p.22-23.

[13] *Jennison* v. Baker, (1972) 1 All ER 997.

[14] Edwin Sutherland and Donald Cressey, Criminology, 10th ed. (New York : J.B. Lippincott,1974), p.4

b. ***Specificity:*** is included as an element in the definition of criminal law because of the contrast in this respect between criminal law and civil law. It gives a strict definition of a specific act.

c. ***Uniformity or Regularity:*** it attempts to provide evenhanded justice without respect to persons. This means that no exceptions are made to criminal liability because of a person's social status; an act described as a crime is crime, no matter who perpetrates it.

d. ***Penal Sanctions:*** refers to the notion that violators will be punished or at least threatened with punishment by the state.

IV- Criminal Justice System

The Indian criminal justice system is based on its colonial legacy; in contrast to the predominantly civil law countries in the European continent; England is a common law country. "The common law" is "the body of principles and doctrines that have emerged implicitly from the history of decision-making by courts rather than explicitly from politically motivated decisions of legislators."[15] Historically, therefore, law in England is judge-made, and legislation has traditionally played only a supporting role. English law has developed in the courts in a piecemeal fashion, in contrast to the much more abstract, systematic civil law systems, with their impressive batteries of codes. Over the last few decades, however, legislation has begun to occupy a more prominent position in the English legal system. Statutes, i.e., Acts of Parliament assented to by the Queen, override the other national sources of law—an Act may not be held to be unconstitutional by a British court.[16] However, "although the rules of common law are subject to legislative alteration and abrogation, there is an important sense in which the common law is superior to statute. As a body of evolving principle, the common law provides stability and continuity. Its settled doctrines and assumptions, though always open to reconsideration and challenge, constitute a framework into which legislation must be fitted."[17] The common law

---

[15] J. Waldron, *The Law*, (London and New York: Routledge, 1992), p. 15

[16] The only situation, in which a British court may override an act, is if it may be held contrary to the European Convention on Human Rights.

[17] T.R.S. Allan, *Law, Liberty and Justice: The Legal Foundations of British Constitutionalism*, (Oxford: Clarendon Press, 1994), p. 79.

encompasses the basic principles of English law, and statute builds on these foundations.[18]

According to Weston and Wells, the primary function of the criminal justice system is; "The prevention, detection, discovery, and suppression of crime; the identification, apprehension, and prosecution of persons accused as criminals; and the incarceration, supervision, and reform and rehabilitation of convicted offenders. These are accomplished primarily through six major functional areas of government: police, prosecution, criminal courts, probation, prisons and other institutions for the care and treatment of offenders, and parole."[19]

In India, the criminal justice system, is also based on the above lines, (as mentioned by Weston and Wells) but is marred by two major problems—the huge number of pending criminal cases and inordinate delay in disposal of criminal cases on the one hand, and the very low rate of conviction in cases involving serious crimes on the other; this trend can be observed as the crime rate arrow is always drifting towards north. With the probabilities of conviction being remote, crime has become a rampant and profitable business. As a consequence, the law and order situation has deteriorated and society has lost confidence in the criminal justice system. Though Article 21 of the Constitution of India[20] ensures protection of life and personal liberty to every citizen, this precious fundamental right is turning out to be a mere dream to those to whom justice is delayed, distorted or denied, rather than it being delivered in accordance with the ideals enshrined in the Constitution. The situation, thus, demands necessary and effective systematic reforms to improve the health of the system, and more specifically, aiming to reduce the level of criminality in society by ensuring maximum detection of reported crimes, conviction of the accused persons without delay, and awarding appropriate punishments to the convicted to meet the ends of justice and to prevent recidivism.

---

[18] P. Derbyshire, *Nutshells: English Legal System in a Nutshell*, (London: Sweet and Maxwell, 1995), p. 13. See also R. Zimmermann, 'Statute Sunt Stricte Interpreted? Statutes and the Common Law: A Continental Perspective', in *The Cambridge Law Journal* 56(2) (July 1997), pp. 315–329, for an analysis of statutes and the common law.

[19] Paul Weston and Kenneth Wells, "The Administration of Justice", 2nd edition (New jersey: Englewood Cliffs: Prentice-Hall, 1973), p.1.

[20] "No person shall be deprived of his life or personal liberty except according to procedure established by law", CRCJS.

The criminal justice system is full of challenges which need to be addressed; and suitable reforms are called for. The Government of India set up the Committee on Reforms of Criminal Justice System, (CRCJS) in 2000, headed by Dr. Justice V.S.Malimath, and the report was submitted in March 2003. Effective criminal justice administration is possible when the various systems are co-ordinated and so able to perform effectively to achieve better results. The machinery includes the public, the police (investigation), prosecution, witnesses, the judiciary, penal sanctions and prison administration.

(a)The Public: The participation of society is a vital component of every justice system, because it is society in which the crime takes place, and it is the same society which can prevent it, as it is duty-bound to assist the system to punish the guilty. The Cr.P.C. imposes a duty on every person to give information of certain offences[21], penalty for the breach of which is

---

[21] Cr.P.C. Sections 39 and 40 impose an obligation on every member of the public to give information of certain offences committed or intention to commit certain offences as covered by I.P.C., to the nearest Magistrate or Police Officer.

Cr.P.C Section 39. reads as follows:

"(1) Every person, aware of the commission of, or of the intention of any other person to commit, any offence punishable under any of the following sections of the I.P.C., namely:—

(i) Section 121 to 126, both inclusive, and section 130 (that is to say, offences against the State specified in Chapter VI of the said Code);

(ii) Sections 143, 144, 145, 147 and 148 (that is to say, offences against the public tranquility specified in chapter VIII of the said Code);

(iii) Section 161 to 165A, both inclusive (that is to say, offences relating to illegal gratification);

(iv) Sections 272 to 278, both inclusive (that is to say, offences relating to adulteration of food and drugs, etc.);

(v) Sections 302,303 and 304 (that is to say, offences affecting life); va Section 364A (that is to say, offence relating to kidnapping for ransom, etc.);

(vi) Section 382 (that is to say, offence of theft after preparation made for causing death, hurt or restraint in order to the committing of the theft);

(vii) Sections 392 to 399, both inclusive, and section 402 (that is to say, offences of robbery and dacoity);

(viii) Section 409 (that is to say, offence relating to criminal breach of trust by public servant, etc.);

(ix) Sections 431 to 439, both inclusive (that is to say, offences of mischief against property);

(x) Sections 449 and 450, (that is to say, offence of house- trespass);

(xi) Sections 456 to 460, both inclusive (that is to say, offences of lurking house-trespass); and

provided in the I.P.C.[22]. Thus, it can be deduced that it is the primary duty of every person to help the state in preventing the commission of crime and identifying the offender, because a betrayal of it is a step towards destabilizing social peace, order and progress. It is the salutary duty of every witness who has knowledge of the commission of crime to assist the state by giving evidence.[23] It is of importance to the public, for the detection of crimes, that the identities of those persons who are the channels by means of which the detection is made should not be unnecessarily disclosed. Thus, on the grounds of public policy, a magistrate or a public officer cannot be compelled to name the source of information received by him as to the commission of a crime.[24] This

---

(xii) Sections 489A to 489E, both inclusive (that is to say, offences relating to currency notes and bank notes), shall, in the absence of any reasonable excuse, the burden of proving which excuse shall lie upon the person so aware, forthwith give information to the nearest Magistrate or police officer of such commission or intention.

(2) For the purpose of this section, the term "offence" includes any act committed at any place out of India which would constitute an offence if committed in India."

[22] I.P.C. Sections 176 and 202 of, punish the illegal omission to give information of offences already committed or intention to commit certain offences (as covered by the I.P.C.), when the person is bound to inform; Section 176 reads as follows:

> "Whoever, being legally bound to give any notice or to furnish information on any subject to any public servant, as such, intentionally omits to give such notice or to furnish such information in the manner and at the time required by law, shall be punished with simple imprisonment for a term which may extend to one month, or with fine which may extend to five hundred rupees, or with both; or, if the notice or information required to be given respects the commission of an offence, or is required for the purpose of preventing the commission of an offence, or in order to the apprehension of an offender, with simple imprisonment for a term which may extend to six months , or with fine which may extend to one thousand rupees, or with both; or, if the notice or information required to be given is required by an order passed under section 356 (1) of Cr.P.C. with imprisonment of either description for a term which may extend to six months, or with fine which may extend to one thousand rupees, or with both."

Section 202 of I.P.C, reads as follows:

> "Whoever, knowing or having reason to believe that an offence has been committed, intentionally omits to give any information respecting that offence which he is legally bound to give, shall be punished with an imprisonment of either description for a term which may extend to six months, or with fine, or with both."

[23] *State of Gujarat* v. *Anirudhsing*, AIR 1997 SC 2780:1997 Cr LJ 3397.

[24] I.E.A. Section 125.

provision in law is important in securing public co-operation, as it encourages the public to come forward with information. The problem with it lies with the fact that these provisions have seldom been invoked by the court of law or the police. An alert and responsible society is always of vital importance to the criminal justice system, but if an individual fails in his obligation, the judiciary and police should invoke the above-mentioned provisions of law, which can make the criminal justice system "as it ought to be".[25]

(b)The Police: The ideal purpose of police in a community should always be as the words quoted below:

> As a law enforcement officer, my fundamental duty is to serve mankind; to safeguard lives and property; to protect the innocent against deception, the weak against oppression or intimidation, and the peaceful against violence against disorder; and to respect the constitutional rights of all men to liberty, equality and justice.[26]

The police in the criminal justice system are comparable to the brain in a human; as human conduct is the reflection of the mind, so an efficient police system is the reflection of a healthy society. Police officers have been armed with extensive powers to prevent the commission of offences.[27] A duty is cast upon every officer in-charge of a police station to register a case on the basis of any information disclosing a cognizable offence[28] and in case of a non-cognizable offence, the police officer is still required to register the information, but cannot investigate the matter without the order of a magistrate.[29] The Supreme Court has also laid down in a number of cases that the police must investigate the matter after registering the case.[30] To make the investigation successful (to help the prosecution in the court of law), the police officer who investigates a case is authorized to require the attendance before himself of any person (within certain territorial limits) who appears to be acquainted with certain

---

[25] The CRCJS has observed in the report that it is the duty of the government to ensure that every citizen of the country is aware of his duty in helping the machinery achieve its goals, so that the government must produce with awareness programmes to this end by various means and especially through mass media.

[26] International Code of Enforcement Ethics.

[27] Cr.P.C. Sections 149 to 153, 156

[28] *Ibid.,* Section 154 (1).

[29] *Ibid.* Section 155.

[30] *Mohindro* v. *State of Punjab*, AIR 2001 SC 2113:2001 Cr LJ 2587; *Naurata Ram* v. *State of Haryana*, 1995 Cr LJ 1568 (P&H).

circumstances of the case,[31] and the police officer may examine witnesses orally and record the statements of such witnesses in writing.[32] Unfortunately, Section 162 of Cr.P.C., prevents the police from using the statements of the accused and witnesses as evidence in the court of law. A person who fails to comply with the order of the police may be prosecuted for disobedience under Section 174 of the I.P.C. Further, every police officer investigating a matter is required to complete the investigation without unnecessary delay,[33] prepare a charge sheet and hand over the documents and evidence collected, to the prosecution. In this context the registration of cases should be prompt (we strongly feel that the registration of complaints should be carried out online and connected to the office of the Superintendent of Police so that Station House Officers (SHOs) cannot meddle with cases and the complainant feels secure and trusts the system), and the Investigation wing should be separated from the Law and Order wing, so that it is given a professional distinction; if the professionalism is improved with the inputs of modern science and technology, it may go a long way in collecting evidence and apprehending criminals.

The police are constantly under tremendous pressure due to workload, lack of staff, and lack of support from the public (the majority believe the police to be their foe rather than their friend), the prosecution and the courts (who always look upon the police with suspicion). This has made the police system a controversial and questionable group.

(c) The Prosecution: H. R. Khanna, J., former judge of the Supreme Court of India, observed,

> The legal profession is designed to be a profession of service...Service to the community. The important duty of the profession is to act as an interpreter, guide and faithful servant of the community. Lawyers have an important role in preserving the confidence of the people in the independence of the judiciary, thereby ensuring the rule of law.

He also opined that a strong bar, an independent judiciary and an enlightened public are the three pre-requisites of the prevalence of the rule of law. The prosecution is expected to act as a liaison between the various

[31] Cr.P.C. Section 160 (1). But, the proviso to this sub-section also provides that no male under 15 years of age or a woman shall be required to attend at any place other than the place in which such male or woman resides.
[32] *Ibid.,* Section 161 (1) and (3)
[33] *Ibid.,* Section 173(1).

components of the criminal justice system, as well as an effective check on the police. Based on the evaluation of the data presented to him, the prosecutor is charged with deciding whether there is sufficient evidence to warrant prosecution or a strong enough case to sustain a conviction, and whether he should accept a plea or reduce the charge against the defendant. The prosecutor has wide latitude in applying the prosecutorial process.

Prosecution is the strength of the Criminal Justice System; it has an onus in assisting the court to establish the truth. An investigation is very often futile without the help of an effective prosecution. To avoid inordinate delay in the trial of cases, the prosecutor is expected to seek the minimum number of adjournments in the examination of witnesses during a hearing. The prosecutors and the lower courts are expected to be courteous towards witnesses, but the present situation is different. Prosecutors seek adjournments on unjustified grounds and personal reasons, which causes grave inconvenience to the witnesses. A lawyer's absence without an alternative arrangement should thus be treated as misconduct.[34] The trend seems to be that lawyers arguing for the prosecution and the defence are more interested in winning the case than assisting the court in establishing the truth before the judge, as a result of which truth is completely lost sight of. This in turn, many times, results in acquittal of the guilty or conviction of an innocent man. Thus, to ensure justice to the victims, which is an important object of the criminal justice system, the prosecution, and the legal profession as a whole, should work towards making the criminal justice system effective by being a bridge between the victim and justice.

(d) The Witness and the Victims: To strengthen the criminal justice system and ensure the delivery of fair justice to the victims, the witnesses (who may also be victims) play a very important role. It is the primary duty of a witness to support the prosecution; if a witness refuses to answer the questions or produce documents, as required to strengthen the prosecution, and has no reasonable excuse for doing the same, then he may be punished with simple imprisonment or can be taken into custody of the court for not more than seven days, unless he agrees to support the

[34] The Supreme Court has laid down in a number of cases that a lawyer should be held guilty of committing professional misconduct if he seeks adjournments repeatedly in the examination of witnesses present for hearing. The Apex Court has also observed that "the legal profession must be purified from such abuses of court procedures. Filibustering tactics, if adopted by an advocate, are also professional misconduct."

prosecution[35]. If the witness persists in his refusal, then the court is empowered to initiate an action for contempt against such person.[36] Further, if the witness, who is summoned by the court, fails to appear without just excuse, then the courts are empowered to try him summarily and sentence him to a fine not exceeding one hundred rupees[37]. The prosecution mainly relies upon the oral evidence of the witnesses to prove the case against the accused. Unfortunately, there is no shortage of witnesses who come to the courts and give false evidence with impunity, which is one of the major causes of failure of the criminal justice system. Thus, to counter the problem of perjury, the courts are empowered to try the witness summarily for perjury and may subject him to imprisonment for a term which may extend to three months or a fine which may extend to five hundred rupees or both.[38] A witness is not excused from answering any question relevant to the matter at issue on the grounds that the answer to such question may incriminate him or expose him to a penalty or forfeiture. However, no answer given by the witness makes him liable to any arrest or prosecution, or can be used against him in any criminal proceeding, though he can be prosecuted for giving false evidence by such an answer[39].

An accused person is a competent witness for the defence and, like any other witness he is entitled to give evidence on oath in disproof of the case laid against him by prosecution.[40] But, the court cannot draw any adverse inference from his non-examination as a witness. Only when the accused volunteers to be examined as a defence witness, the prosecution is entitled to examine him.[41] This provision is based on the cardinal principle of criminal jurisprudence that an accused person cannot be compelled to be a witness. A witness may be punished with imprisonment of either description,[42] which may be extended to a period of seven years, and shall also be liable to a fine, for intentionally giving false evidence or fabricating false evidence for the purpose of being used at any stage of judicial proceeding. If such evidence is used in any other case, then the witness may be punished with imprisonment of either description for a

[35] Cr.P.C. Section 349.
[36] *Ibid.,* According to the procedure laid down under Section 345 and 346.
[37] Ibid., Section 350(1)
[38] *Ibid.,* Section 344(1).
[39] I.E.A. Section 132 and Section 147.
[40] Cr.P.C. Section 315 (1)
[41] *Ibid.,* Proviso to Section 315(1).
[42] Simple imprisonment or rigorous imprisonment.

term which may extend to three years, and shall also be liable to fine.[43] Today, a witness turning hostile has become a common phenomenon; the prosecution and judiciary have been tied down in this respect. Many problems may lead to a witness turning hostile; in order to reduce this, the court should use modern technological innovations such as video conferencing, in important and sensitive cases, as it reduces the risk and burden on police and witness. The victim should be the ultimate beneficiary of the criminal justice system

(e)The Judiciary: "The function of the judiciary is responsible supervision. The judiciary has a high duty and a solemn responsibility to overview the work of the police, the prosecutor, and opposing counsel; to preserve the due process of law throughout the arrest-to-release procedure in the administration of justice; and to translate into living law the sanctions which may be imposed upon the offender after a fair trail."[44] A court is charged with monitoring procedures and with coordinating the activities of those criminal justice practitioners engaged in the prosecutorial and trial processes to insure that justice is carried out in a fair and impartial manner within a constitutional framework, in order to sustain the innocence or prove the guilt of the accused. The court is also responsible for sentencing, based on the protection of the society and the rehabilitation of the offender, i.e., the convicted criminal. An independent judiciary, free from interference by the executive or legislative organs of the government, is an essential prerequisite of a democracy which is wedded to rule of law and public welfare. The criminal justice system makes it clear that the role of the court as an agency of justice and criminal law administration is far more vital and significant than that of other agencies; the primary function of the court is to impart fair and impartial justice. In India there are four classes of criminal courts created under Cr.P.C.[45] besides these courts, the Supreme Court[46] and High Courts,[47] created by the Constitution, wield wide powers in criminal matters.

---

[43] I.P.C. Section 193 of Part XI (Sections 191-229A) deals with giving of false evidence and fabrication of false evidence along with offences against public justice in diverse cases and punishments for the same.

[44] Paul Weston and Kenneth Wells, *The Administration of Justice*, 2nd ed., (Englewood Cliffs, N.J.: Prentice-Hall, 1973), p.105.

[45] Courts of Session, Judicial Magistrates of the First Class and Metropolitan Magistrates, Judicial Magistrates of the Second Class, Executive Magistrates (Cr.P.C. Section 6).

[46] The Constitution of India Article 124.

[47] *Ibid.,* Article 214.

Courts are vested with wide powers (moreover, it is the duty of the court) to call for evidence at any stage of any inquiry, trial or proceedings[48], a necessary adjunct for a just decision in a case. While doing so, the court is enabled to summon any person as witness (excluding the accused), examine any person who is in attendance though not summoned, or recall and re-examine any person already examined. Courts are also empowered to proceed against any person not shown or mentioned as accused if it appears from the evidence that such person has committed an offence for which he could be tried together with the main accused against whom an inquiry or trial is being held.[49] The courts are authorized to issue a warrant of arrest or summons against such a person if he is not attending the court[50]; and if he is so attending, to detain such person for the purpose of inquiring into or trial for the offence which he appears to have committed[51]. The proceedings against such person are commenced *de novo*, and the witnesses reheard. For the purpose of arriving at the truth, the courts are armed with the most extensive powers to put questions to witnesses or parties about any fact, relevant or irrelevant, and may also order the production of any document or thing in the context of a particular matter before the court of law.[52] The effect of this power vested in courts is that in order to get to the bottom of the matter before it, the court will be able to look at and enquire into every fact. While the court exercises this power, none of the parties are entitled to object to any such question or order. It seems that the courts (judges) are not using these powers to their fullest extent to achieve just trial, as is evident from the acquittal rate.

There is a gross inadequacy of judges to cope with the enormous influx of new cases, owing to the imbalanced ratio of judges to population.[53] Apart from this, serious concern has been shown about deterioration of the quality of judges. It is a need of the hour to wipe out the backlog cases by appointing judges specialised in criminal law and to have a transparency in

---

[48] Cr.P.C. Section 311.

[49] Ibid., Section 319 (1).

[50] Ibid., Section 319 (2).

[51] Ibid., Section 319 (3).

[52] I.E.A. Section 165.

[53] The existing judge: population ratio in India is 10.5–13 per million as against 50 judges per million population in many parts of the world. To improve the ratio, the Supreme Court of India gave directions in 2003 to all the states to increase their judge strengths by five times in a phased manner by 2008.

the judgment which brings the confidence in the common man on the criminal justice delivery system.

(f) Penal Sanctions: 'Hate the Sin, not the Sinner': these words of Mahatma Gandhi indicate how penal sanctions should be enforced. Society should see the convict as a victim who has surrendered to his circumstances; as such, punishment should be reformative. Lord Denning, while appearing before the Royal Commission on Capital Punishment, expressed the following views:

> Punishment is the way in which society expresses its denunciation of wrong-doing and in order to maintain respect for law, it is essential that the punishment inflicted for grave crimes should adequately reflect the revulsion felt by the great majority of the citizens. For them it is a mistake to consider the object of punishment as being deterrent or reformative or preventive and nothing else. The truth is that some crimes are so outrageous that society insists on adequate punishment because the wrongdoer deserves it, irrespective of whether it is deterrent or not.

Thus, the punishment should be severe enough to act as a deterrent, but not so severe as to be brutal, and should be moderate enough to be humane, but not so as to be ineffective.

The I.P.C, prescribes the maximum and minimum punishments for offences and the judiciary exercises wide discretion, within the statutory limits, for sentencing. There are no statutory guidelines for regulating this discretion, as a result of which there is a variance in the manner of sentencing. Since the I.P.C. was enacted in 1860, many changes have taken place: new forms of crimes have come into existence, the punishments for some crimes prove to be inadequate, and the need to impose only a fine as sentence for smaller offences is felt. Moreover, as the fines were prescribed more than a century ago, there is a need to enhance the level of fine suitably. There is also a need to have new forms of punishments such as community service, disqualification from holding public offices, confiscation orders, etc. Radical changes in the pattern and intensity of crimes such as terrorism, organized crime, economic offences, cyber-crimes, trafficking in drugs and women and many similar crimes have no boundaries and affect the entire society. We cannot find responses to these changes in the IPC.

(g) Probation: Probation is a sentencing alternative. It permits the convicted offender (if the circumstances warrant) to serve his sentence within the community without going to prison, under the supervision of the probation service. Probation is a judicial act based on the right of the judiciary to suspend the imposition or execution of sentence. The probationer agrees to adhere to certain conditions established by the court. Failure to observe the conditions of probation or the commission of a new offence can result in a revocation of probation. While on probation, the probationer receives treatment, guidance, assistance, and varying degrees of supervision. The use of probation has not been made use of as adequately and properly by the lower courts in India as possible under the Probation of Offenders Act, 1958,[54] and Cr.P.C.[55] The Supreme Court has spelled out the object of the Probation of Offenders Act, 1958, as follows: "The purpose of the Act is to stop conversion of youthful offenders into stubborn criminals as a result of their association with hardened criminals of mature age, in case of youthful offenders being sentenced to undergo imprisonment in jail. Modern criminal jurisprudence recognises that no one is born criminal and that a good many crimes are result of socio-economic milieu. Although not much can be done for hardened criminals, yet a considerable emphasis has been laid on bringing about reform of young offenders not guilty of very serious offences by preventing their association with hardened criminals. The Act gives statutory recognition to the above objective."[56] In *Masa Khan* v. *State of Maharastra*,[57] the Supreme Court pointed out that though the provisions of section 6[58] of the Probation of Offenders Act, 1958 were mandatory, the courts did not appear to make wise use of the provisions, which was necessary to protect the younger generation from becoming professional criminals and therefore, a menace to society. Even the observations made by the Supreme Court have had no impact on the lower courts; until the lower courts act, we will always find on the wrong foot in the justice delivery system, with increasing overcrowding of prisons and with more trouble on our hands by turning young offenders into professional criminals.

(h) Prison Administration: Imprisonment symbolizes a system of punishment; it serves as a deterrent to the offender (to other members of

[54] Section 3—power of courts to release certain offenders after admonition, Section 4—power of courts to release certain offenders on probation of good conduct.

[55] Section 360—"order to release on probation of good conduct or after admonition".

[56] *Ramji Missar* v. *State of* Bihar, AIR 1963 Sc 1088; *Jagdev Singh* v. *State of Punjab*, AIR 1973 SC 2427; *Ram Naresh Pandey* v. *State of Madhya Pradesh*, (1974) 3 SCC 30.

[57] (1977) 1 SCC 733: 1977 SCC (Cri) 164.

[58] Restrictions on imprisonment of offenders under twenty-one years of age.

society also), retributive in some cases (where the death sentence is awarded), preventive, by keeping the criminal away from society, and reformative by providing an opportunity to the convict to readjust to the society as a law-abiding citizen. Prison is an indicator of a sound criminal justice system; the post-sentencing process needs a lot of attention and care as it performs the function of moulding of convicts, so a better administration of prisons results in a better society. The Supreme Court, in *Mohammad Giassudin* v. *State of Andhra Pradesh*,[59] observed: "progressive criminologists across the world will agree that the Gandhian diagnosis of offenders as patients and his concept of prisons as hospitals—mental or moral—is the key to the pathology of delinquency and the therapeutic role of punishment. The whole man is a healthy man and every man is born good. Criminality is curable deviance. Our prisons should be correctional houses, not cruel iron racking the soul." This observation bears upon reforms in prisons and the need for change in the attitudes of society, law-makers, and prison administrators themselves. Reforms in prisons will definitely have a positive bearing on the criminal justice system as they balance the interests of both the victim and the culprit.

(i) Parole: parole is the release of an offender from the prison before the expiration of term of imprisonment. The object of parole is to prepare the prisoner for adjustment to normal social life outside the prison and it therefore signifies the transition phase from imprisonment to normal freedom, where the prisoner lives at liberty subject to the condition imposed by the parole order.[60] The decision to release a prisoner on parole is taken by a parole board and in some cases the courts. The Supreme Court in *Hiralal Mallick* v. *State of Bihar*[61] described the use of parole thus: "One method of reducing tension is by providing for vital links between the prisoner and his family. A prisoner insulated from the world becomes bestial and, if his family ties are snapped for long, becomes dehumanized. Therefore, we regard it as correctionally desirable that this appellant be granted parole and expect the authorities to give consideration to periodically paroling prisoners, particularly of the present type, for reasonable spells, subject to sufficient safeguards ensuring their proper behaviour outside and prompt return inside." The success of parole lies in proper selection of cases and the need to pursue them with all vigor and

---

[59] AIR 1977 SC 1926.
[60] Ahmad Siddique, *Criminology*, 5th ed., (Lucknow: Eastern Book Company, 2005), p.228.
[61] (1977) 4 SCC 44: 1977 SCC (Cri) 538.

the resources at one's command; prison administration needs professionals and officers who are trained to deal with these challenges in their career as professionals.

V-Conclusion

The criminal justice system in India is overdue for a change; the report of Justice V.S.Malimath has emphasized the need for changes in our criminal justice system; he has recommended the changes in police system[62], prosecution[63] (recruitment, training and professionalism for prosecutors), Judiciary[64] (appointment of more judges; ensure objectivity and transparency; changes in the provisions of impeachment of judges; changes in trial procedures; vacation of courts) and witness[65] (benefits for the needs of victims and changes regarding witnesses and perjury), penal sanctions[66] (by introducing special enactments to deal with organised crime, terrorism, economic crimes by bringing in federal laws), in achieving the goal of "quest for truth" which is possible only when the entire law machinery performs its duties with diligence and is prompt, intelligent, informative and imaginative. The present criminal justice system is adversarial (prosecution to prove the guilt against the accused beyond reasonable doubt) which has affected our conviction rate; in contrast, the inquisitorial system (accused is presumed to be guilty and is supposed to prove his innocence) which is practiced in many European countries has a higher conviction rate. It is now necessary to blend both these systems and produce a new system with suitable amendments, so that the victim never suffers (receives justice and reposes faith in the criminal justice system) and the accused gets a chance to protect himself (not compromising his fundamental rights, subject to restrictions).

---

[62] The Report consists of 150 recommendations. Number 15 to 51 - states the changes that are need to be done in connection with the police system.

[63] Number 52 to 62 - recommendations for the changes in the Prosecution.

[64] Number 63 to 99 - recommendations for the changes in the Judicial system and witness.

[65] *Ibid.*

[66] Number 100 to 155 - recommendations for the changes in the penal provisions.

To conclude, it is appropriate to quote the sayings of Henry Peter Broughan with certain adaptations[67]

> it was the boast of Augustus that he founded a Rome of bricks and left it of marble"; "But how noble will be the boast of the citizens of free India of today when they say that they found a law dear and left it cheaper; founded a sealed book and left it a living letter; founded the patrimony of the rich and left it the inheritance of the poor; found the two edged sword of craft and oppression and left it the staff of honesty and the shield of innocence.

[67] As quoted by Justice V.G. Sabhahit in "Public Interest Litigation: Evolution, Growth, Comprehension and Enforcing Limits", in *The Changing Law, Lectures on Current Trends in Jurisprudential Thought, Commemorative Volume in honor of Prof. V.B. Coutinho on his 60th birthday* (2003).

NECESSITY AS A DEFENSE UNDER PENAL CODES: A COMPARATIVE ANALYSIS

SHABER ALI GANDAMAN[1]

> Man cannot be free if he does not know that he is subject to necessity, because his freedom is always won in his never wholly successful attempts to liberate himself from necessity.
> —Hanna Arendt

Introduction

Personal safety, particularly security of life, liberty and property, is of the utmost importance to any individual. Maintenance of peace and order is absolutely essential in any society in order for human beings to live peacefully and without fear of injury to their lives and property. This is possible only in states where the penal law is effective and strong enough to deal with violators of the law. Any state, whatever may be its ideology or form of government, in order to be designated as a state, must definitely have an efficient system of penal laws in order to discharge its primary function of keeping peace in the land by maintaining law and order[2].

Every one of us comes into contact with the criminal justice system at some point in our lives. We do so as the accused in criminal cases, or as victims of crimes, or as relatives or friends of those accused of crime or the victims of crime[3].

Administration of criminal justice is one of the essential functions of the state. Law and order within the state is maintained through the

---

[1] LL.M., (NLSIU, Bangalore), M.L., (SKU) Sr. Lecturer, V.M.Salgaocar Collège of Law, Panaji, Goa.
[2] Pillai, P.S.A., *Criminal Law* (9th ed.) (New Delhi: Butterworth's India, 2000), p. 1
[3] Gonsalves, Rebecca, and Menezes, Ryan, *Criminal Law, Law for Activist Series*. (Vol. 1) (Mumbai: India Centre for HR and Law, HRNL, 2007), p. 1

administration of justice. The present form of administration of justice is the result of passing through various stages. In primitive society, when a wrong was done against an individual, he had to resort to self-help, which was based on private vengeance. During the middle ages the concept of penance or the purification of the soul prevailed. Gradually, society evolved and the state entered the process. The state protects the rights and enforces the duties of citizens[4].

The main purpose of criminal justice administration is to punish the wrongdoer. He is punished by the state. It is one of the main functions of a modern state to protect peaceful and law-abiding citizens from anything which upsets the smooth operation of economic life in society. In certain situations, state aid is not possible and the citizen can follow various defenses to protect himself and his property. In such situations he is not liable, his act is excusable. Criminal law recognizes various circumstances in which the offender is not held liable. These circumstances include accident, necessity, intoxication, insanity, mistake of fact, trivial, duress, right of self defense, etc.

In this article, an attempt is made to explain the concept and importance of necessity as a defense in criminal cases in India in detail. Further, the article analyses and compares the various provisions dealing with the same concept in other countries, such as Portugal, France and Germany.

The Concept of Necessity in India

The word 'necessity,' as we customarily use it, has a special meaning. A particular act is never necessary in the sense that there is literally no option. Some choice is always present, even though one of the alternatives is to meet one's own death. Necessity, in a legal context, involves avoiding a greater evil by committing a smaller evil[5].

Generally, necessity is a good ground to excuse any person morally as well as legally. This concept has been recognized in our society from time immemorial. In an extreme emergency, on the grounds of necessity, if a person kills one innocent person to save the life of a large number of

---

[4] Mani, Tripathi B.N., *Jurisprudence: Legal Theory*, (Allahabad: Allahabad Law Agency, 1997), p. 127

[5] Glanville Williams, *Text Book of Criminal Law* (London: Stevens and Sons Ltd., 1978), p. 553

persons his act is morally excusable. In our present society the act of such a person is also legally excusable under criminal law.

In criminal law, necessity may be either an excuse or an exculpation for breaking the law. Defendants seeking to rely on this defense argue that they should not be held liable for their actions as a crime because their conduct was *necessary* to prevent some greater harm. Most common law and civil law jurisdictions recognize this defense, but only under limited circumstances. Generally, the defendant must firmly show that :

(a) the harm he sought to avoid outweighs the danger of the prohibited conduct he is charged with;

(b) he had no reasonable alternative;

(c) he ceased to engage in the prohibited conduct as soon as the danger passed; and

(d) he did not himself create the danger he sought to avoid.[6]

In India, the necessity defense has long been recognized in common law and has also been made part of most states' statutory law. Although no federal statute acknowledges the defense, the judiciary has recognized it as a part of the common law. The rationale behind the necessity defense is that sometimes, in a particular situation, a technical breach of the law is more advantageous to society than the consequences of strict adherence to the law. The defense is often used successfully in cases which involve a trespass on property to save a person's life or property. It also has been used, with varying degrees of success, in cases involving more complex questions[7].

In almost all common-law and statutory definitions, the concept of necessity as a defense includes the following elements:

(1) the defendant acted to avoid a significant risk of harm;

(2) no adequate lawful means could have been used to escape the harm; and

---

[6] htpp://www.answers.com/topic/necessity dated: 25.08.08

[7] htpp://www.answers.com/topic/necessity dated: 25.08.08

(3) the harm avoided was greater than that which would have been caused by breaking the law.

In addition to the above requirements, the defendant has to prove that the harm would have been imminent and that the action taken could have been reasonably expected to avoid the imminent danger. All these elements reflect the principles on which the defense of necessity was founded:

First, that the highest social value is not always achieved by blind adherence to the law; Second, that it is unjust to punish those who technically violate the letter of the law when they are acting to promote or achieve a higher social value than would be served by strict adherence to the law; and

Third, that it is in society's best interest to promote the greatest good and to encourage people to seek to achieve the greatest good, even if in doing so necessitates a technical breach of the law[8].

The defense of necessity is considered a justification defense, as compared with an excuse defense such as duress. An action that is harmful but praiseworthy is justified, whereas an action that is harmful but ought to be forgiven may be excused. Rather than focusing on the actor's state of mind, as would be done with an excuse defense, the court with a necessity defense focuses on the value of the act. No court has ever accepted a defense of necessity to justify killing a person to protect property[9].

In India, the Penal Law was drafted by Lord MacCaulay during 1860. He drafted the penal law based on English law. It is nothing but the common law. The concept of necessity laid down under Indian penal law is based on the above-mentioned principles, followed under common law.

In India, the Indian Penal Code, 1860, as amended in 2000, is applicable in criminal matters. Chapter IV of this act deals with General Exceptions, in Sections 76 to 106. This chapter provides various exceptions to the accused person. If the act of the accused person is covered by these exceptions, he is not liable: the act of the accused person is either excusable or justified by law. They denote the circumstances in which a man is justified in committing an act which would otherwise be an offence.

---

[8] Ibid
[9] Ibid

Every penal clause is subject to a number of limitations and no offence can be absolute without any exception. An offence committed by a child or by a mentally ill person cannot obviously be treated in the same manner as an offence committed by a sane adult. Similarly, liability cannot be fixed on a person who has committed an offence by accident, under threat, by necessity or in private defense in the same manner as a person who has committed an offence with an evil intention or design[10].

One of the most important exceptions is necessity. Sec. 81[11] of the Act lays down the various grounds on the basis of which the accused can make use of necessity as a defence under general exceptions. In cases of sudden and extreme emergency, it is lawful to cause lesser evils to occur. This embodies the principle that where the accused chooses the lesser evil, in order to avert the greater, then he is immune. The section deals with what one can call inevitable accidents[12]. Inevitable accidents are accidents which are not avoidable by any such precautions as a reasonable man could be expected to take, at the moment they occurred. The doctrine of necessity embodied in Sec. 81 is an indirect recognition of such unavoidable situations.

According to Bentham, an act which would otherwise be a crime may in some cases be excused if the person accused can show that it was done only in order to avoid consequences which could not otherwise be avoided; that if these consequences had followed, they would have inflicted upon him or upon others irreparable evil; and that the evil inflicted by the accused was not disproportionate to the evil avoided. According to him, harm can only be justified if it is established[13]

a. that it was inflicted to avert a greater evil,

b. that other means were less effective or more costly, and

c. that the means employed were the most efficient possible.

---

[10] Supra note.1 at.66

[11] Sec. 81 of the Indian Penal Code, 1860: "Nothing is an offense merely by reason of its being done with the knowledge that it is likely to cause harm, if it be done without any criminal intention to cause harm, and in good faith for the prevention or avoiding other harm to person or property."

[12] Kathuria, R.P., *Supreme Court on Criminal Law*, (Vol. 1, 5th ed.). p. 76

[13] Tandon, M.P., *The Indian Penal Code,* (Faridaba: Allahabad Law Agency, 2005), pp. 116–117

It is clear from the above discussion that if a person causes injury to another without any criminal intention then his act is justified, he will not be held responsible for the result of his act provided the act was done in good faith to avoid or prevent greater harm to persons or property.

If necessity forces a man to do an illegal act, such illegal act is justified because no man can be guilty of a crime without the will and intention of his mind. It must be involuntary. If a man who is absolutely, by natural necessity, forced, his will does not go along with the act[14].

If an evil is done to prevent a greater evil, this is a ground of justification that we must refer to the extreme measures which may become necessary on the occasion of contagious disease, sieges, famines, tempests, shipwrecks, etc. But the more serious a remedy of this nature is, the more evident ought its necessity to be. The welfare of the state has served as a pretext for all crimes[15].

Immunity from criminal liability under this section will be available where an offense is committed without any criminal intention, to cause harm in good faith and if such offense is committed for the purpose of preventing or avoiding other harm to person or property. In *Re Ramaswaami Ayyar*[16], a village magistrate placed a restraint upon a drunkard who was threatening to commit a breach of peace and was a danger to other villagers; it was held the village magistrate, even as a private citizen, was protected by this section. The decision in *Ramaswami Ayyar* was confirmed by a Full Bench of Madras High Court in *Gopal Naidu v. Emperor*[17]; in this case a drunken man carrying a revolver in his hand was disarmed and put under restraint by police officers, although the offense of public nuisance under Sec. 290 was a non-cognizable offense without a warrant. Though the police officers were prima facie guilty of the offense of wrongful confinement, it was held that they could plead justification on the grounds of necessity. Further, the court held that the person or property to be protected may be the person or property of the accused himself, or of others.

---

[14] Ratanlal and Dhirajla, *Law of Crimes,* (26th ed.) (New Delhi: Bharat Law House, 2007), pp. 292–299
[15] Ibid
[16] AIR 1921 Mad 458
[17] AIR 1923 FB 523

Homicide and Necessity

The central question of whether the doctrine of necessity can be applied as a justification for killing another human being is a very difficult question. The general view is that necessity is not an adequate defense to a charge of murder[18].

Killing a person in self-defense may appear to be an example of necessity. While self-defense may overlap with the idea of necessity, the two are not the same. Private defense operates only against aggressors or wrongdoers, while the person against whom action is taken by necessity may not be an aggressor.

In *United States v. Holmes*[19], the accused was a member of the crew of a boat after a shipwreck. On the orders of the mate, he threw out 16 male passengers. The accused, though not convicted of murder, was convicted of manslaughter and sentenced to six months' imprisonment.

In one of the most important landmark English cases, *Regina v. Dudley and Stephens*[20], the crew of a yacht were cast away in a storm and were compelled to put to sea in an open boat, which had no water or food. On the twentieth day, having had nothing to eat for eight days, two of the crew agreed that the cabin boy should be killed with a knife in order that they might feed upon his body. On the fourth day after that, they were rescued by a passing boat. The two men were charged with murder. The question was considered by a divisional court of five judges. They held that the act was murder. However, their sentence of death was commuted by the Crown to six months' imprisonment.

In the above-mentioned cases, it was found difficult to decide which is a matter of greater harm and whether the act was justified. In both the cases, the judiciary held that killing another to save one's own life is not justified and the person is guilty of murder, but taking into account the circumstances and on humanitarian grounds the sentence was reduced.

From the above discussion it is very clear that no one has a right to kill another person on the grounds of necessity. Indian law is also based upon

---

[18] Supra note. 4 at. 558
[19] 1824 Federal Case 360, No 15383
[20] (1884)14 QBD 273 (1884)

the same presumption, that if a person commits a wrongful act to save his life he is liable[21]. He can not take the defense of necessity.

Comparison with Other Countries

Necessity is pleaded as a defense not only in India but also in other countries such as Portugal, France, and Germany. In this section, I attempt to analyze and explain the provisions in other countries relating to necessity as a defense in criminal matters.

The Portuguese Penal Code[22] deals with this issue in Article 1 to Article 130 of its General Part. Part III of the General Part deals with causes for exclusion of the unlawful act of a person. Under these circumstances, if any person commits an act he is not liable criminally, his act is excusable taking into account the whole situation. This applies if one of the following points is applicable:

The act of the accused is excused by legitimate self-defense, he did the act in the exercise of his rights, the act is committed in fulfillment of a duty imposed by law, or in certain circumstances with the consent of the person in the interest of law[23]. Article 34[24] provides for necessity as a right in criminal matters under the Portuguese Penal Code. According to this Article any act, if it is committed to avert a present danger to the agent or a

---

[21] A person starving for lack of food who robs the food of others to save his life is liable. He can not take the defense of necessity. The law states that robbing the food of others without consent is an offense.

[22] htpp://www.verbojuridico.net/download/portuguesepenalcode.pdf dated 24/09/08

[23] Article 31 of the Portuguese Penal Code: "1. The act is not criminally punishable when its unlawfulness is excluded by the legal system considered as a whole, 2. Namely, the act is not unlawful when committed a). In legitimate defense, b). In the exercise of a right, c). In fulfillment of a duty imposed by law or by an order of legitimate authority, or d) with the consent of the holder of the harmed legal interest."

[24] Article 34 of the Portuguese Penal Code: "An act is not unlawful when committed as an appropriate means to avert a present danger that threatens legally protected interest of the agent or of a third person, if the following requisites are verified: a). the dangerous situation must not have been voluntarily created by the agent, save in case of protecting the third person's interest, b). there is a sensible superiority of the interest to be safeguarded relative to the sacrificed interest, and c). it is reasonable to impose on the victim the sacrifice of his interest, considering the nature or value of the threatened interest."

third party, is lawful. The following grounds are required to make such act as lawful:

a. The dangerous situation was not created voluntarily,

b. There was a need to protect a large number of interests rather than a small group of interests, and

c. The injury caused to the victim is justified taking into account the greater benefit to society in general.

Further, Article 35[25] of the Portuguese Penal Code makes it possible to excuse the act of a person on the grounds of exculpatory necessity. It says that a person can show different unlawful behaviour to avert present danger to life, physical integrity, and honour. This unlawful behaviour is necessary to remove the difficult situation.

The above articles clearly prove that if one person kills other persons on the grounds of necessity, if his killing benefits the society at large the offender is not liable. Thus the Portuguese Penal Code justifies the unlawful act of a person if he is trying to prevent danger to a large group of persons.

The Napoleonic Code was based on earlier French laws as well as Roman law. Napoleon set out to reform the French legal system in accordance with the principles of the French Revolution, because the old feudal and royal laws seemed to be confusing and contradictory to the rights of the people. Based on the Napoleonic Code of 1810, French Criminal Law was applied until recently, one of the oldest codified systems in application. Recent reforms (1992–1994), followed in 1997 by further revisions, have brought the system as a whole to national attention and under the scrutiny of anyone interested in comparative criminal law[26].

French Criminal Law is a combination of the Code Penal (Penal Code) and the Code de Procédure Penale (Code of Penal Procedure). These laws deal with the technicalities and philosophy of the criminal justice system in

[25] Article 35 of the Portuguese Penal Code: "Whoever commits an unlawful act appropriate to avert a present danger, not differently removable, that threatens life, physical integrity, honour or freedom of the agent or of a third person, acts without guilt when it is not reasonable to demand, according to the circumstances of the case, a different behaviour."

[26] http://en.wikipedia.org/wiki/Napoleonic_Code dated: 25.08.08

France. The Penal Code defines offenses and assigns sanctions. Its primary function is to protect society as a whole, to ensure social control by categorizing and defining the offenses that disrupt it[27].

French Penal Code consists of four books. Book one summarizes the general dispositions of the Code. It includes the rules of general penal law and most of the rules on sentencing. This general part of the Code, the Partie Générale of the new penal code, recognizes rules that were previously dispersed in various parts of 1810 Code or even in the Procedure Code. Most of these rules had never been modified since 1810. Some of them had remained untouched since 1791[28].

The other three books are referred to as the special part or Partie Speciale. The main focus of book two is the punishment of crimes and misdemeanors against individuals. Book three deals with offenses against property. Finally, book four deals with crimes and misdemeanors against the nation, the state and public order[29].

The French Penal Code[30], Chapter II, deals with grounds for absence or attenuation of liability in Articles 122—1 to 122—8. Article 122—7[31] states that a person is not liable in criminal cases on the ground of necessity. A person can protect himself, his property, any other person and that person's property on the grounds of necessity to ensure the safety of the person or property. The act of the person is excusable if the means employed by him are proportionate to the threat.

German criminal law,[32] that is, the Criminal Code (StGB) as promulgated on 13th November 1998, consists of 358 Sections, divided into 30 Chapters. Under this Criminal Code, heading four deals with necessity as a

---

[27] Ibid

[28] htpp://www.iuscomp.org/gla/statutes/StGB.htm dated 17.08.08

[29] Ibid

[30] htpp://195.83.177.9/code/index.phtml?lang dated 20.09.08

[31] Article 122-7 of the French Penal Code: "A person is not criminally liable if, confronted with a present or imminent danger to himself, another person or property, he performs an act necessary to ensure the safety of that person or property, except where the means used are disproportionate to the seriousness of the threat."

[32] Supra note. 17

defense. This heading consists of four sections. Section 32[33] provides statutory recognition to the concept of necessity. A person can take this defense to avoid an imminent assault on him or on another. This section mainly protects a person with respect to assault alone. If the person exceeds his limits of necessity due to factors like fear or confusion, his act is excusable and he is not liable to punishment[34].

Further, the German Criminal Code holds the act of a person to be justified on grounds of necessity in case of imminent danger to life or limb to avoid greater danger to the community. His act is justified in the following circumstances: his act is lawful, the interest protected outweighs the other interest, or his act is proportionate to avert greater evil[35].

German penal law contains a separate section which deals with necessity as a defense[36]. It states that where the accused person commits an unlawful act he is not guilty if that act was necessary to avoid imminent danger to his life, limb or freedom, or those of a relative or people close to him.

---

[33] Sec. 32 of the German Criminal Code: (1) "Whoever commits an act required as necessary defense does not act unlawfully, (2) Necessary defense is the defense which is required to avert an imminent unlawful assault from oneself or another."

[34] Sec. 33 of the German Criminal Code: "If the perpetrator exceeds the limits of necessary defense due to confusion, fear or fright, then he shall not be punished."

[35] Sec. 34 of the German Criminal Code: "Whoever, faced with an imminent danger to life, limb, freedom, honour, property or another legal interest which cannot otherwise be averted, commits an act to avert the danger from himself or another, does not act unlawfully, if upon weighing the conflicting interests, in particular the affected legal interests and the degree of danger threatening them, the protected interest substantially outweighs the one interfered with; this shall apply, however, only to the extent that the act is a proportionate means to avert the danger."

[36] Sec. 35 of the German Criminal Code: (1) Whoever, faced with an imminent danger to life, limb, or freedom which can not otherwise be averted, commits an unlawful act to avert the danger form himself, a relative or person close to him, acts without guilt. This shall not apply to the extent that the perpetrator could be expected under the circumstances to assume the risk, in particular, because he himself caused the danger or stood in a special legal relationship, however the punishment may be mitigated pursuant to Section 49 subsection (i) if the perpetrator was not required to assume the risk with respect to a special legal relationship. (ii) if upon commission of the act the perpetrator mistakenly assumes that circumstances exist, which would excuse him under subsection (i), he will only be punished, if he could have avoided the mistake. The punishment shall be mitigated pursuant to Section 49 subsection (i)."

All the above four sections highlights the scope of necessity as defense under German penal law. It is clear from the above sections this defense is available to the person himself, to a relative or a person close to him. This concept is not available to a stranger as is laid down under the Indian law.

Under this German Criminal Code, it is difficult to distinguish between the principles of duress and personal necessity. Since the enactment of its first criminal code in 1871, German law has clearly recognized both excuses. Indeed, the 1975 code unites duress and personal necessity in one overarching provision (§ 35). It follows that in *Dudley and Stephens*, German courts would have considered the possibility of excusing the homicide. Despite some signs to the contrary, Anglo-American courts persist in distinguishing between duress, which they recognize, and personal necessity, which they have yet to recognize as an excuse[37].

A critical examination of the above penal provisions of Portuguese, German and French law proves that killing a person on the grounds of necessity is justified, and the offender is not liable in such situation. But Indian law being Anglo-Saxon law, it does not protect the offender's killing due to starvation on the grounds of necessity. French and German law would endorse starvation and other natural circumstances as excuses even for homicide. The situation in Indian, England and America is different; the judiciary played an important role in these countries and it was held that killing due to starvation under natural circumstances could neither excuse nor justify homicide, and influential opinion ruled out starvation as an excuse for theft.

Conclusions

> In all human institutions, a smaller evil is allowed, to procure a greater good.
> —Oliver Goldsmith[38]

Necessity in legal contexts involves the judgment that the evil of obeying the letter of the law is socially greater in the particular circumstances than the evil of breaking it. In other words, the law has been broken to achieve a greater good[39]. The above discussion highlights that necessity cannot be a defense in certain natural circumstances such as killing out of starvation

[37] http://law.jrank.org/pages/1112/Excuse-Theory-range-excuse.html dated 25.08.08
[38] The Vicar of Wakefield
[39] Supra note.16 at. 553

or theft out of hunger. But morally, such natural circumstances are also excusable and justifiable.

Common law does sometimes permit private parties to assert the defense of public necessity; as for instance, to justify the destruction of private stores of liquor before an invading army enters a city or, presumably, in the example presented in the comments to the *Model Penal Code*, the destruction of a dike to save a city, although its destruction might lead to the inundation of a farm[40].

In my opinion, a person making a decision whether to kill one innocent person in order to save the lives of a greater number of other people would be correct in a belief that it is necessary to kill the one to save the others. In the real world, however, people do make mistakes. From the perspective of law and practical morality, the privilege to kill innocent people to save a greater number of lives would have to include the privilege to kill innocent people on the reasonable but unfortunately mistaken belief that such action was absolutely necessary in order to save a greater number of lives. The fact that this makes us feel uncomfortable is another reason why it is not permissible to intentionally kill an innocent person in order to save a larger number of other people.

Morally, there is a difference between action and inaction; it is permissible intentionally to kill an innocent person in order to save a larger number of other people. This proposition is without legal foundation and the proposition also lacks an adequate moral foundation. The proposition seems to violate Kant's injunction that one must treat people as ends in themselves and never as means[41].

We regard the right to life as almost a supreme value, and it is very unlikely that anyone would be held to be justified in killing for any purpose except the saving of other life, or perhaps the saving of great pain or distress. Our revulsion against a deliberate killing is so strong that we are loath to consider utilitarian reasons for it[42].

Personal necessity is not recognized as an excuse in Indian, England and America: for example killing due to starvation, escape from prison to avoid threatened violence. There is a need to change and follow the

---

[40] htpp://ww.law.duke.edu/shell/cite.p1?48+Duke +L.+J.+975 dated 20.08.09
[41] Ibid
[42]Supra note. 4 at.559

situation in other countries, that is, to provide the defense of personal necessity to the offender in certain natural circumstances, even though the offender kills another person.

REVISION OF THE PORTUGUESE CODE OF CRIMINAL PROCEDURE[1]

PAULO DE SOUSA MENDES

Introduction

The Portuguese Code of Criminal Procedure (CPP), approved by Decree Law 78/87, of 17 February, has been considered by the majority of those operating within the national justice arena to be a notable piece of legislation, despite the criticisms of some specific aspects which are so often heard.

As a result of these criticisms, it is not hard to understand that the CPP has been amended fourteen times, always surgically and with none of these amendments disfiguring the Code itself.

Recently, further amendment was made to the CPP. Indeed, on 20 December 2006, the Government presented the National Parliament with Bill 109/X, which would lead to the fifteenth amendment to the CPP. This Bill was based on the work of the Mission for Penal Reform Unit (UMRP), created by Council of Ministers Resolution 138/2005, of 17 August. The PSD, CDS-PP, BE and PCP Parliamentary Political Parties also presented draft proposals with the purpose of amending the CPP.

The Bill and draft proposals warranted discussion in Parliament. The Bill was approved by a majority, on 15 March 2007, with favourable votes from PS and PSD and abstention by BE, CDS-PP, PCP and PEV. In addition, the "Pact of Justice" between the Parliamentary Political Parties of PS and PSD, signed on 8 September 2006, guaranteed that the Bill would be approved in practice.

---

[1] Translation from the Portuguese by Michelle L. Wells.

The Bill underwent further amendment during the detailed analysis stage, and the amendment of the CPP was finally approved by Law 48/2007, of 29 August[2]. After a short period of *vacatio legis* (15 days), the CPP came into force on 15 September 2007, at the same time as the amendments to the Criminal Code (CP) and with Law 51/2007, of 31 August, which defines the Objectives, Priorities and Direction of Criminal Policy.

The process of revision of the CPP was carefully prepared and benefited from the participation of many, insofar as the work of the UMRP was supplemented by frequent meetings of a Council created on the initiative of the Coordinator of the UMRP, Mr Rui Pereira, and which included representatives from the various sectors of justice as well as university professors. The solutions resulted from a consensus whenever possible, although discussion of diverging opinions was never dispensed with.

The UMRP's draft bill proposed amendment of more than a third of the Code. Despite the vast number of amendments presented, the UMRP was careful to safeguard the essence of the Code, seeking only to improve it based on the experience of its application and on the case-law of the Constitutional Court. There were also amendments which resulted directly from the need to transpose international obligations of the Portuguese State into the national legal order.

Improving legislation on criminal procedure is never, however, an issue which is merely technical and axiologically neutral. On the contrary, improvement occurred within the framework of certain criminal policy objectives, which were, on the one hand, increasing the protection granted to victims and, on the other, strengthening the guarantees of defence of the defendant, yet making these compatible with the aim of improving the efficiency of the criminal procedure, also recalling that Article 32(2) of the Constitution consecrates the presumption of innocence alongside the right to a speedy trial.

Our purpose here is not, of course, to detail all the amendments produced, but rather to refer to the most important ones.

---

[2] Amended by Declaration of Rectification 105/2007, of 9 November.

1. Protection of the Victim

The CPP is not sparing with regards to protection granted to the victim, yet, nevertheless, some new measures are established:

—The injured party will now be informed of the crime notification, whenever the Public Prosecutor's Office (MP) has reason to believe that s/he is unaware of this (Art. 247(1));
—The position of the private prosecutor (*assistente*) is strengthened, and it is expressly provided that s/he may be accompanied by a lawyer in all activities in which s/he intervenes (Art. 70(3));
—To make criminal proceedings viable in cases of anonymous submission of a complaint, the competent judicial authority or organ of the criminal police (OPC) will now inform those entitled to present a complaint or to report a crime of the existence of the submission of a complaint, as long as this provides evidence of the practice of a crime or itself constitutes a crime (Art. 246(6));
—Bearing in mind the vulnerability of the injured party, the law provides that the court shall inform him/her of the date on which the defendant is to be released, when this may give rise to danger, with this rule being extended to cases of the release and escape of prisoners (Arts. 217(3), 480 (3) and 482(2)).

2. Protection of the Defendant

There are many amendments which seek to strengthen the guarantee of the defence of the defendant. The following are particularly significant:

—The defendant will now be informed of the facts with which s/he is charged before providing a statement to anybody (Art. 61(1)c)), in order to bring to an end inquisitorial questioning in which the defendant had to guess the meaning of the questions, even running the risk of incriminating him/herself by offering new facts in addition to those which were already being investigated;
—In particular, in the first judicial questioning of the detained defendant, the judge must inform the defendant of the reasons for his/her detention, of the facts with which s/he is charged and of the means of evidence, unless, in the latter case, revelation of these seriously jeopardizes the investigation, discovery of the truth or fundamental rights (Art. 141(4));
—If the detained defendant is presented before the MP without having been questioned by the judge of instruction following his/her detention, the MP must inform him/her in the same way (Art. 143(2));

—Furthermore, all statements of detained defendants may only be obtained in the presence of a lawyer (Arts. 64(1)a), and 144(3));
—Besides this, when a defendant who is not detained is called to provide a statement, s/he shall now have the right to be aided by a lawyer, and shall be informed of this right at an opportune moment by the body calling him/her for questioning (Art. 144(4));
—Bearing in mind that a witness may, at any moment, become a defendant, s/he may now be accompanied by a lawyer whenever s/he is required to provide a statement (Art. 132(4));
—In addition, the defendant, on request, shall be given access to the statements during the inquiry, except where there is the possibility of harm to the investigation or to the rights of those reporting the crime or of the victims (Art. 89(1)).

These amendments were welcomed, amongst other bodies, by the Bar Association, which, in addition, was represented in the Council of the UMRP.

Many other measures for the protection of the defendant could also be mentioned, but a selective review of the reform is required here. Nevertheless, two others must certainly be noted:

—The amendments to the system for remanding defendants in custody, which hereafter may only be applied to cases of crimes involving intent punishable with a prison sentence of five years or more, except for certain phenomena of terrorist, violent or highly organized criminality (Art. 202(1)b)). In addition, the periods of remand are reduced. However, in the case of a defendant who has already been convicted in two successive hearings, the maximum period is increased to half of the sentence that has been fixed (Art. 215(6)). To avoid the continuation of remand, it is established that the periods provided for may not be surpassed when there is a plurality of cases (Art. 215(7));
—The creation of the possibility for the defendant to request compensation for harm suffered when it is proved that s/he did not commit the crime or acted justifiably (Art. 225(1)c)). The State assumes a kind of objective civil liability, paying no attention to costs when it is a question of compensating the innocent defendant who has suffered deprivation of freedom, even though there has been no procedural error in this.

3. Strengthening of the powers of the Public Prosecutor's Office

The powers of the MP are significantly strengthened, in several aspects:
—In the system of the CPP, the MP is in charge of the inquiry, but its domain has diminished in practice. Nowadays it is not uncommon for the MP to only come into contact with the case at the end of the inquiry, when all that remains is to accuse or to file the case. With the revision, there are several actions by the police that will have to be validated or otherwise simply checked by the MP, such as the conferring of the status of defendant, if this is performed by the OPC (Art. 58(3)), or telephone tapping, the recordings and reports of the content of which must be handed over to the MP, which then has 48 hours to take these to the judge of instruction (Art. 188(1),(3) and (4)). The aim of this is to improve communication between the MP and the police, while still respecting the technical and tactical autonomy of the latter, as set out in the Law of Criminal Investigation (Law 21/2000, of 10 August);
—At the beginning of inquiries, the MP may now assess whether the submission of a complaint constitutes a crime notification, and must decide accordingly whether the inquiry should be opened or not (Arts. 58(1) a) and d), and 246(5)a)), notwithstanding the fact that all submissions of complaints shall be recorded, even those which are clearly unfounded. The assessment of the submission of the complaint must not, however, be confused with the judgement of opportunity, unless the idea of the MP is that of a robot which records submissions of complaints and automatically opens inquiries.

4. Strengthening of the effectiveness of the criminal procedure

The special forms of procedure have undergone amendments of considerable scope, with a view to expanding and improving their application, thus promoting maximum speed in procedures, so long as this is compatible with the guarantee of defence. For examples, we may see that:

—The scope of the summary procedure has been extended, making it compulsory in cases of arrest *in flagrante delicto* of a crime punishable with a prison sentence of not more than five years, rather than the current three years (Art. 381(1));
—Besides this, the summary procedure now covers cases of arrest *in flagrante delicto* by a private individual, so long as the detained person is

handed over to a judicial authority or police body within a time limit of no more than 2 hours (Art. 381(1)b)). The intention here is to include the numerous situations of theft, amongst others, which cannot currently be tried using this procedural format, despite the fact that the inquiry, which is compulsory in the format of the common procedure, is sometimes a useless ritual here, particularly since the means of evidence are all already known;

—The pre-trial case management disappears in the accelerated procedure (Arts. 286(3) and 391-C);

—Actions related to the summary and accelerated procedures may now take place on non-working days (Art. 103(2)c)) and the respective deadlines continue throughout the judicial holidays (Art. 104(2).

Conclusion

To sum up, one might say that all those involved in the procedures have cause to celebrate following the revision of the CPP, since the position of all of them is strengthened. This is not at all surprising, nor, much less, paradoxical: the Portuguese criminal procedure is not a procedure of parties, purely accusatorial in nature. In fact, the MP does not have the status of a party, but of an authentic magistrate, who is subject to the strict duty of objectivity. For this reason, the strengthening of the powers of the MP does not have to occur at the expense of the rights, freedoms and guarantees of the citizens, whether injured parties, suspects or defendants.

PART IV:

CONTRACTS

STANDARD FORMS OF CONTRACT IN GERMAN AND COMMON LAW

SAIRAM BHAT[1]

Standard forms of contracts fulfill an important role in business dealings. Statutes and doctrines of contract law are generally drafted broadly in order to cover a large number of contracts. Therefore certain contracts, for example concerning usage of parking lots, dry cleaning or the placing of vending machines, are unlikely to be governed by a specialized provision. However, in those contracts questions may arise that are not foreseen by the general provisions, or certain provisions may be unfitting to the contract at hand. It would be inefficient for a party engaging in a great number of such contracts to negotiate detailed terms and provisions every time. In economic terms, the transaction costs would be too high. Nevertheless, certain problems arise through the usage of standard form contracts.

Naturally, the party using the standard terms will draft them as favorably to himself as possible. This can cause problems, as in many cases those terms will not be negotiable, thus the weaker party might have no choice but to accept the terms. Furthermore, the standard terms are rarely read and are much less important than the price or quality of the good or services provided. Therefore competition does not lead to usage of reasonable standard terms as it does, for example, in the case of prices. Also, it is often reasonable not to read standard terms. The effort required to read and compare several different standard terms is disproportionate to their relatively small significance. The chances that something will go wrong are often slim and even if it does, the damages expected will commonly not be too high. Because of all this, laws are required that on one hand do not unduly hinder the usage of standard term contracts, but on the other hand offer protection for the other party (the consumer). This paper attempts to analyses the position of standard forms of contract in

[1] Assistant Professor of Law, National Law School of India University, Bangalore, India.

German law and in common law, while also highlighting the striking similarities and difference.

History and Development in Germany

Standard form contracts were being used increasingly from the late 19th century onwards. The Reichsgericht[2] applied #138 BGB[3] to determine whether such agreements were valid, thus offering some basic protection. # 138 BGB renders agreements void which are contrary to public policy (literally 'against the good mores'; another translation might be 'common decency,' for example usury). The Bundesgerichtshof (BGH) established a tighter and more specific control of standard business terms[4] based on # 242 BGB which establishes a duty to perform according to the requirements of good faith.[5] In a leading case the BGH rules:

> 'as far as regulations of dispositive law are not merely created out of convenience, but due to a commandment of justice evolving from the nature of the substance matter, alteration through standard business terms has to be backed by reasons which, in the cases to be governed by those terms, question the underlying commandment of justice of the dispositive law and make an alteration appear in accordance with justice and equity. The amount of justice in dispositive regulations made by the legislator can vary. The greater this amount, the stricter the scale with which the standard business terms' accordance with the principle of good faith is measured. The needs of honest business dealing that shall be governed by standard business terms demand that those terms are within the frame of what thinking persons deem equitable and just to be appropriate.'[6]

This test established by the court provides following steps in order to determine the validity of standard business terms:

- Do the terms differ from the regulation of the code?
- If yes, are those regulations merely choosing one of several equally acceptable solutions in order to provide clarity (created

---

[2] Court of the Empire, German Supreme Court from 1879 to 1945.

[3] Burgerliches Gesetzbuch, German Civil Code. English translation available at http://www/gesetze-im-internet.de/english_bgb/index.html.

[4] Note that German law uses the term 'standard business terms' when referring to standard terms of contracts.

[5] Note that # 242 BGB is subject to wide interpretation and establishes a general principle of good faith not restricted to performance only.

[6] BGH, judgment of 17.2.1964, BGHZ 41, 151 (154 ff.)

out of convenience) or are they based on the view that this particular approach is more just than others?
- If the latter applies, are there reasons that justify the aberration through standard business terms?

If no to all, the term is void.

Based on this general test, the courts have provided numerous case examples concerning the validity of concrete clauses. In 1976 the Act for the regulation of the law of standard business terms[7] was passed, codifying most of the principles established by the BGH. The European Council Directive 93/13/EEC of 5 April 1993 on Unfair terms in Consumer Contracts brought only minor changes, as the German Act was more detailed than the directive. In 2002 the Act was incorporated into the civil code.[8]

Scope of Application

The law of standard business terms generally applies to all kinds of contract. # 310 IV 1BGB provides an exception for contracts relating to the law of succession, family law and company law[9] and for collective agreements and private sector works agreements for public-sector establishment agreements; these contracts are not considered to be 'standard' contracts. When applied to employment contracts, reasonable account must be made of the special features that apply in labour law.[10] To what extent protection is granted depends mainly on whether a party is an entrepreneur or a consumer.[11] The ## 305 ff BGB apply to unmodified contracts between two consumers. If the other party[12] is an entrepreneur

[7] Gesetz Zur Regelkung des Rechts der Allgemeinen Geschaftsbedingungen (AGB-Gesetz) vom 9. Dezember 1976.
[8] Compare with Florian Faust, *Recht der Allgemeinen Geschaftsbedingungen* (Hamburg: Bucerius Law School, 2007), pp. 1 and 2.
[9] Note that in special cases some basic protection may be provided through ## 138, 242 BGB, e.g. if public companies with many shareholders use standard terms in the Articles of association.
[10] # 310 IV 2 BGB.
[11] For legal definition of entrepreneur and consumer see ## 13, 14 1 BGB.
[12] By 'other party', I refer to the party which is not the user of the standard terms in question.

the provisions regarding incorporation (#305 II and III BGB) and the catalogues of prohibited clauses (## 308, 309 BGB) do not apply.[13]

Where the standard form contract is a contract between an entrepreneur and a consumer, # 310 III BGB modifies the definition of standard business terms and extends to the application of certain provisions to terms that are not standard business terms and the factors to consider when determining validity.

Definition of standard business terms

305 1 BGB defines standard business terms as 'all contract terms pre-formulated for more than two contracts which one party to the contract [the user] presents to the other party upon the entering into the contracts.' Terms are not standard business terms if they have been negotiated in detail between the parties.

With regard to the number of times contract terms have to be used to be deemed standard business terms, the actual number of uses is immaterial. What is decisive is the intention of the person drafting the terms. Thus standard business terms can already be given with the first usage of the respective terms.

It is immaterial how often the actual user intends to use the terms (what is decisive is the intention of the drafter). Standard business terms can also be given if the user intends to use a certain set of terms only once, but has, for example, used a sample contract from the internet.

In the case of consumer contracts, most provisions apply regardless of the number of intended uses.[14] It is only required that due to the preformulation the consumer had no influence on the terms.

Terms also have to be 'presented' by the user. This means that the user demands the incorporation of the terms into the contracts. If the terms are preformulated, but the user is honestly ready to negotiate the terms and expressly states so, the terms can be individually agreed terms in the sense of # 305 1 3 BGB even if they remain unchanged. It is, however, not sufficient for the establishment of individually agreed terms that the user

---

[13] # 310 1 BGB.
[14] # 310 III No. 2 BGB.

explains the terms and the other party acknowledges and accepts them.[15] In the case of consumer contracts, the terms are deemed to be presented by the user as long as they are not presented by the consumer.[16] Therefore terms can also constitute standard business terms if they are proposed by a neutral third party such as a notary or broker.

Incorporation of standard business terms into the contract

The requirements with regard to incorporation of standard business terms into the contract are laid out in # 305 11 BGB.[17]

The user, when entering into the contract, has to:

- explicitly refer the other party to the standard terms.

If such reference is disproportionally difficult (e.g. where there is no direct contact between the parties as is the case when driving into a car park, or in mass transactions of daily life as in a supermarket), a clearly visible notice is sufficient.

If the contract is formed orally, the reference should be oral. In written contracts, the reference must be contained in the text in such a manner that an average customer will not overlook it even if only skim-reading the text.[18]

The reference must be made when entering into the contract. A prior reference without direct connection to the contract at hand (e.g. made in connection with an earlier contract) is insufficient. So is a reference made after formation of the contract (e.g. when a notice is printed on ticket, because at the time the ticket is handed over, the contract has already been closed).[19]

---

[15] *Supra at n. 7*, at 6.

[16] # 310 111 No. 1 BGB.

[17] Except if the other party is an entrepreneur or the contract at hand is an employment contract: # 310 1, IV 2 BGB. In those cases general contract law provisions apply.

[18] Note that such a reference only makes sense when the standard terms are not part of the main body of the contract document anyways, see Florian Faust, *Recht der Allgemeinen Geschaftsbedingungen*, p. 7.

[19] Dominant opinion: see Ulmer in *Ulmer/Brandner/Hensen*, AGB-Recht, 10th Edition., #305 at 3\134.

- Give the other party, in an acceptable manner, the opportunity to take notice of the standard terms.

If the contract is formed in the presence of both parties, it is sufficient that the text of the standard terms is displayed in the place of formation. If the contract is formed through correspondence, the text has to be sent with it.[20]

- The other party also has to agree to the applying of the terms

This need not be done explicitly.

Surprising clauses

305c 1 BGB offers protection against surprising clauses. Clauses are surprising when they are so unusual that an average customer involved in the type of dealing involved could not reasonably expect such a clause. Regard shall also be paid to the outward appearance of the contract. Thus a clause is not surprising if it has been pointed out to the other party. An evaluation of a clause's surprising nature is done on a case-by-case basis. Therefore highlighting such a clause in bolder print may be sufficient if it constitutes merely a variation from usual clauses, but will not be enough if the customer will not expect it due to the course of dealings.[21]

Battle of forms

When two businesses form a contract, often both parties refer to their standard business terms. An acceptance with alterations is a refusal in connection with a new offer.[22] Therefore one possible solution would be to declare those standard terms to be incorporated into the contract that has lastly been referred to, the final acceptance often lying within the performance of the contract (the theory of the last work, equivalent to the last shot rule). However, this approach can lead to arbitrary results. Therefore, another approach sees such a situation as an overt lack of agreement. In doubt this will, according to # 154 1 BGB, lead to the ineffectiveness of the whole contract. But frequently the intention of the parties will be to uphold the contract, in which case the contract remains effective excluding those parts in which the standard terms are contradictory. The gap will be filled by application of the regular statutory provisions.[23]

---

[20] *Supra* at n. 7, at 8.
[21] BGH, judgment of 21.6.2001, NJW-RR 2002, at 485 [487].
[22] # 150 11 BGB.
[23] Supra at n. 7. at 10, compare also # 306 1 and 11 BGB.

Interpretation

Standard business terms are subject to the general rules of interpretation for legal acts.[24] But considering that they are preformulated for many contracts, a uniform and objective interpretation is required. The horizon for interpretation is the capacity of understanding of an average customer without legal education.

Individually agreed terms overwrite standard business terms, even in cases of indirect contradiction. For examples if a certain price is agreed upon (considering German business customs this price will be understood to include taxes) and the standard business terms declare that taxes are to be added to the price, this clause will be overwritten by the price agreement. Orally individually agreed terms are also effective if the standard business terms require all terms to be recorded in writing. The orally agreed term mutually contains the setting aside of the written-form requirement.[25]

If the clause is ambiguous, doubts will be resolved against the user (contra proferentem rule).[26] This does not always mean that the interpretation that is fairest for the customer will be chosen. If one possible interpretation renders the clause so unfair that it would become ineffective, this interpretation will be chosen and the clause at hand will drop out of the contract completely.[27]

The most unfair interpretation can thus be best for the other party.

Control of Unfair terms

Provision of standard business terms can only be tested for unreasonableness if they depart from or supplement the statutory provisions.[28] Hence clauses that merely repeat statutory provisions or concern the essentialia negotii are not subject to the test. # 307 I and II BGB represent the general test to determine reasonableness of terms, which applies to all standard form contracts. Standard business terms are

---

[24] See ## 133, 157 BGB.
[25] *Supra* at n. 7. at 10.
[26] # 305c 11 BGB.
[27] Supra at n. 7, at 10.
[28] #307 III 1 BGB, other provisions may however be unreasonable due to their unclarity and incomprehensibility, # 307 111 2 BGB.

ineffective if they, contrary to the requirement of good faith, unreasonably disadvantage the other party.

Such an unreasonable disadvantage may also arise from unclear and incomprehensible provisions.

The test is general and abstract, taking into account the effect of validity/invalidity of the clause on typical parties and whether a party can avoid or insure against the risk distributed by the clause.[29]

In case of doubt, the existence of an unreasonable disadvantage is assumed if a provision in standard terms:

- Is incompatible with essential principles of the statutory provision from which it departs; or
- Limits essential rights or duties inherent in the nature of the contract to such an extent that attainment of the purpose of the contract is jeopardized.

308 and 209 BGB apply to contracts where the other party is a consumer. #308 BGB contains a catalogue of prohibited clauses with the possibility of value judgment of the court (generally through the usage of words that require evaluation such as 'unreasonable' or 'undue') and # 309 BGB contains a catalogue of clauses that are absolutely void. If a certain clause does not fall under ## 308 or 309 BGB that does not mean it is automatically effective.[30]

Examples of important provisions are:
309 NO 7 BGB: Exclusion of liability for injury to life, body or health and in case of gross fault
Provisions are void that exclude or limit liability for damage from injury to life, body or health due to negligent breach of duty by the user or intentional breach of duty by a legal representative or a person employed to perform an obligation of the user.[31]

So is an exclusion or limitation of liability for other damage arising from a grossly negligent breach of duty by the user or from an intentional or

[29] Supra at n. 7. at 14.
[30] See the wording of the section: 'following [terms] are in particular ineffective…'.
[31] Note that liability for intentional breach of duty by a party is invalid even in individually agreed terms. # 276 111 BGB.

grossly negligent breach of duty by a legal representative of the user or a person used to perform an obligation of the user.

309 No. 8a BGB: Exclusion of the right to free oneself from the contract
A provision is void which, where there is a breach of duty for which the user is responsible and which does not consist in a defect of the thing sold or the work, excludes or restricts the right of the other party to free himself from the contract.

#308 No. 3 BGB: Reservation of the right to withdraw
The agreement of a right of the user to free himself from his obligation to perform without any objectively justified reason indicated in the contract is void. This does not apply to continuing obligations.

308 No. 4 BGB: Reservation of the right to modify
The agreement of a right of the user to modify the performance promised or deviate from it is void, unless the agreement of the modification or deviation can reasonably be expected of the other party to the contract when the interests of the user are taken into account.

The ## 308, 2309 BGB do not apply if the other party is an entrepreneur. But that does not mean that such terms would be valid per se. The validity then has to be determined using the test of # 307 BGB. If a standard business term would be invalid according to ## 308 or 309 BGB then this can serve as an important factor indicating its unfairness. The provision would be invalid unless justified by the needs of business dealings.[32]

Consequences of void terms
If a clause is void it will be deleted completely, its place is taken by the statutory provision.[33] It will not be redrafted or reinterpreted so as to make it valid and serve its original purpose as far as possible (geltungserhaltende Reduktion: effect-conserving reduction). The reason behind this is that otherwise the user of the standard business terms could simply draft harsh clauses without any risk, because the clause would simply be reduced to the content most unilaterally beneficent to the user that is still enforceable by law. The rest of the contact remains valid.[34] A rare exception is made in

[32] BGH, judgment of 8.3.1984, BGHZ 90, 273 [278].
[33] # 306 11 BGB.
[34] # 306 1 BGB overwrites the general rule of # 139 BGB.

cases where enforcement of the contract lacking the ineffective clause would constitute an unbearable hardship for one party.[35]

Standard forms of contract in the common law

In common law there is no legal definition as to what exactly constitutes standard form contracts; the term is interpreted widely.[36] On the other hand, although the German definition is narrower and the laws require the existence of standard business terms in order to apply, the practical implications are small. The question of whether terms qualify as standard business terms is rarely debated.[37]

The focus in the common law is shifted more towards unfair contract terms in general; practically, however, they appear mostly in standard forms of contracts in any case. German law, however, has focused on standard forms of contracts as such. As such the protection basically consists of two main approaches:

- The control of unfair contract terms; and
- The rules regarding incorporation into the contract (the requirement of explicit reference to surprising clauses).

In common law, however, with regards to incorporation into the contract, principally the general contract rules apply. As established in *L' Estrange v Graucob Ltd.*[38] standard terms can be incorporated into a contract even if they have not been read, there is no general requirement as to express reference.[39] However, in many cases dealing with exclusion clauses[40] parallels can be drawn between German and common law.

In *Olley v Marlborough Court Hotel*[41] it was established that in order for a term to be included into the contract, the representation has to be made at

---

[35] # 306 111 BGB.

[36] Lawson, *Exclusion clauses and Unfair Contract terms* (London: Sweet and Maxwell, 2003), p. 134.

[37] See the United Kingdom, Unfair Terms in Consumer Contracts Regulations 1999 and sec. 3 of the Unfair Contract Terms Act 1977.

[38] [1934] 2 KB 394.

[39] Note that the requirement of express reference does not apply under German law either in the case of the other party being an entrepreneur.

[40] Which are almost always part of standard business terms; in the following case they would constitute such terms under German law.

[41] [1949] 1 KG 532.

the time the contract is entered into. This is in line with the German rule that the reference to the standard business terms has to be made when entering into the contract.[42]

In *Thornton v Shoe Lane Parking*[43] it was established that an exclusion clause may only incorporated into the contract if sufficient notice is given. Lord Denning ruled that terms which are exceeding what normally would be expected 'would need to be printed in red ink with a red hand pointing to it before the notice was sufficient'. This relates to the German principle that when express reference is not (or only with disproportionate effort) possible, a clearly visible notice must be displayed. The judgment also shows similarities with the concept of surprising clauses, as Lord Denning refused to incorporate unexpected terms without sufficient notice.

Still, the concept of surprising clauses has no direct equivalent. However, in schedule 2 of the Unfair Contract Terms Act 1977 one of the factors to be considered in the reasonableness test is:

- Whether the customer knew or ought reasonably to have known of the existence and the extent of the term having regard, among other things, to any custom of the trade and any previous course of dealing between the parties.

Hence, if the customer has been referred to the standard terms (as required under German law)[44] the standard term is less likely to be unreasonable. If the term is out of line with the customs of the trade and is not be expected[45] (and thus potentially considered a surprising clause under German Law) the term is more likely to be unreasonable. Therefore the underlying principles of the German law are not foreign to the common law, but are applied to a lesser extent, being factors rather than having effects just by themselves.
Both legal systems employ the *contra proferentem* rule when interpreting standard terms. The control of unfair terms is similar in German and common law. The decisive statutes in the UK are the Unfair Contract Terms Act 1977 and the Unfair terms in Consumer Contracts Regulation 1999. The Unfair Terms Act also distinguishes between businesses[46] and

[42] The same principle would apply in general German contract law also.
[43] [1971 1 All ER 686.
[44] In the case of the other party being a consumer.
[45] Note that this test is concrete, thus considering the actual customer, whereas the German test is an abstract test considering the typical customer.
[46] Essentially equivalent to the German 'entrepreneur'.

consumers. Certain clauses are also absolutely void, others subject to a test of reasonableness.[47] However, the Act deals with exemption clauses only, whereas the German law provides a greater scope of unfair terms.[48]

The Unfair Terms in Consumer Contracts Regulation 1999 applies specifically to standard forms of contract where the user is a business and the other party a consumer,[49] thus also presenting a smaller scope than the German law, as business contracts and contracts between two consumers are excluded. The test provided in the Regulation is quite similar to the test laid down in # 307 BGB.[50]

Terms are unfair according to regulation 5(1) if they are:

- Not individually negotiated[51]
- Causing significant imbalance in the parties rights and obligations; and
- are contrary to the requirement of good faith.[52]

Unfair terms are not binding upon the consumer.[53] The rest of the contract remains unaffected.

Conclusion

The German and the common law approaches to resolving the problem presented by standard form of contracts are similar in many ways. However, when compared, the German law offers greater protection to the consumer. In both legal systems, the characterization of the problem, such as unequal bargaining positions[54] and the other party's unawareness of the content of the standard terms, is comparable.

---

[47] Compare with sec. 11 and schedule 2 of the Act.

[48] Cheshire, Fifoot and Furmston, *Law of Contract* (Oxford: Oxford University Press, 2007), p. 253.

[49] *Ibid*, p. 254.

[50] Note that both statutes implement the European Council Directive 93/13/EEc of April 1993.

[51] Compare with # 305 1 3 BGB.

[52] Compare with # 307 1BGB, the Significant imbalance' is similar to the 'unreasonable disadvantage.

[53] Regulation 8.

[54] See Lord Diplock in *A. Schroeder Music Publishing Co. Ltd. v Macaulay* [1974] 3 All ER 616.

Still, the UK courts historically attach great value to the principle of freedom of contract and were thus reluctant to overrule terms agreed upon by the parties. They also consider the uncertainty that is caused through the control of contact terms, as the parties do not know which provision will be valid, before the question has been answered by the courts. German courts, in contrast, were less hesitant. To quote: 'But there is nothing like the power which the German Courts have felt themselves free to exercise based on Arts. 138 and 242 of the BGB'.[55] The courts have considered that when an offer is 'take it or leave it,' and standard business terms are not heavily taken into account by customers, freedom of contract only exists to a smaller degree.[56] They have emphasized the difference between imposed standard terms and freely negotiated terms to a greater extent than their British colleagues. Furthermore, the principle of good faith is fundamental to German law. The courts found it easier to demand that contract terms shall generally be 'fair'.

Despite the differences, both systems offer sound protection against the dangers of standard forms of contract, and yet do not unduly restrict their effective use in business dealings.

---

[55] Marsh, *Comparative Contract Law* (Hampshire: Gower), p. 292.

[56] For an evaluation of this trends in the common law, see Iyer, *The Law of Contracts and Tenders* (Hyderabad: S Gogia and Co.), pp. 9–10.

The Formation of Contracts: A Comparison between the Indian Contract Act of 1872 and the Portuguese Civil Code of 1966

Luís Manuel Teles de Menezes Leitão

1. Introduction

The subject of this article refers to the rules of the formation of contracts, intending to establish a comparison between the Indian Contract Act of 1872, and the Portuguese Civil Code of 1966.

The Indian Contract Act of 1872 (ICA) applies throughout India, except the State of Jammu and Kashmir (ICA, § 1), and has been in force in Goa since 1963. Although it is a statutory law, it is in fact a codified reformulation of the common law of contracts. It originally covered the topics of general principles of the law of contract, law relating to sale of goods, contracts of indemnity and guarantee, contracts of bailment and pledge, contracts of agency and law relating to partnership. However, later on, chapters VII and XI, referring to sale of goods and partnership were revoked by the Indian Sale of Goods Act, 1930, and the Indian Partnership Act, 1932[1].

The Portuguese Civil Code of 1966 codifies the rules of Portuguese private law[2]. Portugal belongs to the civil law system, so the rules of contract law are mostly based in the Roman Law. The former Portuguese Civil Code of 1867 was influenced by French Law, but the present Civil

---

[1] See Ishwar C. Saxena, in Rudolf R. Schelsinger (ed.), *Formation of Contracts: A study of The Common Core of the Legal Systems*, I, (London and New York: Steven and Sons/Oceans Publication, 1968), p. 281.

[2] A brief overview of Portuguese law can be found in Carlos Ferreira de Almeida, Assunção Cristas and Nuno Piçarra, *Portuguese Law: An Overview* (Almedina: Coimbra, 2007).

Code of 1966 is based on German Law. It uses the German classification of private law, referring after a General Part to the branches of Law of Obligations, Real Rights, Family Law and the Law of Successions.

2. The rules of formation of contracts, according to the Indian Contract Act, 1872

To perform a contract, according to the ICA, it is necessary that two parties express a proposal and an acceptance, and the existence of a consideration.

The definition of the proposal is established in § 2 (a) of the ICA, which states that "when one person signifies to another his willingness to do or to abstain from doing anything, with a view to obtaining the assent of that other to such act or abstinence, he is said to make a proposal". Therefore, the ICA defines "proposal" as synonymous with "offer" in the Anglo-American sense[3].

The definition of acceptance comes in § 2 b) of ICA which states that "when the person to whom the proposal is made signifies his assent thereto, the proposal is said to be accepted. A proposal, when accepted, becomes a promise".

The definition of a consideration appears in § 2 d) of the ICA which states that "when, at the desire of the promisor, the promisee or any other person has done or abstained from doing, or does or abstains from doing, or promises to do or to abstain from doing something, such act or abstinence or promise is called a consideration for the promise".

§§ 2 e) and f) of the ICA state that "every promise and every set of promises, forming the consideration for each other, is an agreement" and "promises, which form the consideration or part of the consideration for each other, are called reciprocal promises".

A contract is an agreement enforceable by law (§ 2 h) ICA). When an agreement is not enforceable by law, it is said to be void (§ 2 g) ICA), which also occurs when the agreement ceases to be enforceable (§2 j) ICA). An agreement which is enforceable by law at the option of one or more of the parties thereto, but not at the option of the other or the others, is a voidable contract (§ 2 i) ICA).

---

[3] See Ishwar C. Saxena, in Rudolf R. Schelsinger (ed.), *Formation*, p. 375.

Referring to communication, acceptance and revocation of proposals, § 3 ICA states that "the communication of proposals, the acceptance of proposals, and the revocation of proposals and acceptances, respectively, are deemed to be made by any act or omission of the party proposing, accepting or revoking, by which he intends to communicate such proposal, acceptance or revocation, or which has the effect of communicating it".

§ 4 ICA indicates when the communication is complete, referring firstly to the completion of the communication of the proposal. "The communication of proposals is complete when it comes to the knowledge of the person to whom it is made". There is an illustration (a) about this rule, which says that if A proposes, by letter, to sell a house to B at a certain price, the communication of the proposals is complete when B receives the letter. Therefore we must conclude that although the ICA refers to reception, it requires knowledge of the proposal[4].

Considering now the acceptance, § 4 states that its communication is complete:

—as against the proposer, when it is put in the course of transmission to him, so as to be out of the power of the acceptor:
—as against the acceptor, when it comes to the knowledge of the proposer.

Illustration b) explains this rule with an example:
"B accepts A's proposal by a letter sent by post. The communication of the acceptance is complete,
—as against A, when the letter is posted,
—as against B, when the letter is received by A.

Referring at last to the revocation, its communication is considered complete:
—as against the person who makes it, when it is put into a course of transmission to the person to whom it is made, so as be out of the power of the person who makes it;
—as against the person to whom it is made, when it comes to its knowledge.

Illustration c) explains this rule with this example:

---

[4] See Ishwar C. Saxena, in Rudolf R. Schelsinger (ed.), *Formation*, p. 705.

"A revokes his proposal by telegram. The revocation is complete as against A when the telegram is dispatched. It is complete as against B when B receives it.

B revokes his acceptance by telegram. B's revocation is complete as against B when the telegram is dispatched and as against A when it reaches him".

§ 5 of the ICA refers to the revocation of proposal and acceptance. It states that a proposal may be revoked at any time before the communication of its acceptance is complete as against the proposer but not afterwards. An acceptance may be revoked at any time before the communication of the acceptance is complete as against the acceptor but not afterwards.

The illustrations give us the following example:
"A proposes, by a letter sent by post, to sell his house to B.
B accepts the proposal by a letter sent by post.
A may revoke his proposal at any time before or at the moment when B posts his letter of acceptance, but not afterwards.
B may revoke his acceptance at any time before or at the moment when the letter communicating it reaches A, but not afterwards".
§ 6 of the ICA describes how a revocation of a proposal is made. It states that a proposal is revoked:

(1) by the communication of notice of revocation by the proposer to the other party;
(2) by the lapse of the time prescribed in such proposal for its acceptance, or if no time is so prescribed, by the lapse of a reasonable time without communication of the acceptance;
(3) by the failure of the acceptor to fulfill a condition precedent to acceptance; or
(4) by the death or insanity of the proposer, if the fact of his death or insanity comes to the knowledge of the acceptor before acceptance.

§ 7 ICA deals with the characteristics of the acceptance, expressing that, in order to convert a proposal into a promise, it must:

(1) be absolute and unqualified;

(2) be expressed in some usual and reasonable manner, unless the proposal prescribes the manner in which it is to be accepted. If the proposal

prescribes a manner in which it is to be accepted, and the acceptance is not made in such manner, the proposer may, within a reasonable time after the acceptance is communicated to him, insist that his proposal shall be accepted in the prescribed manner, and not otherwise; but if he fails to do so, he accepts the acceptance.

§ 8 ICA deals with acceptance by performing conditions, or receiving consideration. It states that performance of the conditions of the proposal, or the acceptance of the consideration for a reciprocal promise which may be offered with a proposal, is an acceptance of the proposal.

§ 9 ICA distinguishes between express and implied promises. In so far as the proposal or acceptance of any promise is made in words, the promise is said to be express. In so far as such proposal or acceptance is made otherwise than in words, the promise is said to be implied.

3. The rules of formation of contracts according to the Portuguese Civil Code

To perform a contract in the Portuguese law, it is simply required that two parties express a proposal and an acceptance, and that the parties have agreed in all the matters subject to negotiation. According to art. 217 of the Portuguese Civil Code (PCC), proposal and acceptance can be either express, when they are made in words, letters, or signs, directly expressing the intention of its author, or implied, when they result from the interpretation of his behaviour[5]. The silence of an addressee can also be interpreted as a declaration, but only when such interpretation is established by law, use or convention (PCC, art. 218).

Art. 224 PCC states that the proposal and the acceptance, or their revocations, are considered in force as soon as they are received by the other party or he or she has knowledge of them. Besides that, proposal and acceptance, or their revocations, can also be considered in force if they are not received only by fault of the addressee. Proposal, acceptance and their revocations can also be made by public announcement, published in a local newspaper, if they are addressed to an unknown person or one whose residence is unknown (art. 225 PCC).

---

[5] Portugal uses the subjective theory in relation to this distinction. See Paulo Mota Pinto, *Declaração Tácita e Comportamento Concludente no Negócio Jurídico*, (Almedina: Coimbra, 1995), p. 438, and Carlos Mota Pinto, *Teoria Geral do Direito Civil*, 4th ed. (Coimbra: Coimbra Editora, 2005), p. 422.

According to Portuguese legal writers[6], a proposal must have three characteristics: it must be complete, certain and it must observe the form required by the contract. The completion of the proposal means that all questions considered essential by the parties must be answered. The certainty of the proposal means that it cannot be ambiguous, as the proposer has to express clearly his willingness to perform the contract. Finally, the observance of the form legally required is necessary, because proposals which do not observe that form would be considered null and void (art. 220 PCC). If the declaration does not have all these characteristics, it will be considered only as an invitation to contract.

The proposal is binding to its author, and he cannot revoke it after its reception or knowledge by the addressee (art. 230, 1, PCC). Therefore its rescission can only occur, if the addressee receives that declaration before or at the same time of the proposal (art. 230, 2, PCC). If the proposal is addressed to the public in general, its rescission is effective when declared in the same form as the proposal or in a similar form (art. 230, 3, PCC).

The proposal cannot stay in force forever, so its acceptance must occur within a short time. Art. 228, 1, PCC proposes these three rules for the time in which the proposal must be accepted:

a) if the proposer refers to a term, or it was previously established by the parties, the proposal remains in force during that term;

b) if a term was not established, but the proposers asks for an immediate answer, the proposal stays in force until the period necessary for the reception of proposal and acceptance:

c) if a term was not established and the proposal was made to an absent person or in writing to a present person, the proposal will stay in force for five days after the term referred in b).

If the acceptance is not received within these periods of time, the proposal ceases to have force. However, if the proposer receives the acceptance after these periods, but has no grounds to believe it was sent with delay, he must inform the acceptor that the contract was not concluded, or he will be liable for damages (art. 229, 1, PCC). The proposer, however, may consider the acceptance as effective, if it was sent in time. In all other cases, the contract will only be formed after a new proposal and a new acceptance (art. 229, 2, PCC).

---

[6] See António Menezes Cordeiro, *Tratado de Direito Civil*, I, 1, 3rd ed. (Almedina: Coimbra, 2005), p. 552 ff., and Pedro Pais de Vasconcelos, *Teoria Geral do Direito Civil*, 3rd ed.(Almedina: Coimbra, 2005), p. 304 ff.

The acceptance has to be absolute. In fact, art. 233, PCC establishes that if an acceptance is made with amendments, limitations or other modifications, it would be considered as a refusal of the proposal. However, if the modification has enough precision, it would be considered as a new proposal, unless it has another meaning.

In certain cases, depending on the circumstances or the uses, acceptance can result simply from the interpretation of the addressee's behaviour. In this case, the contract is considered concluded as soon as he shows the intention of accepting the proposal (PCC, art. 234).

If the addressee in the first place rejects the proposal, but accepts it afterwards, the acceptance will prevail, if its communication reaches the proposer at the same time as or before the refusal (PCC, art. 235, 1). The acceptance can also be revoked, if that revocation reaches the proposer at the same time as or before the acceptance (art. 235, 2, PCC).

4. Results of the comparison

Although India and Portugal belong to different legal systems, there are many similarities between India and Portugal regarding formation of contracts. We can only point out a very few differences.

The main difference lies in the concept of contract itself. In India, a contract needs a consideration, otherwise it would be considered as a promise. In Portugal, the law does not require a consideration to form a contract, so a promise would be considered as such[7].

Another difference refers to when the communication of a proposal is complete. In Portugal, according to art. 224 PCC, the communication is complete not only with its knowledge but also with its reception by the person to whom is made. Besides that, the communication is also considered complete when the reception is frustrated due to the addressee's fault. On the contrary, in India § 4 ICA only considers the communication complete when it comes to the knowledge of the

[7] It is normally said that the concept of contract is not the same in civil law and common law countries. See the comparative analysis of Antonio Silva, "The role of consent in the formation of contract in comparative private law", in *International Journal of Baltic Law*, 2/2004, pp. 117–127, at http://www.ceeol.com

addressee, giving no relevance to its reception or to the fault of the addressee.
Another difference lies in the completion of the communication of acceptance and revocation. § 4 ICA establishes a different rule as to the proposal, distinguishing its completion in relation to proposer and acceptor, while art. 224 of PCC establishes precisely the same rule as to the proposal.

In conclusion, the solutions regarding to the formation of contracts do not differ in essence between India and Portugal.

PART V:

FAMILY LAWS

LAW RELATING TO MARRIAGE IN INDIA

RANJANA FERRAO[1]

"A man leaves his father and mother and is united with his wife, and they become one."
—Genesis, Chapter II verse 26

Lord Westbury stated, in his dictum in Shaw V. Gould[2], "Marriage is the very foundation of civil society, and no part of the laws and institutions of a country can be of more vital importance to its subjects than those which regulate the manner and conditions of forming and if necessary of dissolving the marriage contract."

"When a man marries he has fulfilled half of his religion, so let him fear Allah regarding the remaining half." These words of Prophet Mohammad mark the importance of marriage, thus it could be well concluded that marriage in Islam is an obligation. Christians and Hindus are also of a similar belief.

All religions view marriage as a divine union. With changing times, marriage is no longer a divine union that requires celestial blessings included in the various religious rituals associated with it. This has far-reaching legal consequences too. The growing number of divorce cases, cases regarding custody of children and maintenance, polygamy, and dowry deaths reveal that marriage is no longer considered as a divine union by society. The consequences of a breakdown of marriage could be irreparable.

There is no law governing marriage in India which is common to all communities. There is multiplicity in personal laws, based on various factors such as religion, caste, tribe, domicile, etc. Hindus, Sikhs, Jains and Buddhists are governed by the Hindu Law, Muslims by the Muslim Law. Some communities are wholly or partly governed by customs, e.g. Jews.

---

[1] Lecturer, V.M.Salgaocar College of Law, Miramar

[2] (1868) L.R. 3 H.L. 55, 82

In Goa, the provisions of the Portuguese Civil Code of 1867, together with some other laws of the pre-Liberation period, are in force in the area of family law and succession[3]. The Civil Code was a result of historic ties. This nineteenth-century Portuguese Code—which, together with the Old Napoleonic Code, is still considered to be one of the great legislative masterpieces—was greatly influenced by Roman law.[4] These laws are to a great extent uniformly followed by Catholics, Hindus and Muslims, and have proved to be a powerful tool in creating a well–knit, homogeneous society. Thus the Code sets a precedent in family law by upholding the values enshrined in the Preamble of the Constitution of India and also fulfilling the demands of Article 44 of the Constitution. The Portuguese Civil Code, coupled with other related laws, contains comprehensive provisions dealing with marriage in Goa.

The Family Law Curriculum

The academics of Goa perceived the imperative need to ensure that students are familiar with the Portuguese Civil Code and other related laws and at the same time are not ignorant of the family laws prevalent in the rest of India. To fulfill this need, students are also taught the other enactments necessary and relating to laws of marriage in India. Some of the enactments which the author wishes to compare with the Portuguese Civil Code are:

1. The Hindu Marriage Act, 1955
2. The Special Marriage Act, 1954
3. The Indian Christian Marriage Act, 1872
4. The Parsi Marriage and Divorce Act, 1936

Viewing Marriage as a Contract

Marriage is in a sense a contract, and thus it will follow that there can be no valid marriage unless each party consents to marry the other.[5] Marriage is a contract of a very special kind. Marriage being a contract, importance is given to the free consent of each party to the contract at the time the

[3] For example the law of divorce of 1910 and the law of marriage of the same year.
[4] Prof. Dr. Pires De Lima and Prof. Dr. Joao De Matos Varela, *Fundamental Concepts in Civil Law—Family Law and Succession,* Volume II (Mirandela)
[5] Under common law a marriage is void for lack of consent.

contract is entered into, and this is why it takes the central place in the celebration of marriage. In Hindu Law the marriage is void if consent is obtained by fraud, force or coercion. The contract cannot be rescinded by the mutual consent of the parties as a rule; it may be dissolved by a formal public act, usually an order or decree of the court.[6]

Marriage in Christianity

Marriage is a permanent, irrevocable contract between a man and woman to live together on terms of the deepest human friendship and start a family. The fact that the same contract becomes a sacrament by ceremony further strengthens this bond of union.

Context of Marriage in Hinduism

In Hinduism, marriage is not a custom or contract of partnership simply between two individuals as in the Western culture. There is a belief among the Hindus that the marriage relationship extends beyond one's life. Two souls come together and get married because their Karmas are intertwined and they have to resolve many things together on earth in order to ensure their mutual salvation. More than that, it is a union of two families with each and every member of the extended family on both sides related to the husband and wife being responsible for their action and their future lives. The extended family referred to here consists of paternal grandparents, sons, daughters-in-law, unmarried daughters and future generations on both sides.[7]

The term "Hindu," in post-independence Hindu law governing marriage, divorce, adoption, maintenance, guardianship and succession, describes not only persons who are Hindu by religion, but also those who are Sikh, Buddhist, and Jain. The term "Hindu" encompasses those Indians who are not Christian, Parsi, Muslim, or Jewish for the purposes of the law.

---

[6] In Canon Law annulment of marriages was carried out by the church, but today the law requires the annulment to be approved by the High Court.

[7] The unique feature of Hindu society is the institution of the joint family .Within this unit of joint family there is another unit called Coparcenary. S.6 of the Hindu Succession Act, 2005 defines coparcenary as a narrow body of a Hindu joint family. Unmarried daughters and other females are now included in coparcenary.

Hindu Marriages :Ceremonies

Betrothalor sagai is a contract marriage. Most Hindu marriages precede a sagai. If a girl is promised in marriage to one man a good man does not give her to another. Only the father has the right to annul betrothal. Performance of Shastric ceremonies is necessary for a valid Hindu marriage[8].

In India, various communities have different customs and ceremonies; the law states that a marriage can be performed or "solemnized" according to the customary rituals and ceremonies of the community to which either the bride or the groom belongs. It is very important to understand that the rituals and ceremonies carried out must be recognized and accepted by the community concerned as being the proper ones for formalizing a marriage. The performance of certain Shastric ceremonies is still necessary for a valid Hindu Marriage. There are 4 ceremonies laid down in minute detail in the Grihya Sutras. They are the sampradana, the vivaha-homa, the agni-parinayana, and the saptapadi. The law makes it very clear that in a Hindu marriage, where the ceremony includes the saptpadi, the ritual of circling the sacred fire seven times, the ceremony becomes complete and the marriage binding[9].

The Madras High Court, in a catena of cases, stated that there are in fact two ceremonies which are necessary: a secular ceremony, Kanyadanam, and a religious one, Panigrahana and Saptapadi. There are a few differences between the castes, but in general saptapadi is still absolutely necessary for validity .

The presumption of marriage is covered by section 114 of the Evidence Act, which states that if evidence of the solemnization of marriage is not available, it will be presumed to be a valid marriage by continuous cohabitation between the parties, unless the contrary is proved[10].

Section 7 of the Hindu Marriage Act, 1955, deals with the ceremonies of marriage. It states that a Hindu marriage may be solemnized in accordance

---

[8] Paras Diwan, *Hindu Law* (Central Law Agency , 2007)

[9] Section 7 of the Hindu Marriage Act states that the marriage may be solemnized according to customary rites and ceremonies and when such rites and ceremonies include saptapadi.

[10] Ratanlal and Dhirajlal, *Indian Evidence Act*, (Universal Publishing House, 1999).

with the customary rites and ceremonies of either party . It states that where such rites include Saptapadi (that is , the taking of seven steps by the bridegroom and the bride jointly before the sacred fire), the marriage becomes complete and binding when the seventh step is taken. Thus the Marriage Act permits customary rites and ceremonies of either party to the marriage. It is to be noted that Sikhs, Jains and Buddhists are considered Hindus for these purposes.

Hindu Marriage: Capacity to Marry

Section 5 of the Hindu Marriage Act lays down the conditions for a Hindu marriage. The section reads as follows:

> "A marriage may be solemnized between any two Hindus, if the following conditions are fulfilled, namely:
> (i) neither party has a spouse living at the time of the marriage;
> (ii) at the time of the marriage, neither party,—
> (a) is incapable of giving a valid consent of it in consequence of unsoundness of mind; or
> (b) though capable of giving a valid consent has been suffering from mental disorder of such a kind or to such an extent as to be unfit for marriage and the procreation of children; or
> (c) has been subject to recurrent attacks of insanity or epilepsy;
> (iii) the bridegroom has attained the age of twenty-one years and the bride the age of eighteen years at the time of the marriage;
> (iv) the parties are not within the degrees of prohibited relationship unless the custom or usage governing each of them permits of a marriage between the two;
> (v) the parties are not sapindas of each other, unless the custom or usage governing each of them permits of a marriage between the two".

Thus bigamy is prohibited, one should not be in prohibited degrees of relationship or sapindas to each other unless the custom or usage permits them. It is to be noted that age is also prescribed, which can make marriage voidable and attracts punishment for child marriages. A party should not be incapable of giving consent in consequence of sound mind. Insanity and epilepsy are grounds for invalidating consent.[11] .Consent should not be obtained by fraud or force in Hindu and Canon Law. Under Muslim law an insane person can marry with the consent of the guardian. In Canon Law idiocy or lunacy are grounds for declaring nullity of marriage. It is to be noted that consanguinity, affinity and fosterage are

---

[11] Sec. 5, Hindu Marriage Act.

prohibitions under Muslim law, while consanguinity and affinity are also prohibitions in Canon Law.

Context of Marriage in Islam[12]

Marriage is a religious duty of every Muslim, and it is considered to be a moral safeguard and a social need. The Prophet has also said "Marriage is my tradition; whosoever keeps away therefrom is not from amongst me[13]." Marriage is not a sacrament but in the nature of a civil contract[14].

> Marriage is a legal process by which the sex process and procreation and legitimation of children between man and women is perfectly lawful and valid.[15]

A Nikah in Arabic means "Union of the series" and carries a civil contract for the purposes of legalizing sexual intercourse and legitimate procreation of children[16].

Marriage is an organization for the protection of society, made to protect society from foulness and unchastity[17].

Under Section 2 of the Muslim Women (Protection of Rights on Divorce) Act, 1986, Marriage or Nikah among Muslims is a 'Solemn Pact' or 'Mithaq-e-ghalid' between a man and a woman, soliciting each other's life companionship, which in law takes the form of a contract[18].

Whether Muslim marriage is only a civil contract or an Ibadat and Muamlat is a pertinent question. While unleashing the various definitions, one is unable to comprehend and say which one is the most appropriate. It is submitted here that although the essentials of a contract are fulfilled, yet marriage can never be said to be a contract because marriage always creates a bond between the emotions and thinking of two persons.

---

[12] Paras Diwan and Peeyush Diwan, *Muslim Law in Modern India* (Allahabad Central Agency, 2001),pp. 39–40 deal with the concept of marriage.
[13] Aquil Ahmed, *Mohammedan Law*, pp. 41,42.
[14] Abdul Qadir .V. Salima (1986) 8 All 149 Justice Mahmood observed
[15] Hedaya
[16] Bailies Digest
[17] Ameer Ali
[18] Aquil Ahmad, *Mohammedan Law* (Central Law Agency, 2001).

Muslim marriage compared with Hindu marriage:

1. Muslim marriage is a civil contract, whereas Hindu marriage was a sacrament. At present Hindu marriage too has elements of a contract.
2. Payment of a consideration in any form is not essential in Hindu law, as required in Muslim marriages.

The following points may be noted of Muslim Marriage[19]:

1. Muslim law does not insist upon any particular form of marriage.
2. There has to be a proposal from one side, and its acceptance on the other.
3. No writing is necessary.
4. The Sunnis insist on the presence of two witnesses[20].
5. Ithna Ashari law recognizes muta[21] (temporary) marriage.

Classification of Muslim Marriage

All schools of Sunnis classify marriages into: (a) valid i.e. sahih , (b) void i.e batil and , (c) irregular i.e. fasid. The Ithari Ashari school of the Shias does not recognize the irregular marriage, and therefore among them, marriages are either valid or void[22].

The marriage is Sahih or valid when it is performed between parties having full capacity to marry and with all the necessary formalities. It is Batil or null and void when the marriage is performed in violation of absolute impediments or perpetual impediments. The marriage is irregular or fasid if the impediment or prohibition is temporary or remediable.

A fasid marriage is not a valid marriage at first, but it can be validated by removing the impediment. For instance, on marrying a wife's sister the marriage is irregular, but it can be validated by pronouncing divorce, i.e. Talak, to the wife. Similarly, if a Sunni marries an idolater, the marriage is irregular, but on the wife's conversion to Islam, the marriage becomes valid.[23]

---

[19] See Paras Diwan and Peeyush Diwan, *Muslim Law in Modern India,* p.41.
[20] Two male witnesses or one male and two female witnesses.
[21] Paras Diwan and Peeyush Diwan, *Muslim Law in Modern India,*deals with muta marriage in pp. 41–43
[22] Paras Diwan and Peeyush Diwan, *Muslim Law in Modern India,*p. 44.
[23] Ibid, pg .45.

Categories of Prohibited Degrees.
In Muslim law various categories of prohibited degrees are laid down. They are: (1) consanguinity, (2) affinity, (3) fosterage and (4) unlawful conjugation . The first three among them are absolute impediments whereas the last one results in irregular or fasid marriage[24].
Formalities
All that is necessary for a Muslim marriage is that there is a proposal (ijab) of marriage made by or on behalf of one of the parties and that it is accepted (qubul) by or on behalf of the other party at one and the same meeting. Among the Sunnis the proposal and acceptance must be made in the presence and hearing of two adult male witnesses (or one male and two female witnesses)[25].

The Portuguese Civil Code of 1867 and Related Laws (Family Laws of Goa)

Under the original Civil Code of 1867, marriage was a perpetual contract. Article 1056 of the Civil Code of 1867 stated: "Marriage is a perpetual contract made between two persons of different sex with the purpose of legitimately constituting a family"[26]

This position was changed by the Decree of 25 December 1910. Article 1 of the decree states: "The marriage is a contract solemnized between two persons of different sex with the purpose of legitimately constituting a family"[27]. It is to be noted that the word "perpetual" was dropped.

Article 2 of the same decree states: "Such a contract is purely civil and is presumed to be perpetual, without prejudice to its dissolution by way of divorce as per the provisions of the Decree with the force of law, dated 3rd November 1910"[28].

Further, the concept of a purely civil contract was reinforced in Article 3 of the Decree. It stated, "All Portuguese shall solemnize their marriage before the respective officer of Civil Registration, under the conditions

---

[24] Ibid , pg.46
[25] Ibid.
[26] M. S. Usgaocar, *Family Laws of Goa, Daman and Diu*, Vol. I (Vela Associates), p. 1.
[27] Ibid , pg.39
[28] Ibid.

and in the manner established in civil law, and only such marriage is valid".

Thus solemnization of marriage was moved only to the Civil Registration. This meant that Catholic religious marriage was no longer recognized as legally effective. It is to be noted that the Catholic Church in Portugal had already established the system of registers for Catholic marriages and thus Catholic marriage was well established in society. Thus with the decree of 1910 we have recognition for civil marriages only.

This situation was changed with Decree no. 35461, put in force in the territories of Goa, Daman and Diu with effect from 4/9/1946, dealing with marriages in Portuguese colonies[29].

The Decree referred to Article 22 of the Treaty with the Holy See. By this article, the Portuguese Government was bound to acknowledge civil effect to marriages solemnized in conformity with Canon Law as per the stipulated terms. Though the said article was implemented in Portugal by the decree with force of law No. 36615, dated 25 July 1940, this could not be extended to the colonies as conditions in the colonies were different. Hence Decree no. 35461 was promulgated to give civil effect to canonical marriages in the colony . Thus we have religious marriage restored and accepted under due conditions.

The above law stated in Article 1, "The marriage may be solemnized in the presence of Government employee for the work of civil registration as per the civil law, or before the ministers of the Catholic Church as per the canonical laws and under the conditions imposed by the Civil law for such cases". Thus, though this law acknowledged the effectiveness of civil marriage as well as Catholic marriage, it gave persons the option to marry as per religious rites after meeting the requirement of law, or choose civil marriage. It is to be noted that one had to meet the requirements of civil law before he could proceed with the Catholic marriage. It is to be noted that canonical marriages did not permit divorce.

In order to prevent the religious beliefs and feelings of some individuals leading them to celebrate religious marriages without civil marriage, thus giving rise to situations of concubinage in the eyes of the civil law, the 1911 Civil Registry Code prohibited the celebration of religious marriage

---

[29] Ibid. pg. 55.

without the prior celebration of civil marriage. Article 220 of the Civil Registry Code required that religious marriage only be celebrated on the production of a bulletin, birth certificate or marriage certificate proving that the civil wedding had already taken place.[30] Religious marriage may be celebrated only after the completion of civil marriage[31]. The code supersedes religious rules. If a marriage is not registered, the court does not recognize it. At this time, marriage was a permanent bond; the concept of divorce did not exist[32]. Today, it is necessary to produce a certificate of no objection from civil registration before one enters into Catholic marriage.

The civil code insists that all couples must register their intent to marry as well as the marriage itself. The fiancées can make an ante-nuptial agreement to establish the matrimonial disposition of property.[33] The engaged couple can agree what they wish with regard to their assets prior to the celebration of marriage and within the law[34]. This ante–nuptial agreement must be a notarial deed, failing which it is null and void[35].
In a pre-nuptial agreement, the couple should choose any of the systems which deal with property distribution. This contract cannot be changed after the marriage has taken place.

Should marriages be registered?

Registration of marriage is one of the vital facets in the field of the law of marriage. Due to the absence of registration records of the registration of marriage, unscrupulous spouses, despite the existence of marriage, dispute the status. Registration of one's marriage provides proof of it for legal

[30] The State's consent to the marriage—it is not only to witness the marriage, to certify that it has been celebrated and to ensure that there are no legal impediments and all formalities required by law are observed.
[31] Article 1075 "Whosoever desires to contract marriage as per the procedure prescribed by the Civil Law shall present to the official of Civil Registration of his domicile or of his residence a declaration signed by both the contracting parties."
[32] In Portugal divorce was introduced by a Decree only on 3rd November 1910. This enabled marriages to be dissolved. Conditional marriages and alteration as legal conditions by agreement were avoided.
[33] Article 1096 states "It is lawful for the spouses to stipulate before the solemnization of the marriage and within the bounds of law whatever they think fit in respect of their property."
[34] Article 1097 "Such Contracts shall not be valid unless they are recorded by way of a public deed."
[35] Article 1096 of the Civil Code.

purposes and is a safety measure. In Smt. Seema v. Ashvani Kumar,[36] the Supreme Court took the matter into consideration and issued directions to the states to make registration compulsory.
Section 8 refers to the registration of Hindu marriages. It reads:

> "For the purpose of facilitating the proof of Hindu marriages, the State Government may make rules providing that the parties to any such marriage may have the particulars relating to their marriage entered in such manner and subject to such condition as may be prescribed in a Hindu Marriage Register kept for the purpose.
> (2) Notwithstanding anything contained in sub-section (1), the State Government may, if it is of opinion that it is necessary or expedient so to do, provide that the entering of the particulars referred to in sub-section (1) shall be compulsory in the State or in any part thereof, whether in all cases or in such cases as may be specified and where any such direction has been issued, and person contravening any rule made in this behalf shall be punishable with a fine which may extend to twenty-five rupees.
> (3) All rules made under this section shall be laid before the State Legislature as soon as may be after they are made.
> (4) The Hindu Marriage Register shall at all reasonable times be open for inspection, and shall be admissible as evidence of the statements therein contained; and certified extracts therefrom shall, on application, be given by the Registrar on payment to him of the prescribed fee.
> (5) Notwithstanding anything contained in this section, the validity of any Hindu marriage shall in no way be affected by the omission to make the entry.

S. 8 (1) & (2) of Hindu Marriage Act, 1956 states that the state government may make rules for parties intending to marry. The registration of Hindu and Muslim marriages is not compulsory. In a vast country like India with its variety of customs, religions and level of literacy there are reservations about making registration of marriage compulsory.

Under the Portuguese Civil Code, all marriages must be registered[37]. These provisions come under Chapter VI, and the heading is "Proof of Marriage". Article 3 of Decree No 1 of 25thNovember, 1910 states: "All Portuguese shall solemnize their marriages before the respective officer of the Civil Registration under the conditions and in the manner established

---

[36] 2006(2) SC 378
[37] Hindu, Muslim and Christian.

in civil law, and only such marriages are valid."[38] The procedural aspects of the registration of marriage are contained in Articles 1075 to 1081 of the Portuguese Civil Code. The aforesaid provisions were repealed by a law enacted as the Code of Civil Registration[39]. The Chapter dealing with marriage is contained in Articles 180 to 248 of the Code of Civil Registration.

The institution of marriage being secular and not connected with religion, it is mandatory that the officer of civil registration verifies whether there are no impediments for the marriage and objections to that effect are called by the public. The marriage is to be performed before the officer of the Civil Registrar and only such marriages established from the record of civil registration are valid.

Catholics can perform their marriages in the Church. Article 1069 states ,"Catholic marriage will produce civil effects only when solemnized in conformity with the canonical laws followed in the country or recognized by them." For others the essence of marriage is that it is disassociated from religion[40]. Without the "no objection certificate" from the Office of the Civil Registrar and without undergoing all the ceremonies of publication, it is not possible even for Catholics to perform marriage. They must follow the prescribed procedure of the Civil Code. The transcript which is made before the Church must to be re-submitted to the Officer of the Civil Registrar, and has to be produced as per the forms of the civil registration. When the parties wishing to marry submit their declaration before the civil registry, the civil registration officials shall affix the declaration in a public place at the entrance of their offices as a notice of the intention of the contracting parties and their respective details[41]. After the lapse of fifteen days, provided there are no impediments to the marriage, the Civil Registration Official shall solemnize the marriage in accordance with Article 1081. The solemnization of marriage contracted shall be proved by a certified copy of the competent registration.

---

[38] Article 3 – The solemnization of marriage before a marriage officer is similar to that under Special Marriage Act, 1952

[39] Passed on 9/11/1912.

[40] Article 1072: "Marriages between non- Catholic Portuguese subjects shall have civil effects where the essential requirements of contract are followed and satisfied."

[41] Article 1076 discusses the mentioned para. Article 1058 and contains legal impediments which may be bought to the notice of those who consent to marry.

Implementation of The Law

Certain state governments have made the registration of marriage compulsory, thus giving legal status to wedlock and strengthening the institution of marriage:

- The Bombay Registration Marriages Act, 1953, which is applicable to the state of Maharashtra.
- The Karnataka Marriages Act, enacted in 1976 and in force since 1983.
- The Himachal Pradesh Registration of Marriage Act, 1997.
- The Andhra Pradesh Compulsory Registration of Marriage Act, 2002.

Advantages Of The Law

Compulsory registration of marriages has many advantages for women.

- Married couples are given a Government certificate as a marriage document; it becomes a valuable indisputable evidence of marriage.
- This would be a valid evidence while accompanying the wife/husband to a foreign country. It would also facilitate the easy processing of passport and visa applications.
- When a person happens to die without leaving a will for disposal of their bank deposit or life insurance policy, it will be helpful for the husband/wife to inherit such money.
- Compulsory legal registration of marriages prevents child marriages and also the sale of girls and trafficking.
- Since the Registrar is supposed to verify whether the marriage has in fact taken place in accordance with the personal law applicable to the spouses, he would have to specifically mention in a special column the presence of the spouses before issuing the marriage certificate.

Economic Rights of Women Within Marriage

In an advancing India it is necessary to specifically protect the rights of women within marriage. The economic rights of married women during the subsistence of marriage and on dissolution of marriage must be protected by law. The following points can be noted within a discussion of family law:

- All endowments pledged to a woman at the time of her marriage, whether by parents, parents-in-law or her husband, and gifts given to her, shall be her absolute and separate property.
- Adequate maintenance, including interim maintenance, shall be provided to the dependent spouse during the subsistence of the marriage.
- During the subsistence of the marriage, the wife's access to matrimonial assets must be guaranteed, including her right to reside in the matrimonial home.
- Laws against domestic violence shall empower the courts to grant injunctions restraining a violent spouse from entering the matrimonial home.
- In case of dissolution of a marriage, the courts shall decide all related matters, e.g. divorce/dissolution, maintenance/alimony or dower/ financial settlement and provision of shelter simultaneously, except disputes relating to custody of minors. In doing so, separate procedures shall be laid down in order to provide for expeditious disposal of suits.
- Assets movable or immovable accumulated during the subsistence of the marriage shall be distributed equally on the termination of the marriage.
- Inheritance laws shall be changed to ensure that the share of male and female heirs of the same class of kinship shall be equal. The children shall inherit in equal proportion a share of their mother's assets.

Conclusion

There is a need for comparative research on family laws in India. The laws also need to be analyzed on the basis of the economic rights of women within marriage.

DIVORCE: COMPARATIVE ANALYSIS OF THE FAMILY LAWS OF GOA AND HINDU AND MUSLIM FAMILY LAW

MRUNMAYI MUKUND VAIDYA[1]

Introduction

The State of Goa enjoys a special status as far as the application of the law in the sphere of family matters is concerned. The family laws which are prevalent in Goa have the distinctive feature of being applicable to all the communities to whom the law applies, irrespective of their religion except for certain differences. This is in contradistinction to the personal laws applicable to the whole of India which allow every religion to be governed by its own personal laws.

This article aims to carry out a comparative analysis of the family laws of Goa[2] and those of the Hindu law and the Muslim law of divorce applicable in India. An attempt is made to study the provisions of all three sets of laws and to make suggestions for improvement if required, in order to make the law more comprehensive and effective.

Tracing the roots of the Family Laws of Goa

The Portuguese Civil Code of 1867 was made applicable to Portuguese citizens and also to overseas provinces, whereby it came to be applied in the State of Goa. Thereafter, various Statutes were passed which had the effect of altering the form of the Civil Code and repealing certain

---

[1] Lecturer in Law, V.M.Salgaocar College of Law, Miramar, Panaji,Goa.

[2] The term refers to Portuguese laws which were applicable to Goa in the area of family laws and which still continue to be in force. They include some provisions of the Civil Code of 1867 and other statutes.

provisions in it. The Decree of 3rd Nov 1910[3] was one such important statute which provided for alterations in the law of divorce. Even after the Liberation of Goa, these family laws have continued to apply and are largely uniform in the sense that they do not discriminate on the grounds of religion.

Comparative Analysis of the Family Laws of Goa with Hindu and Muslim Law of Divorce

The Hindus are governed by the Hindu law[4] in the sphere of personal matters. Secs. 13 and 13.B of the Hindu Marriage Act, 1955, provides for divorce among Hindus. They recognize a wide variety of grounds for divorce, such as the fault of one party, including the special grounds of divorce available to the wife; irretrievable breakdown of marriage; and mutual consent of the parties.

Divorce for Muslims is provided for by Muslim personal law. This law is largely uncodified[5]. This uncodified portion of the law provides for the unilateral right of the husband to divorce his wife, even in the absence of any specific reason, without a justification or her consent[6]. It also contains rare provisions for divorce by the wife. However, specific provision for divorce at the initiation of the wife is made in the form of the Dissolution of Muslim Marriage Act, 1939. It is this Act which will be our subject of analysis in comparison with the family laws of Goa and the Hindu law.

The Decree of 3rd November 1910 provides for divorce under the Family Laws of Goa[7]. All these three laws recognize various grounds for divorce. Some of these grounds are community-specific, especially in case of the Hindu law. There are a few grounds which are available in all the three set

---

[3] Better known as the 'Divorce Law'.

[4] Legislation such as The Hindu Marriage Act,1955; Hindu Adoption and Maintenance Act,1956; Hindu Minority and Guardianship Act,1956; Hindu Succession Act,1956, etc.

[5] The source of the uncodified Muslim personal law is the Koran (the sacred book); Sunna (the tradition); Ijmma (the consensus of jurists),and Qiyas (analogical deductions).

[6] See, Asaf.A.A.Fayzee, *Outlines of Muhammadan Law*, 4th ed. (Oxford India Paperbacks, 1999), p. 150

[7] Provisions of the Decree of 3rd November 1910 are referred from *Family Laws of Goa,Daman and Diu*, Volume I (Vasco da Gama, Goa: Devi Shreevani Education Society, 1979).

of laws, but we find fine differences in the nature, interpretation and application of the same. Some of the grounds, though differently titled, are in substance similar to others when it comes to application.

The grounds of divorce can be classified into five categories generally, viz. a) Guilt ground, b) Fault ground, c) Irretrievable breakdown of marriage, d) Mutual consent and e) other grounds. Our comparative analysis will be on the basis of this classification.

Guilt grounds of Divorce

These grounds of divorce are based on an element of guilt of one of the spouse of the marriage, who is considered to have committed an offence against marriage.

1. Adultery

Adultery signifies consensual sexual intercourse between one of the spouses of the marriage and another person who is not his or her spouse. The Hindu Marriage Act, 1955 provides that:

> "Any marriage solemnized, whether before or after the commencement of the Act, may, on a petition presented by either the husband or the wife, be dissolved by a decree of divorce on the ground that the other party has, after the solemnization of the marriage, had voluntary sexual intercourse with any person other than his or her spouse"[8].

The provision of the family laws of Goa is similar. Article 4 of the Decree of Nov 1910 mentions "adultery by the wife" and "adultery by the husband"[9] as grounds of contentious divorce. Though these are two different grounds, they are equally available to both spouses.[10] Originally, under the family laws of Goa, adultery by the husband could only be invoked as a ground of separation of persons and assets when it was accompanied by public scandal or complete failure to support his wife, or where the correspondent was maintained in the matrimonial home. However, wives' adultery was treated very harshly. But this position was altered by the Decree of 3rd November 1910, clauses 1and 2 of which make the ground equally available to both parties.

[8] Sec.13 (1)(i)

[9] Clause (1) &(2)

[10] Art 1204, para 2

The Muslim law does not specifically recognize adultery as an independent ground of divorce. However, under the Dissolution of Muslim Marriage Act, 1939, in the ground of cruelty, the husband's associating with women of ill-repute[11] is included. But the act of associating with women of ill-repute may or may not include the act of sexual intercourse. Also, the word used in the Act is 'women' and not 'woman'. Thus it is possible to draw an inference that when the husband associates with a single woman of ill-repute, this does not amount to cruelty. This kind of an interpretation may lead to injustice.

Under Hindu law, a single instance of extramarital sexual intercourse is sufficient, provided it can be proved by preponderance of probabilities. In cases of adultery the parties are not required to prove the fact beyond doubt; rather the court will conclude it on basis of probabilities, considering the nature of the act and the difficulty of proving it. Even under the family law of Goa, the nature of this wrong would be the same as under Hindu law. The Muslim law, however, does not provide any sufficient redress, and the above-mentioned provision under the ground of cruelty, which includes husbands' associating with women of ill-repute, is generally worded; it cannot be safely concluded that it will cover cases of adultery. It is desirable, therefore, to include a specific ground of the nature of 'Adultery' in the Muslim legislation.

Desertion

Desertion signifies the act of completely forsaking one spouse by the other, by cessation of cohabitation. The family laws of Goa provide a ground of divorce where there is

> "…complete abandonment of the conjugal domicile for a period of not less than three years"[12].

The Hindu law has a similar ground which provides redress in the case that the:

> "…respondent has deserted the petitioner for a continuous period of not less than two years immediately preceding the presentation of the petition"[13].

The Act defines 'Desertion' as

---

[11] Sec,2(viii)(b)

[12] Clause 5, Art 4 ,Decree of 3RD November, 1910.

[13] Sec. 13(i-b), Hindu Marriage Act, 1955

> "Desertion of the petitioner by the other party to the marriage without reasonable cause and without the consent or against the wish of such party, and includes the willful neglect of the petitioner by the other party to the marriage, and its grammatical variations and cognate expressions shall be construed accordingly".

However, under the Dissolution of Muslim Marriage Act, 1939, the ground available to the wife is worded differently. The word 'Desertion' or 'abandonment' is not used, but it states that

> '...the husband has failed to perform, without reasonable cause, his marital obligations for a period of three years"[14]

This can be construed to mean an act of desertion, as it in fact amounts to abandonment of matrimonial obligation. Another clause of the same Act provides a ground where:

> "...the husband has neglected or has failed to provide for her maintenance for a period of two years"[15].

This too may amount to desertion if it is viewed as failure to fulfill marital obligations. We do not find any mention of this ground in the other two laws specifically, though under the ground of 'desertion' under the Hindu law 'willful neglect' is mentioned in the explanation of 'desertion,' which will include the willful act of neglecting to maintain the wife.

On comparative analysis of the three provisions, it can be said that there is a difference between the Hindu law and the family laws of Goa with regards to the duration of desertion. Another distinction is the specific requirement of the Hindu law that the desertion should be without just cause. The provision of the family laws of Goa does not mention anything similar and is rather plainly worded. It is more appropriate to allow desertion as a ground only when it is without a reasonable cause, or else it may tend to injure the interest of the party, who may have a just excuse for withdrawal.

Cruelty

The term 'Cruelty' has not been defined in any of the laws. But it has been recognized as a ground of divorce in all three sets of laws. The ground under the family laws of Goa is defined as

---

[14] Sec 2.(iv).

[15] Sec.2(ii),

> "...ill-treatment or serious injuries"[16].

Ill-treatment would include physical harm or threat of harm, unreasonable restriction, etc. It may also include indignity by acts or words that are offensive to the honour, dignity and reputation of the other spouse, in which both the words and the acts are characterized by the intention to cause harm, to degrade, i.e. by *animus injuriandi*[17]

The Hindu law too does not explain what 'cruelty' is, but simply mentions that the other party

> "...has, after the solemnization of the marriage, treated the petitioner with cruelty"[18].

It is through judicial interpretation that the word is accorded an explanation. It is not accompanied by any qualifying term such as 'serious', as used in the family laws of Goa. The word has been understood to mean physical as well as mental cruelty, and seems to have a wider ambit than in the family laws of Goa.

Under the Muslim law also, husbands' cruelty is a recognized ground. Clause (viii) of Sec.2 of the Dissolution of Muslim Marriage Act, 1939, specifically mentions acts which would be considered as amounting to cruelty. The wife is entitled to divorce if

> "the husband treats her with cruelty, that is to say, (a) habitually assaults her or makes her life miserable by cruelty of conduct even if such conduct does not amount to physical ill-treatment, or (b) associates with women of evil repute or leads an infamous life, or (c) attempts to force her to lead an immoral life, or (d) disposes of her property or prevents her exercising her legal rights over it, or (e) obstructs her in the observance of her religious profession or practice, or (f) if he has more wives than one, does not treat her equitably in accordance with the injunctions of the Quran".

Whether this widens the scope of availability of the ground by making it more specific, or restricts the ambit, is a question to be considered.

---

[16] Clause 4, supra No. 10

[17] Prof Doutor Pires de Lima & Prof. Doutor Joao de Matos Antunes Varela, *Fundamental Concepts Of Civil Law*, Vol II (Fundacao Oriente,1997), p. 250

[18] Sec.13(1)(i-a), supra No. 11

Sentencing of a spouse for an offence

The family laws of Goa[19] provide for divorce on the final sentencing of any spouse to any of the penalties under arts. 55 and 57 of the Penal Code[20]. A similar ground is found in the Dissolution of Muslim Marriage Act, 1939[21], which allows divorce on the ground that the husband has been sentenced to imprisonment for a period of seven years or upwards. The sentence has to be a final sentence. But the Hindu law recognizes no such ground specifically.

Chronic vice of gambling[22]

This ground is provided under the family laws of Goa and has come under heavy criticism. Such a specific provision is not found in either the Hindu law or the Muslim law, though under Hindu law, gambling may probably be understood to amount to cruelty to the other spouse. In case of Muslim law, it may be used as a ground if it results in the use and disposal of the wife's property by the husband for the purpose of gambling, as disposing of the wife's property may amount to cruelty to her.[23]

Rape, Sodomy and Bestiality by the husband

This ground is recognized under Hindu law[24] exclusively for the wife. These are sexual acts committed by the husband against the wife or any other. Rape on the wife is available as a ground in the case that she is below the age of fifteen.[25]

Fault Grounds of Divorce

The grounds available for divorce on basis of the fault of a spouse include any fault which a party suffers from which may be a conscious act or accidental, where guilt cannot be attributed to such act. It therefore needs to be studied as a different class in itself.

---

[19] Clause 3,supra No.10

[20] The articles referred are of the Portuguese Penal Code, which is no longer in force.

[21] Sec.2(iii)

[22] Clause 9,supra No.10

[23] Sec 2.(viii)(d),Dissolution of Muslim Marriage Act,1939

[24] Sec.13(2)(ii), supra No.11

[25] Sec. 375, Indian Penal Code ,1860: Exception: Sexual intercourse by a man with his own wife, the wife not being under fifteen years of age, is not rape.

Insanity

The family laws of Goa provide for insanity as a ground of divorce in the words:

> "...Incurable unsoundness of mind, when at least three years have elapsed after its pronouncement by judgment, becomes final for want of appeal, as per article 419 onwards of the Code of Civil Procedure"[26].

According to the Hindu law, incurable mental disorder constitutes a ground of divorce. The Hindu Marriage Act, 1955 provides for divorce if the respondent:

> "...has been incurably of unsound mind, or has been suffering continuously or intermittently from mental disorder of such a kind and to such an extent that the petitioner cannot reasonably be expected to live with the respondent."[27]

The explanation to the clause states that

> "(a) the expression 'mental disorder' means mental illness, arrested or incomplete development of mind, psychopathic disorder or any other disorder or disability of mind and includes schizophrenia;
> (b) the expression 'psychopathic disorder' means a persistent disorder or disability of mind (whether or not including sub-normality of intelligence) which results in abnormally aggressive or seriously irresponsible conduct on the part of the other party and whether or not it requires or is susceptible to medical treatment".

The Dissolution of Muslim Marriage Act, 1939,[28] contains a ground similar to the family laws of Goa, viz, the insanity of the husband. However, the duration required is of a continuous period of two years, where as under the Goa law it is three years.

The situation may sometimes amount to hardship when the parties are required to wait for a certain duration in spite of the mental illness being confirmed. Under the Hindu Marriage Act, 1955, there is no qualifying time-limit for such disorder. It would result in better justice if the parties were allowed to file a petition immediately, in cases where the unsoundness of mind has been determined to be incurable, as waiting for a particular duration will not serve any purpose in such a situation.

---

[26] Clause 7,supra No.10.
[27] Sec 13(1)(iii)
[28] Sec.2(vi)

Leprosy and Venereal diseases

The Hindu law and the Dissolution of Muslim Marriages Act, 1939, recognize suffering from leprosy and venereal diseases as a ground of divorce. Clause (iv) if Sec. 13(1) of the Hindu Marriage Act,1955, states that a divorce petition may be filed if the other party

> "…has been suffering from a virulent and incurable form of leprosy".

Clause (v) of the same section states that a petition may be filed if the other party

> "…has been suffering from venereal disease in a communicable form".

The ground under the Dissolution of Muslim Marriage Act, 1939, is worded as

> "…suffering from leprosy or a virulent venereal disease"[29].

The family laws of Goa provide for this ground in the case of a

> "Contagious disease found incurable or an incurable disease involving sexual aberration"[30].

In this explanation, leprosy and venereal disease as mentioned under Hindu and Muslim law will be included. But this ground appears to be much more comprehensive as it includes various kinds of incurable contagious diseases, which are not covered in the grounds of Hindu and Muslim law. The Hindu and Muslim laws only recognize leprosy. Then again, under the Hindu law, leprosy has to be virulent and incurable, but the Muslim Law does not impose such a condition. The provision of the family laws of Goa appears to be better placed as it has a wider ambit to include all diseases which are incurable and contagious, and will include venereal diseases as well. Under the Hindu and Muslim laws, diseases other than leprosy or venereal diseases cannot serve as grounds of divorce, though they may be contagious. There is a need for amendment to these provisions, especially considering the new kinds of diseases that are developing all the time.

---

[29] Sec.2(vi)

[30] Clause 10. supra No.10

Impotence of the Husband[31]
This ground for divorce is recognized only under the Muslim law. The Dissolution of Muslim Marriage Act,1939, provides a ground where

> "...the husband was impotent at the time of the marriage and continues to be so".

The decree does not, however, take effect immediately. If, after the petition, the husband applies to the courts, the court can issue an order asking him to satisfy the court within one year that he has ceased to be impotent.

Irretrievable breakdown of marriage as a ground of divorce

In certain cases, from the conduct of one of the spouses it is apparent that the marriage has miserably failed and that there are no hopes of restoring conjugal relations. This is termed irretrievable breakdown of marriage ties. In such cases, the law finds no sense in retaining the marriage tie and therefore allows its dissolution. Some grounds are recognized by the law which project the breakdown of a marriage.

Non-compliance with a Decree of Restitution of Conjugal Rights.
The Hindu law[32] provides that, in cases where the court has passed an order of Restitution of Conjugal Rights[33] between the parties, and it is not complied with up to the period of one year, then it becomes a ground for divorce. This ground is available even to the non-complying spouse, as it signifies the fact that the marriage has broken down beyond repair. No such ground is found under the other two laws.

---

[31] Sec.2(v) ,id

[32] Sec. 13(1-A)(ii),supra No.11

[33] Sec 9, supra no.11 (Restitution of Conjugal Rights):—(1) When either the husband or the wife has, without reasonable excuse, withdrawn from the society of the other, the aggrieved party may apply, by petition to the district court, for restitution of conjugal rights, and the court, on being satisfied of the truth of the statements made in such petition and that there is no legal ground why the application should not be granted, may decree restitution of conjugal rights accordingly.

Non-resumption of cohabitation after a Decree of Maintenance[34]
This is an exclusive ground under the Hindu Marriage Act, 1955. The Hindu law provides for maintenance to the wife under the Hindu Adoption and Maintenance Act, 1956, as well as under Sec.125 of the Code of Criminal Procedure, 1974. Where an order for maintenance under the Hindu Adoption and Maintenance Act or Sec. 125 of the Code of Criminal Procedure is passed against the husband, but the parties do not resume cohabitation up to the period of one year after the date of passing of the order, the wife can seek divorce. Maintenance is available to a wife irrespective of her residing separately from the husband, but requires reasonable grounds. In cases where the wife claims maintenance from the husband when they reside together, it is possible that the husband may refuse to cohabit for the reason that the wife had recourse to the law. This provision is made to provide relief to the wife faced with such a situation.

Divorce by Mutual Consent

In this kind of divorce, both parties to the marriage wish to dissolve the marriage tie and therefore by mutual consent may apply for divorce.

Divorce by mutual consent may be applied for under Art.1472 of the Portuguese Civil Code, 1867, by parties who have been married for more than five years and the age of both the parties is more than 25 years. Before granting a decree nisi for divorce, the court calls the parties and their parents and children above the age of eighteen years and attempts to effect reconciliation. In cases where the decree is granted and reconciliation fails, the parties have to reappear before the court for reconciliation. It is at this stage that the divorce becomes final if reconciliation fails. In cases where the parties reconcile before the final decree of divorce, they cannot seek divorce by mutual consent again, but may apply for contentious divorce.

The Hindu and Muslim laws also provide for divorce by mutual consent. The divorce provision under the Muslim law is available by virtue of the uncodified Muslim personal law[35], which involves an act of freeing each other, having an irrevocable effect.

---

[34] Sec. 13(2)(iii), id
[35] Supra n.5,163 Known as 'Mubarra'/'Mubarrat' and 'khul'.

Divorce by mutual consent under the Hindu law can be granted on a petition of both the parties

> "…on the ground that they have been living separately for a period of one year or more, that they have not been able to live together and that they have mutually agreed that the marriage should be dissolved"[36].

There are differences in the provisions of all three laws which provide for divorce by mutual consent. The family laws of Goa and the Muslim law do not require separation between parties prior to the application by mutual consent like, as is the case with the Hindu law. Under the Muslim law, divorce can be taken by following the mode stated in accordance with the personal law. But under the family laws of Goa, the provision requires the parties to wait for a period of one year for the decree to take effect, when they are expected to appear before the court, where the divorce becomes final if the parties still do not wish to reconcile. This is similar to the position under the Hindu law, where the parties, after six months from the date of petition, have to move a motion to the court within eighteen months, whereafter the court grants divorce. Under both these laws the period of waiting is aimed at reconciliation.

Other Grounds of Divorce

The present heading of 'Other grounds' has been made to cover all those grounds which do not involve the guilt or the fault of either party to the marriage, nor is there consent to divorce by both, and therefore stand on a different footing..

Separation between the spouses
The family laws of Goa provide a ground where there is

> "…De facto separation, freely consented to, for ten consecutive years, whatever may have been the cause of that separation"[37].

The reason for separation is not material. In addition, this law also allows divorce in cases where the petitioner in cases of proceedings for separation of persons and assets, on ground of para 1 to 4, 9 and 10 of Art. 4 of the Decree of Nov 1910, is unsuccessful. This fact alone shall be deemed to be grave harm[38]

---

[36] Sec 13-B, supra No.11
[37] Clause 8, supra no.10
[38] Supra no.15, at 234

Absence of a spouse without any news

The family laws of Goa recognize a ground of divorce where there is

> "...absence, where nothing has been heard of the absentee, for a period of not less than four years"[39].

The Hindu law mentions a similar ground where the other party has

> "...not been heard of as being alive for a period of seven years or more by those persons who would naturally have heard of it, had that party been alive"[40]

thus raising a presumption of death of the missing spouse.

The Dissolution of Muslim Marriage Act,1939, also raises a similar presumption where

> "...the whereabouts of the husband have not been known for a period of four years"[41].

However, the decree does not take effect until the expiry of six months. If the husband appears personally or through an agent, and satisfies the court of his willingness to resume cohabitation, the decree will be set aside.

In all these three sets of laws, the ground is recognized for the purpose of divorce, but under the family laws of Goa and the Muslim law the duration required is four years, whereas under the Hindu law it is as long as seven years. It would be desirable to reduce this term of seven years under the Hindu Marriage Act, 1955, as it causes undue hardship to the petitioner.

Renunciation of the world[42]

This is a typically Hindu ground recognized on the basis of the sanyasashrama system that the Hindu philosophy provides. This is the act of one spouse giving up the worldly life. It resembles 'desertion' in the sense that there is non-performance of marital obligations. But what makes it different is the requirement of giving up worldly life and entering a religious order. It is available immediately on the fact of renunciation, and there is no qualifying duration like that in case of desertion.

---

[39] Clause 6, supra no.10

[40] Sec.13(1)(vii),supra No.11

[41] Sec.2(i)

[42] Sec.13(1)(vi),supra no.11

Conversion

Hindu law mentions conversion of the respondent as a ground of divorce. The clause makes it a ground when a party

> "…has ceased to be a Hindu by conversion to another religion".[43]

Conversion includes not only the act of renouncing one's own faith, but also embracing another faith. Conversion to a non-Hindu faith becomes a ground of divorce, as the Hindu law allows marriage between two Hindus only. The family law of Goa does not recognize this as a ground as it is applicable to all, irrespective of religion. The Muslim law also does not provide this as a ground of divorce as husbands' conversion to another faith automatically results in the dissolution of the marriage.

Repudiation of the marriage by the wife

The Hindu law and the Muslim law nowhere affect the validity of child marriages, but in such cases the law recognizes divorce. In the case of the Hindu law, the wife is entitled to claim divorce on the ground that

> "…her marriage (whether consummated or not) was solemnized before she attained the age of fifteen years and she has repudiated the marriage after attaining that age but before attaining the age of eighteen years"[44].

Muslim law recognizes the same ground but only in cases where the wife, having been given in marriage by her father or other guardian before she attained the age of sixteen years, repudiated the marriage before attaining the age of eighteen years provided that the marriage has not been consummated[45]. Consummation of marriage does not exclude the relief under the Hindu Marriage Act,1955, as it does under the Dissolution of Muslim Marriage Act,1939.

This exclusive relief under the Hindu law is available only to the wife but not to the husband. However, under the uncodified Muslim personal law, a minor male who was married by his guardians during minority has the option of repudiating his marriage on attaining puberty, depending on his nearness of relationship to the guardian who contracted his marriage; a welcome provision indeed.

---

[43] Sec.13(1)(ii), id

[44] Sec 13(2)(iv),id

[45] Sec.2(vii), supra No.20

Pre-Act polygamous marriages[46]
This is a particular ground recognized under the Hindu Marriage Act, 1955. But it has lost much of its significance due to the lapse of time since the passing of the Act in 1955. It allows all the wives of pre-Act polygamous Hindu marriages to seek divorce on the ground of subsistence of another marriage of the husband. Polygamous marriages performed after the commencement of the Act are made void by the Act.

Delegated divorce and Khul
These are grounds recognized under Muslim personal law whereby the husband may delegate the right of divorce to the wife or other relatives where she will be entitled to divorce herself on his behalf. In the Khul kind of divorce the husband releases the wife from the bond of marriage in exchange for some consideration. Such a type of divorce is not recognized by the Hindu and Goan laws.

Conclusion

A Uniform Civil Code is a mandate of the Indian Constitution under Art.44, which directs the State to provide for a Uniform Civil Code throughout the territory of India. In addition, there have been recommendations from various sectors to enact the same.

But the demand is still unfulfilled. To date we do not have a unified system as far as personal laws are concerned. Different communities are governed by their own laws. Problems thus arise when the law deals with every case differently, even where the facts are similar, and this is on basis of religion. This system causes injustice as it places certain people at a disadvantage when it comes to the claiming of rights, due to the incomprehensive provision of law applicable to them. For example, the Hindu Marriage Act, 1955, does not prescribe any duration in cases of unsoundness of mind as a ground of divorce, but the family laws of Goa and the Dissolution of Muslim Marriage Act,1939, state it as three years and two years respectively. Thus a Hindu spouse is entitled to immediate relief, whereas spouses subject to the family laws of Goa or Muslim legislation cannot receive the same remedy though they face the same situation. Thus the situation leads to according different treatment to different parties due to the different laws applicable to them due to different religions, though their cases may be the same or similar.

---

[46] Sec. 13(2)(i) supra no.11

At such a time what is required is to introduce a Uniform Civil Code which will be applicable to all irrespective of religion, so that all are governed by the same provisions and there is equality in the true sense. The application of uniform law in the state of Goa is given as a standard example to be followed by the rest of the country. But it can be concluded from the present study that even the Goa law, though it succeeds in attaining uniformity, is not in fact a comprehensive law. Rather, it can be said that none of the three sets of laws are comprehensive enough to cover all the possible grounds of divorce. What would be ideal, therefore, is to pool all the relevant grounds of divorce from all three sets of laws in a single Code and make it applicable to the whole of India, including the State of Goa, irrespective of the religion of the parties. Only then will we be able to implement a unified law of divorce to all without discrimination.

INDIRECT CALLINGS UNDER THE CIVIL CODES OF 1867 AND 1966

JORGE DUARTE PINHEIRO[1]

1. Introduction

The expression "indirect callings" is used to refer to in English a group of entities which are known in Portuguese as *"vocações indirectas"*.

In Portugal, "indirect callings" are an important issue in Succession Law.

Succession Law governs the transfer of the estate of a deceased person. The process of succession, or transfer of the estate of a deceased person, comprises three main phases: the opening of succession; the *calling of successors*; and the acquisition of inheritance (which includes partition).

The opening of succession occurs at the time of death of the person leaving the estate (see Article 2009 CC1867 and Article 2031 CC1966)[2].

Calling of successors is the expression used to translate the Portuguese word "vocação" or "chamamento". After the death of the estate-leaver, his/her successors are "called". This means that they acquire the right to succeed, *i.e.*, the right to accept or repudiate the succession in question.

---

[1] Professor of the Faculty of Law, University of Lisbon.

[2] In this study, "CC1867" is an abbreviation for "Portuguese Civil Code of 1867"; "CC1966" is an abbreviation for "Portuguese Civil Code of 1966".

Unless otherwise stated, we will follow the translation of the CC1867 made by M. S. Usgãocar, *Family Laws of Goa, Daman and Diu*, volume II, reprint (of the 1st edition 1988) (Panaji (Goa): Vela Associates, 2007).

We are responsible for the translation of the articles of CC1966 quoted in this paper.

Article 2009 CC1867 declares: "The inheritance opens by the death of the estate-leaver". The contents of Article 2031 CC1966 are similar.

The *calling*, or acquisition of the right to succeed by the successor, implies that three conditions have been satisfied[3]: personality of the successor (he/she has to survive the deceased); capacity, or competence, of the successor (for instance, a disinherited or unworthy person cannot succeed); priority in succession (*e.g.*, priority of class and degree of relationship, in cases of legal succession).

The calling to succession can be direct or indirect[4]. Direct calling, which is the most common, happens when someone acquires the right to succeed solely because of his/her relationship with the deceased. In *indirect calling*, the successor acquires the right to succeed due to two relationships: the relationship between him/her and the deceased and the relationship between him/her and another successor who could not accept the succession, or did not want to accept it.

The notion of indirect calling is not very simple, which is a sign of the technical difficulty of this matter. This difficulty of the theme of "indirect callings" is one of the reasons that has led us to write about it. We aim to provide a clearer understanding of this matter. An additional reason is the lack of a basic study in English dealing globally with all types of indirect callings. In fact, Succession Law books and articles (translated in English, or written originally in English) study the different types of indirect callings separately[5]. The common logic of these types and the connections between them are not very visible. Last, but not least, understanding indirect callings is important for solving practical problems. For instance:

---

[3] See Carlos Pamplona Corte Real, *Direito da Família e das Sucessões*, vol. II, *Sucessões* (Lisbon: Lex, 1993), pp. 197–217; Jorge Duarte Pinheiro, *Direito da Família e das Sucessões*, vol. IV, *Parte geral dinâmica: Da abertura da sucessão à partilha. Parte especial: a sucessão legitimária*, 1st edition (2005), 2nd reprint (Lisbon: AAFDL, 2008), pp. 16–20; José de Oliveira Ascensão, *Direito Civil—Sucessões*, 5th ed. (Coimbra: Coimbra Editora, 2000), pp. 151–154.

[4] See Carlos Pamplona Corte Real, *op. cit.*, pp. 224–231; Jorge Duarte Pinheiro, *op. cit.*, pp. 31–33; José de Oliveira Ascensão, *op. cit.*, pp. 171–175.

[5] See Mário Bruto da Costa, *Law of Succession*, bound edition (previous edition of 1997 *(?)*) (Panjim *(*Goa*)*: Author's edition, sponsored by Fundação Oriente, 2000 *(?)*), pp. 89–91, 132–134, 215–225; Pires de Lima and João de Matos Antunes Varela, *Fundamental Concepts of Civil Law*, vol. II, *Lectures to the 1st Year Law Course of 1944-45 (Family Law and Succession)*, bilingual edition (sponsored by Fundação Oriente and Ordem dos Advogados Portugueses), including Portuguese version [*Noções Fundamentais de Direito Civil, vol. II, Lições ao Curso do 1º ano jurídico de 1944-45 (Família e Sucessões)*] and its translation into English (Lisbon *(?)*, 1997 *(?)*), pp. 394–398, 510–512, 538–542.

A made a will, leaving all his property to a friend, *B*; *A* died; he was survived by a sister, *C*, his friend *B* and *E*, *B's* daughter. *B* repudiated the succession of *A*. Who is called to succeed? *C* or *E*? The correct answer depends upon an understanding of indirect callings.

In order to help the reader find the correct solution to the question presented above and to other important questions, the following pages will be organized as follows: the next section will demonstrate the unity between the different types of indirect callings; sections 3, 4 and 5 will analyze each of the three types of indirect callings separately (section 3 for common substitution, section 4 for right of representation, section 5 for right of accretion); section 6 will refer to the hierarchy of indirect callings; and section 7, the last, will be dedicated to some brief remarks on indirect callings.

2. General requirements and effects of indirect callings

There are three types of indirect callings: common substitution, right of representation and right of accretion. These types are subject to different rules, but they have a certain unity, based upon two general requirements and one general effect[6].

The indirect calling of a successor involves the existence of another successor who cannot or does not want to accept the succession. A successor is unable to accept the succession if he/she did not survive the estate-leaver, or if he/she is unworthy to succeed[7] or has been disinherited[8]. A successor does not want to accept if he/she repudiates the inheritance or legacy[9].

---

[6] See footnote 4.

[7] On unworthiness to succeed, see Articles 1749 and 1782 CC1867, Articles 2034-2038 CC1966. For instance, a person convicted of the act of taking the life of the estate-leaver is deprived of his/her right to the inheritance.

[8] On disinheritance see Articles 1875-1884 CC1867, Articles 2166-2167 CC1966. Disinheritance may be declared only in the will and with indication of a cause specifically enshrined in the law (*e.g.*, an offence committed against the estate-leaver that is punishable with imprisonment of more than six months). Disinheritance deprives the mandatory (or legitimary) heir of all his/her rights to the inheritance, including the right to legitime (see Jorge Duarte Pinheiro, *op. cit.*, p. 23; Pires de Lima and João de Matos Antunes Varela, *op. cit.*, pp. 524–528).

[9] The law makes the vesting of the estate in the successor dependant on the acceptance of the inheritance or legacy (paragraph 1 of Article 2050 CC1966; for

However, the aforementioned requirement—the existence of a successor who cannot or does not want to accept the succession—is not sufficient. For instance, let us imagine *A* died intestate. *D*, his daughter, and *I*, his brother, survived *A*. Having priority in the legal succession of *A* (Articles 1969 CC1867 and 2133 CC1966), *D* is called to succeed, but repudiates. Now, *I* is called to the succession. Nevertheless, he does not benefit from an indirect calling. His entitlement is the result of another mechanism: the *calling of a subsequent successor.*

A second requisite is indispensable: indirect calling is based upon a relationship between its beneficiary and the successor who could not or did not want to accept the succession. This relationship may be a family tie or may result from a testamentary provision.

In the previous example, *I* was called to the succession of *A* only because he had a certain relationship with the deceased; the relationship between him and *D* was of no consequence.

Let us imagine another case. *A* died intestate. His brother *I* died before him. *X* and *Z* survived *A*. *X* is *A's* uncle and *Z* is *I's* son. *Z* will be called to succeed *A* in representation of *I* (Articles 1982 CC1867 and 2042 CC1966). The calling of *Z* is an indirect one. The acquisition of the right to succeed by *Z* is the result of a double relationship: the relationship between himself and *A* and the relationship between himself and *I*.

We can highlight one more example. Imagine *A* made a will, in which he appointed *B* to inherit half of the estate and *C* to inherit the other half. *B*, *C* and *I* survived *A*. *B* and *C* were mere friends of *A*. *I* was his brother. *B* and *C* are called. *B* repudiates. If *C* accepts, he will acquire all the inheritance: he is entitled to half of the inheritance, to which he was directly called, and he is entitled to the other half, by right of accretion, an indirect calling. The entitlement of *C* in this second half was produced by two relationships: a relationship between *A* and *C* and a relationship between *C* and *B*. The first relationship was brought into existence by the will that appointed *C* to inherit half of *A's* estate. The second relationship was also created by the same will, in which *B* and *C* were both designated heirs of *A*.

CC1867, see Pires de Lima and João de Matos Antunes Varela, *op. cit.*, p. 532). The successor is free to accept or repudiate (Article 2021 CC1867; for CC1966, see Inocêncio Galvão Telles, *Direito das Sucessões: Noções fundamentais*, 6th ed. (Coimbra: Coimbra Editora, 1991), p. 128.

Besides the two above-mentioned requirements, all the three indirect callings have an identical effect: the beneficiary of the indirect calling occupies the position of the successor who could not or did not want to accept. The person indirectly called to the inheritance or legacy shall have the same rights and obligations as the one who could not or did not want to accept.

3. Common substitution

Common substitution is an indirect calling provided for in Articles 1858, 1864, 1865 CC1867, and in Articles 2281–2285 CC1966.

According to law, common substitution is a testamentary clause by which a person is appointed to replace the designated heir or legatee where such heir or legatee cannot or does not want to accept the inheritance or legacy (see Article 1858 CC1867 and Article 2281, § 1, CC1966)[10].

Common substitution is normally drafted as follows: "I appoint F as my universal heir (or my legatee to *such* and *such* assets); but if he is unable or unwilling to accept the estate (or legacy), my assets (or these my assets) shall pass to C... (or I appoint C to replace him...)"[11].

Common substitution is also known as *direct substitution* because there is no intermediary between the estate-leaver and the beneficiary of the substitution (substitute), *i.e.*, if the substitute is entitled, the property passes directly from the testator to him[12].

Common substitutions are conditional provisions and, consequently, they lapse if not activated during the substitute's lifetime[13], *i.e.*, the substitute has to survive the testator and be alive when the withdrawal from succession of the substituted heir or legatee occurs.

The testator may appoint several substituted heirs or legatees and provide for one substitute only or, inversely, appoint several substitutes for only

---

[10] Nevertheless, a common substitution may be made in a donation *mortis causa* (see, *e.g.*, Article 1700, § 2, CC1966). For this reason, the legal notion is inaccurate (see Jorge Duarte Pinheiro, *op. cit.*, p. 39).

[11] Pires de Lima and João de Matos Antunes Varela, *op. cit.*, p. 512.

[12] See Pires de Lima and João de Matos Antunes Varela, *op. cit.*, p. 510

[13] See Pires de Lima and João de Matos Antunes Varela, *op. cit.*, p. 512, footnote 1; Jorge Duarte Pinheiro, *op. cit.*, p. 41.

one substituted heir or legatee (plural substitution, admitted expressly in Article 2282 CC1966).

The testator may appoint successive substitutes. In contrast to fide-commissary substitution (see Articles 1867 CC1867 and 2287 CC1966), common substitution for more than one degree is not forbidden.

The testator may stipulate reciprocal substitutions (Articles 1865 CC1867, 2283 and 2285, § 2, CC1966).

The substitutes shall succeed to the rights and obligations to which the substituted heirs and legatees would succeed, unless the testator has provided otherwise (Articles 1864 CC1867 and 2284 CC1966).

4. Right of representation

Right of representation is an indirect calling mainly provided for in Articles 1980-1984 CC1867 and Articles 2039-2045 CC1966.

According to Article 2039 CC1966, "there is right of representation when the law calls the descendants of a certain heir or legatee to occupy the position of the one that could not or did not want to accept the inheritance or legacy".

According to Article 1980 CC1867, "there is right of representation when the law designates certain relatives of a deceased person to succeed to all the rights to which such person would have succeeded, if living". Taking into account Articles 1981 and 1982 CC1867, the right of representation exists solely in a descending line. Article 1984 adds: "the representatives shall only inherit, as such, what the person represented would have inherited, if living".

In both Codes, right of representation is conferred by law (not by a will), and benefits the descendants of a person designated to succeed who did not acquire the right to succeed, and entitles/lays upon the beneficiary of the right of representation (representative) the rights and obligations that would have belonged to the person represented, if he/she had succeeded[14].

[14] When there are two or more representatives, "they shall succeed by stirpes or by forming branches, amongst whom the inheritance shall be distributed, and subdivided in the branches where there is more than one heir, always observing the

The existence of a person designated to succeed who did not acquire the right to succeed is a requirement that draws a clear distinction between the right of representation and transmission of the right to succeed[15].

A transmission of the right to succeed takes place when a person called to the inheritance dies without accepting or repudiating it. In that case, the right to accept or repudiate passes to his/her heirs (Articles 2032 CC1867 and 2058, § 1, CC1966). The beneficiary of the transmission of the right to succeed may be a descendant or any legal heir of the person who died before accepting or repudiating the inheritance.

The death of a person designated to succeed is a prerequisite for transmission of the right to succeed and it is also a possible requirement for the right of representation. Nevertheless, the effects of transmission of the right to succeed and of right of representation are not identical. The right of representation exists in favour of descendants; the transmission of the right to succeed benefits legal heirs of the person designated to succeed, who may or may not be his/her descendants. A person may acquire assets by virtue of the right of representation, even if he/she has repudiated the inheritance of the represented person[16]; in the transmission of the right to succeed, an acquisition of assets presupposes acceptance of the inheritance opened by the death of the person designated to succeed (Articles 2033 CC1867 and 2058, § 2, CC1966).

Therefore it is crucial to know which of the two will operate. If a person designated to succeed predeceases the estate-leaver, right of representation is applicable. If that person dies after the estate-leaver, transmission of the right to succeed will apply. For instance, *A* died intestate; *C* and *D* survived *A*. *C* is *A*'s son. *D* is the daughter of *B*, another son of *A* who died before him. *D* is called to succeed to half of A's inheritance as representative of *B*. Another situation: *A* died intestate; *B*, *C* and *D* survived *A*. *B* and *C* are sons of A. *D* is the daughter of *B*. *B* dies without accepting or repudiating the inheritance of A. If *D* accepts the inheritance of *B*, she will be called to inherit half of what *A* left by virtue of transmission of the right to succeed.

---

same rule of equality" (Article 1987 CC1867; the same solution results from Articles 2044 and 2136 CC1966).

[15] See Jorge Duarte Pinheiro, *op. cit.*, pp. 49–51.

[16] See Article 2043 CC1966. For CC1867, see Luiz da Cunha Gonçalves, *Tratado de Direito Civil em comentário ao Código Civil Português*, vol. X (Coimbra: Coimbra Editora, 1935), pp. 380–381.

Now, we shall point out differences in regulation between the two Portuguese Codes concerning the right of representation.

In the Civil Code of 1867, the aforementioned right exists only in legal succession[17]. Previous death and incapacity to succeed are possible requirements for right of representation (Articles 1980 and 1979). Repudiation is not a cause of it (Article 2035).

Right of representation exists in a descending direct line and in favour of the descendants of siblings of the estate-leaver (Articles 1981 and 1982 CC1867).

In the Civil Code of 1966, right of representation may operate in legal or testamentary succession (Article 2040). Repudiation and previous death of a successor are common causes of it (see Articles 2039 and 2041, § 1). Unworthiness and disinheritance may give rise to right of representation in legal succession (see Articles 2041, § 1, 2037, § 2, and 2166, § 2).

Right of representation benefits in a descending direct line, including descendants of siblings of the estate-leaver and descendants of a person adopted by him/her (Articles 2042, 1986, § 1, and 1999, § 2, CC1966).

5. Right of accretion

Right of accretion is another indirect calling, the rules of which are set out in Articles 1852-1856, 1972 CC1867 and in Articles 2301-2307 and 2137, § 2, CC1966.

There is right of accretion when two or more persons are designated to succeed to the same inheritance (or to the same specific and certain thing included in the inheritance) and one of them cannot or does not want to succeed. In that case, the former is also entitled to the right to succeed to the portion initially destined for the latter[18].

It is useful to recall a previous example. *A* made a will, in which he appointed *B* to succeed to half of the estate and *C* to succeed to the other

---

[17] The right of representation is regulated in a division included in the chapter of intestate succession (Articles 1980-1984).

[18] See Jorge Duarte Pinheiro, *op. cit.*, p. 53; Luiz da Cunha Gonçalves, *op. cit.*, p. 23.

half. *B* and *C* survived *A*. *B* repudiates. *C* accepts, acquiring all the inheritance. *C* is entitled to half of the inheritance, to which he was directly called, and is entitled, by right of accretion, to the half that *B* did not want to accept.

The person who has accepted the portion to which he/she was directly called cannot repudiate the portion under accretion, unless this portion carries special encumbrances created by the testator (Articles 1856 CC1867 and 2306 CC1966). In the last example, *C* cannot accept half of the inheritance and repudiate the other. By accepting the half to which he was directly called, he automatically acquires the other half. However, *C* could accept the half to which he was directly called and repudiate the other half if, *e.g.*, the testator had burdened this second half with a legacy.

Accretion has the same effect as any other indirect calling: regarding the portion under accretion, the beneficiary shall succeed to all the rights and obligations of the one who could not or did not wish to accept the inheritance (or the legacy), had it been accepted by him/her[19].

Right of accretion may operate in testamentary or legal succession.

In testamentary succession, the right of accretion can be caused by previous death, incapacity to succeed and repudiation of a person who was designated to succeed. It is more common among heirs (Articles 1852 CC1867 and 2301 CC 1966).

There is one possibility of accretion between heirs and legatees, where the beneficiary is a legatee: if an heir repudiates a portion burdened with a legacy and the portion under accretion is repudiated by another heir, the said portion shall pass to the person in whose favour such encumbrance has been created[20].

The right of accretion among heirs and legatees, in benefit of heirs, is admitted in the Civil Code of 1867[21] and denied in the Civil Code of

---

[19] See Articles 1855 CC1867 and 2307 CC1966.

[20] See the second part of Articles 1856 CC1867 and 2306 CC1966; and Jorge Duarte Pinheiro, *op. cit.*, pp. 58–59. In the opinion of Luiz da Cunha Gonçalves (*op. cit.*, pp. 26 and 33), the second part of Article 1856 CC1867 establishes a case of reversion (in favour of the legatee), not of accretion.

[21] See Article 1853: "The right of accretion shall also pass on to heirs if the legatees do not want or are unable to receive the respective legacy".

1966.[22] The right of accretion is excluded amongst co-legatees in the Civil Code of 1867 (Article 1854), but it is possible in the Civil Code of 1966, in favour of persons designated to succeed to the same legated thing (Article 2302).

In legal succession, the Civil Code of 1867 mentions only repudiation as a cause of accretion (Article 1972). In Article 2137, § 2 of the Civil Code of 1966 accretion is said to occur if some of the called heirs cannot or do not want to accept. In spite of that, previous death of a successor is not a requirement of the right of accretion[23].

Since the right of accretion in legal succession and in testamentary succession is ruled separately, we can conclude that this right does not apply between legal and testamentary successors[24].

6. Articulating the three indirect callings

Some requirements are identical for the three indirect callings (*e.g.*, in testamentary succession, previous death is a cause of common substitution, right of representation and right of accretion). Nevertheless, the beneficiaries of the three indirect callings may be different.

For example: *A* made a will, appointing *B* to succeed to half of his inheritance and appointing *C* to succeed to the other half; the testator added that if *B* died before him, the portion left to *B* should pass to *D*. *B* predeceased *A*. *C*, *D* and *E*, the daughter of *B*, survived *A*. Which indirect calling should operate? Common substitution? In that case, the beneficiary of the previous death of *B* would be *D*. Right of representation? The beneficiary would be *E*. Right of accretion? The beneficiary would be *C*. What is the correct solution?

The criterion results from the hierarchy of indirect callings[25].

---

[22] See Article 2303, where the benefit of the heir (discharged from the burden) is considered a mere consequence of the lapse of the legacy.

[23] See Carlos Pamplona Corte Real, *op. cit.*, pp. 226–227; Jorge Duarte Pinheiro, *op. cit.*, p. 54.

[24] See Carlos Pamplona Corte Real, *op. cit.*, pp. 252, 254, 257; Jorge Duarte Pinheiro, *op. cit.*, pp. 56–59.

[25] See Jorge Duarte Pinheiro, *op. cit.*, p. 59.

In the field of the indisposable portion (the legitime), common substitution is not admissible[26]. Only right of representation and right of accretion may operate, with right of representation prevailing (Articles 2137, 2138 and 2157 CC1966).

In the field of the disposable portion[27], the will of the estate-leaver has to be respected. So, common substitution is in first place. Second place belongs to right of representation, and last is right of accretion.

Looking again at the last example given, the beneficiary is *D*, because common substitution precedes the two other indirect callings.

7. A final idea

The occurrence of certain events that are prerequisites of indirect callings, *e.g.*, repudiation or death of a successor prior to the opening of the inheritance, is not particularly unusual. To avoid mistakes it is important to know the rules and principles governing these issues. Ignorance can give rise to high costs for lawyers and interested parties. Paying attention to the issue of indirect callings avoids erroneous options.

In fact, several types of confusion with practical consequences are possible: confusion between one type of indirect calling and another, *e.g.*, right of representation instead of common substitution, in a case of testamentary substitution; confusion between right of representation and transmission of the right to succeed; and confusion between opening of intestate succession and applying one indirect calling.

By the way, the solution to the case presented in the first section of this text is the following: *E* is called to succeed to all of *A's* inheritance, as the representative of *B*. The sister of the deceased will not inherit because there is no reason to open the intestate succession.

---

[26] The testator cannot dispose of the legitime (Articles 1784 CC1867 and 2156 CC1966).

[27] It is easier to find articles that justify our conclusions about a hierarchy of indirect callings in the Civil Code of 1966 than in the Civil Code of 1867: for the hierarchy in testamentary succession, see Articles 2041, § 2, a), and 2304 CC1966.

PART VI:

JUDICIAL CULTURE

SELF-REGULATION OBLIGATIONS OF AN AUTONOMOUS PROFESSION

CHIDANANDA REDDY SANNABASANA GOUDA PATIL[1]

I. Introduction

Law is universally described as the great profession par excellence. Its greatness lies not in the wealth it brings or the prospects of high political office which it affords to its members, but in its code of professional ethics. It may, however be asked what a lawyer gains by scrupulous observance of the etiquette of his vocation.[2] Answering this question involves diverse important considerations, especially when the profession is at the cross roads.

The science of professional etiquette, over and above the ordinary rules of morality which bind all men in general, was first given to the world by lawyers and it would be very strange indeed if those who were the pioneers in this field did not respect the professional ideals which have come down to them from ages. The *Shastras* enjoin that success in life is measured, not by the riches one is able to collect or the power wielded, but by the faithful and efficient performance of duties according to one's capacities, and there is no greater virtue than living up to one's *dharma*. Sir Gooroodas Bannerji said many years ago in his address delivered at the Calcutta University Institute on the moral aspects of the Legal Profession[3]:

> Do your duty to the best of your ability, knowledge and judgment, and then, though you may not earn wealth and distinction, you will have earned that self-satisfaction, that peace of mind, which is the Crown of

---

[1] B.Sc., LL.M., Ph.D., Principal, University College of Law, Dharwad.

[2] C.L.Anand, *Professional Ethics of the Bar*, (Allahabad: The Law Book Co.(P) Ltd., 1987), p.23.

[3] *Ibid.*, pp.23-24.

> Crowns, which no wealth can buy, no patronage can bestow, and which no calamity, not death itself, can take away."

Public interest also demands that professional ideals be respected by the members of the Bar. Lord Bolingbroke once said of the legal profession that it is "in its nature the noblest and most beneficial to mankind, and in its abuse the most sordid and most pernicious."[4] Similarly, Daniel Webster has said, "Our profession is good if practiced in the spirit of it; it is a damnable fraud and inequity when its true spirit is supplanted by mischief-making and money-making."[5] A decline in ethical observance is therefore a matter of grave concern to the Bar, and it cannot but affect public confidence in the administration of justice.

Professions are noble. The movement of all professions, hitherto, has been from chaos to organization, organization to consolidation and consolidation to autonomy and monopoly[6]. The same is true of the legal profession also. The prime reason for society conferring autonomy and monopoly on professionals is the fact that they are a body of learned persons and the interests of society and individuals are safe in their hands. An attempt is made in this article to appreciate the obligation on the part of the profession to regulate itself if it wants to avoid an external agency monitoring its members. Part I deals with the importance of professional etiquette; Part II touches upon the meaning and standing of professions; Part III analyses the *pro bono publico* commitment of professions; Part IV explains the legal regime applicable to professions; the limited role of the courts in regulating professions is traced in Part V, and Part VI assesses the self-regulation obligations of professions.

II. Meaning and Standing of Professions

"Professions" are a select body of superior occupations where commercialism cannot be tolerated, and which are pursued not for pecuniary gains but out of a sense of duty to serve society[7]. According to Roscoe Pound, professions are callings in which men pursue a learned art and are united in the pursuit of it as a public service—no less a public service because they may earn a livelihood out of it. He writes in *The*

---

[4] Quoted by C.L.Anand, *op.cit.*

[5] Quoted by C.L.Anand, *op.cit.*

[6] O.Chinnappa Reddy, "Accountability of Professions", *Ind.Bar.Rev.* 14 (1987), p.623.

[7] M.K.Ramesh, "Consumer Interest in Legal Profession: Problems and Perspectives", *CULR* 1989 pp. 405 ff. (408).

Lawyer from Antiquity to Modern Times: "There is much more in a profession than a traditionally dignified calling. The term refers to a group of men pursuing a learned art as a common calling in the spirit of public service—no less a public service because it may incidentally be a means of livelihood. Pursuit of the learned art in the spirit of public service is the primary purpose"[8].

Justice Brandeis of the U.S. Supreme Court applied three criteria to professions, viz[9]:

> "First: A profession is an occupation for which the necessary preliminary training is intellectual in character, involving knowledge and to some extent learning, as distinguished from mere skill;
> Second: it is an occupation which is pursued largely for others and not merely for one's self;
> Third: it is an occupation in which the amount of financial returns is not the accepted measure of success."

The Father of the Nation, Mahatma Gandhi, wanted the members of the bar to spiritualise the legal profession. The following observations made by him while addressing a bar association deserve to be noted:

> "The duty of lawyers is always to place facts before the judges and help them to arrive at the truth. It is up to you to maintain the dignity of your profession. You young men claiming to be the fathers of tomorrow should be the salt of the nation. If the salt was to lose its savour, wherewith shall it be salted?"

Sharing the same rationale, Justice V.R.Krishna Iyer of our own Supreme Court has observed in *Bar Council of Maharastra v. M.V.Dabholkar*[10] as follows:

> "The Bar is not a private guild, like that of barbers, butchers, and candlestick makers, but, by bold contrast, a public institution committed to public justice and *pro bono publico* service. If these are the high expectations of what is described as a noble profession, its members must set an example of conduct worthy of emulation".

---

[8] Quoted by V.R.Krishna Iyer, "Professions for the People: A Third World Perspective", *Ind.Bar.Rev.* 15 (1988), pp. 219 ff.(221).
[9] *Ibid.,* pp.221–2
[10] AIR 1975 SC 2092

III. Professions are not for oneself

A profession differs from a business in that it is committed to public service, and the earnings resulting from such a service are only incidental. There cannot be any doubt that the lawyer's calling is a profession. Theoretically, in a profession, public service motivation and intellectualised expertise for the community's good are dominant, with a spirit of discipline and high ethics to guide their exercise, and income for the practitioner and material success for one's client being of lesser value in the scale. As in other professions, the legal profession also has a monopoly over practice, which society has historically surrendered to it in return for self-limitation and regulation by it so as to protect citizens from exploitation and inadequate service. That is, professional peers are authorized to sit in judgment on allegations of professional misconduct by the clients. The professions are expected to evolve their own rules for upholding professional standards and enforce them against those guilty of professional misconduct.

The legal profession touches human life at many more points than any other profession. It has always been held in high esteem and its members have played an enviable role in public life. It is different from other professions in that what lawyers do affects not only the individual but also the administration of justice, which is the foundation of any civilized society. Canons of professional ethics are the most prestigious heritage of the Bar. The greatness and honour of the legal profession is due to the canons of conduct governing the relations of lawyers *inter se* and with others in their professional capacities.[11]

It is through adherence to the highest standards of professional ethics that the stature of the Bar can be enhanced. Unless a lawyer observes the highest standards of professional ethics he cannot earn the respect of the community, nor will his peers in the profession accept him as an outstanding lawyer. Although entry to the profession can be gained by merely acquiring the qualifications prescribed, honour as a professional has to be maintained by its members by exemplary conduct both inside and outside the courts.[12]

---

[11] G.Geethisha, "Disciplining the Lawyers: Law and Professional Ethics", *CULR* 2003, pp.153 ff. (153).
[12] *Ibid.*

To expect the profession to abide by its part of the bargain in full is utopian, but society also needs a framework of the law that can act as a watchdog and as a deterrent to those few who cannot help being incompetent or unethical. Here the law needs to be laid down and enforced with unerring accuracy.[13] Dean Swift was right when he observed in *Gulliver's Travels*, of the bar, that "… they were a society of men bred up from their youth in the art of proving by words multiplied for the purpose, that white is black and black is white according as they are paid"[14]. The barbed remark by Bernard Shaw, that "all professions are conspiracies against laity," contains a real and relevant truth[15]. The *quid pro quo* for professional monopoly can never be less than a *pro bono publico* commitment.

It is legitimate on the part of society to trust professions. If a profession becomes a career rather than a public service, it will be disastrous to society. If people lose confidence in the profession on account of the deviant ways of some of its members, it is not only the profession which will suffer but also the administration of justice as a whole. The legal profession in India is passing through a critical phase, and the declining standards of lawyers are the talk of the day. The present trend, unless properly checked, is likely to lead to a situation where the system will be found wrecked from within before it is wrecked from outside.[16]

IV. Legal regime applicable to professions

In India, before the *Advocates Act, 1961*[17], breaches of rules of professional etiquette were subject to the disciplinary jurisdiction of the High Courts. According to its gravity, misconduct was punishable by permanent disbarment or temporary suspension, or reprimand, or fine. The primary reason for which the courts were armed with this power was the conception that advocates were officers of the court. That being so, the court, in maintenance of its purity and the dignity of the administration of justice, must enjoy the authority to remove its unfit officers. Its existence was necessary for the orderly discharge of its judicial functions. If the

[13] Madan Mohan, "Accountability of Medical Profession", *Ind. Bar. Rev.* 15 (1988), pp. 227 ff.(229).
[14] Quoted by Justice V.R.Krishna Iyer, *Salvaging Democracy: Some Reflections*, (Delhi: Konark Pub. Pvt. Ltd., 1990) p.52.
[15] Justice V.R.Krishna Iyer, *op.cit.*, p.219.
[16] G.Geethisha, *loc.cit.*
[17] Act No. 25 of 1961.

Courts had authority to decide who were qualified to become its officers and counselors, it must also have power to remove them from that position[18]

Indian society created an exclusive right on the part of advocates to appear on behalf of others in courts, and created a monopoly in favour of them by enacting the *Advocates Act, 1961*. As per this Act, advocates are the only class of persons who are entitled to practice the profession of law.[19] The Act further debars all other persons from practicing law unless they are enrolled as advocates under this Act.[20]

With the coming into force of the *Advocates Act, 1961*, the power of enrolment of legal practitioners and the disciplinary jurisdiction in respect of them are now vested in the State Bar Councils[21] and the Bar Council of India[22]. It is now the function[23] of the State Bar Council, *inter alia*, to admit persons as advocates on its roll, to prepare and maintain such a roll and to hear and decide cases of misconduct against advocates on its roll. The functions[24] of the Bar Council of India include, *inter alia*, preparing and maintaining a common roll of advocates, laying down standards of professional conduct and etiquette for advocates, and laying down the procedure to be followed by its disciplinary committee and the disciplinary committees of State Bar Councils. Any person aggrieved by an order of the disciplinary committee of the State Bar Council may prefer an appeal to the Bar Council of India.[25] Further, any person aggrieved by an order of the disciplinary committee of the Bar Council of India may prefer an appeal to the Supreme Court of India and the Supreme Court may pass such an order, including an order varying the punishment awarded by the disciplinary committee of the Bar Council of India as it sees fit.[26] Thus, it is the professional bodies, the State Bar Council and the Bar Council of India, which have power to decide who shall be on the rolls and who shall be disbarred.

---

[18] C.L.Anand, *Professional Ethics of the Bar*, (Allahabad: The Law Book Co.(P) Ltd., 1987), p.26.
[19] Sec.29, *The Advocates Act, 1961.*
[20] Sec.33, *The Advocates Act, 1961.*
[21] Sec.35, *The Advocates Act, 1961.*
[22] Sec.36, *The Advocates Act, 1961.*
[23] Sec.6, *The Advocates Act, 1961.*
[24] Sec.7, *The Advocates Act, 1961.*
[25] Sec.37, *The Advocates Act, 1961.*
[26] Sec.38, *The Advocates Act, 1961.*

The Bar Council of India has framed rules exercising its power under the *Advocates Act* titled 'Standards of Professional Conduct and Etiquette.'[27] The preamble of the rules provides that 'An advocate shall, at all times, comport himself in a manner befitting his status as an officer of the Court, a privileged member of the community, and a gentleman, bearing in mind that what may be lawful and moral for a person who is not a member of the Bar, or for a member of the Bar in his non-professional capacity, may still be improper for an Advocate. Without prejudice to the generality of the foregoing obligation, an Advocate shall fearlessly uphold the interests of his client, and his conduct shall conform to the rules hereinafter mentioned both in letter and spirit. The rules hereinafter mentioned contain canons of conduct and etiquette adopted as general guides; yet the specific mention thereof shall not be construed as a denial of the existence of others equally imperative though not specifically mentioned."

V. Limited role of courts

It is to be noted that even after the *Advocates Act, 1961*, the status of an advocate has not changed from being an officer of the court, as Sec.30 of the Act, which confers a right on advocates to practice before courts and tribunals throughout the territory of India, has not come into force yet.[28]

By contrast Sec.34 (1) of the *Advocates Act* empowers the High Court to make rules laying down the conditions subject to which an advocate shall be permitted to practice in the High Court and the courts subordinate thereto. Further, Article 145 of the Constitution of India empowers the Supreme Court to make rules for regulating generally the practice and procedure of the court, including rules as to the persons practicing before

---

[27] Rules framed under Sec.49(1)(c) of the *Advocates Act, 1961* read with the proviso thereto; Part VI Chapter II, The Bar Council of India Rules.

[28] Sec.30 of the Advocates Act, 1961, is a crucial article. It confers a right to practice in courts on an advocate. The text of the section is as follows:

> "30. Right of advocates to practice.—Subject to the provisions of this Act, every advocate whose name is entered in the State roll shall be entitled as of right to practice throughout the territories to which this Act extends—
>
> i. in all courts including the Supreme Court;
>
> ii. before any tribunal or person legally authorized to take evidence;
>
> iii. before any other authority or person before whom such advocate is by or under any law for the time being in force entitled to practice."

the court. Therefore, an advocate's right to practice before a court is subject to the rules made by the High Court under Sec.34(1) of the *Advocates Act* and Art.145 of the Constitution of India. Hence an advocate has no absolute right to practice before courts.

A dent in the prerogative of the Bar Councils to discipline its members was made by the decision of the Supreme Court in *Re Vinay Chandra Mishra*[29]. In this case, the Court found the contemner, an advocate, guilty of committing criminal contempt of court for interfering with and "Obstructing the course of justice by trying to threaten, overawe and overbear the Court by using insulting, disrespectful and threatening language". The Court suspended him for a period of three years from practicing as an advocate.

Aggrieved by the decision of the Court in *Re Vinay Chandra Mishra* that the "contemner shall stand suspended from practicing as an Advocate for a period of three years", the Supreme Court Bar Association, through its Honorary Secretary, filed a writ petition under Art.32 of the Constitution before the Supreme Court in the case of *Supreme Court Bar Association v. Union of India*[30], and argued that the disciplinary committees of the Bar Councils, set up under the *Advocates Act, 1961,* alone have exclusive jurisdiction to inquire into and suspend or debar an advocate from practicing law for professional or other misconduct, arising out of punishment imposed for contempt of Court or otherwise. It appealed to the Supreme Court to declare that the Supreme Court of India or any High Court, in exercise of its inherent jurisdiction, has no such original jurisdiction, power or authority in that regard.

The question for consideration was whether the Supreme Court of India, while dealing with contempt proceedings and exercising power under Art.129 read with Art.142 of the Constitution or under Art.142 of the Constitution, can debar a practicing lawyer from carrying on his profession as a lawyer for any period whatsoever. Taking note of the importance of the question involved, the petition was placed before a Constitution Bench of the Supreme Court. Overruling *Re Vinay Chandra Mishra,* the Court held:

> "The power of the Supreme Court to punish for contempt of Court, though wide, is yet limited and cannot be expanded to include the power to

---

[29] (1995) 2 SCC 584.
[30] AIR 1998 SC 1895.

> determine whether an advocate is also guilty of "professional misconduct" in a summary manner, bypassing the procedure prescribed under the Advocates Act. The power to do complete justice under Art.142 is, in a way, corrective power, which gives preference to equity over law, but it cannot be used to deprive a professional lawyer of the due process contained in the Advocates Act, 1961 by suspending his licence to practice in a summary manner while dealing with a case of contempt of Court. The Supreme Court cannot in exercise of its jurisdiction under Art.142 read with Art.129 of the Constitution, while punishing a contemner for committing contempt of Court, also impose a punishment of suspending his licence to practice, where the contemner happens to be an Advocate. Such a punishment cannot even be imposed by having recourse to the appellate powers under Sec.38 of the Act while dealing with a case of contempt of Court and not an appeal relating to professional misconduct as such."[31]

Thus the Court recognized that the disciplinary jurisdiction of the State Bar Council and the Bar Council of India to take action for professional misconduct is different from the jurisdiction of the Courts to take action against advocates for contempt of Court; the Court cannot invest itself with the jurisdiction of the disciplinary committee of the Bar Council.[32] Acknowledging the prerogative of the Bar Councils, the Court made the following observations:

> "...the powers conferred on the Court by Art.142, being curative in nature, cannot be construed as powers which authorize the Court to ignore the substantive rights of a litigant while dealing with a cause pending before it. This power cannot be used to "supplant" substantive law applicable to the case or cause under consideration of the Court. Art.142, even with the width of its amplitude, cannot be used to build a new edifice where none existed earlier by ignoring express statutory provisions dealing with a subject and thereby to achieve something indirectly which cannot be achieved directly. Punishing a contemner advocate, while dealing with a contempt of Court case by suspending his licence to practice, a power otherwise statutorily available only to the Bar Council of India, on the ground that the contemner is also an advocate, is, therefore, not permissible in exercise of jurisdiction under Art.142."[33]

By this judgment, the Supreme Court restored the power of the Bar Councils over their members. Even the appellate authority vested in the Supreme Court under Sec.38 of the *Advocates Act* cannot enable the Court

---

[31] *Ibid*, pp.1907 – 1917.
[32] *Ibid.*, p.1908.
[33] *Ibid.*

to award punishments prescribed for professional misconduct under the *Advocates Act* while deciding a contempt case. The Court explained the courses of action open to the High Court and Supreme Court in such circumstances thus:

> "...It is, therefore, not permissible for Supreme Court to punish an advocate for 'professional misconduct' in exercise of the appellate jurisdiction by converting itself as the statutory body exercising 'original jurisdiction'. Indeed, if in a given case the concerned Bar Council, on being appraised of the contumacious and blameworthy conduct of the advocate by the High Court or Supreme Court, does not take any action against the said advocate, the Supreme Court may well have jurisdiction in exercise of its appellate powers under Sec.38 of the Act read with Art.142 of the Constitution to proceed *suo motu* and send for the records from the Bar Council and pass appropriate orders against the concerned advocate. In an appropriate case, Supreme Court may consider the exercise of appellate jurisdiction even *suo motu* provided there is some cause pending before the concerned Bar Council, and the Bar Council 'does not act,' or fails to act, by sending for the record of that cause and passing appropriate orders".[34]

Except in the above-mentioned situation, wherein a Bar Council fails to act upon a complaint of professional misconduct, the Supreme Court cannot interfere and the exclusive power to regulate the profession and professionals remains with the Bar Councils as intended by the society.

In *Ex-Capt. Harish Uppal v. Union of India,*[35] asserting its power to regulate the right of appearance, the Supreme Court held:

> "The right of appearance in Courts is still within the control and jurisdiction of Courts. Section 30 of the Advocates Act has not been brought into force and rightly so. Control of conduct in Court can only be within the domain of Courts. Thus Article 145 of the Constitution of India gives to the Supreme Court and Section 34 of the Advocates Act gives to the High Court power to frame rules including rules regarding conditions under which a person (including an Advocate) can practice in the Supreme Court and/or in the High Court and Courts subordinate thereto....Such a rule would be valid and binding on all. Let the Bar take note that unless self-restraint is exercised, the Courts may now have to consider framing specific rules debarring Advocates, guilty of contempt and/or unprofessional or unbecoming conduct, from appearing before the Courts. Such a rule, if framed, would not have anything to do with the disciplinary

[34] *Ibid.*, p.1917.
[35] AIR 2003 SC 739.

jurisdiction of Bar Councils. It would concern the dignity and orderly functioning of the Courts."[36]

VI. Self-regulation Obligations

India has an organized Bar with adequate statutory power to set and enforce professional standards. It has the distinction in its sphere of heading the independence movement successfully. It is distasteful to note that the reports of the disciplinary committee decisions published in the *Indian Bar Review*, the journal of the Bar Council of India, bear testimony to the fallen standards of professionals. Definitely, the society that has created a monopoly in favour of the Bar cannot endure this deterioration. It expects that the Bar should set high standards of ethics and adhere to them. It is too good of the society to trust the learned body of the professionals to regulate themselves and not to empower an outsider to sit in judgment over their activities. The trust reposed by the society in profession is to be lived up to.

It will be deeply regrettable for the professionals to have rules framed by the Supreme Court and High Courts to regulate their conduct in the Courts. They should regulate themselves in such a way that there should be no room for such rules. It is to be borne in the mind by all professionals that autonomy and self-regulation bind the professions with accountability. Their performance is subject to social audit. If they fail to live up to the professional standards expected of them, the same society which has conferred monopoly on the profession may be compelled to reconsider its decision and withdraw that monopoly, or try to circumvent the profession by creating forums which are open to all persons, as has already been done under several statutes. If this happens, it will neither be for the good of the society nor for the good of the professions. Given the track record of the legal profession in India, from the pre-independence years, in providing leadership to society, it is hoped that the profession will firmly regulate itself and make every member of the Bar proud of his fraternity.

[36] *Ibid.*, p.757.

PART VII:

HISTORY

THE PROCLAMATION OF THE PORTUGUESE CONSTITUTION AND ITS EFFECT ON THE ESTADO DA INDIA PORTUGUESA

MARIA DE LOURDES BRAVO DA COSTA RODRIGUES

Introduction

The revolutionary movement of 24th August 1820, which began in Oporto under the leadership of Fernandes Tomas, Ferreira Borges and Silva Carvalho, spread to Lisbon, the capital of Portugal, where a *Junta Provisional do Governo Superior do Reino* and a *Junta Provisional Preparatoria das Cortes* were constituted. The movement decided to draw up a constitution, for which an assembly, elected by the nation, held discussions and promulgated the Constitution in 1822.

Did this revolt and the constitution have any repercussions on the Estado da India Portuguesa?

In order to understand better the effect that the revolt had on the territories, it is important to understand the circumstances at the time.

D. Diogo de Sousa, Count of Rio Pardo, took over control of the Estado da India from Bernardo Jose Maria de Lorena, Count of Sarzedas, on 29th November 1816[1]. At the time of his taking over as Viceroy, political relations were not good with the neighbouring dessais of Uspa, Harya Apa Gaunco, who, despite signing an agreement, violated it by helping the Ranes of Nadora, Revora and Pirna. This forced the Count of Sarzedas to order the military commanders of the outposts of Pernem and Bardes to take strict action against them. However, the Count of Rio Pardo tackled this problem with the Dessais by force and diplomacy, by seizing the house and headquarters of Uspa Dessai, who fled and hid in the jungles.

---

[1] Gabriel Saldanha, *Historia de Goa (Politica e Arqueologica)*, Vol.1, p.237.

Another troublemaker, the dessai of Zambotim, who had also attacked and robbed in Verem, was successfully tackled by Count of Rio Pardo.

The sar-dessaina Durga Bai had also defied the government, being offended because the Portuguese wanted to build a fort at Manerin, in the territory of the dessai of Uspa. The sar-dessaina felt that she was the ruler of this area and sent her dessai Sammbaji Saunto to rob and commit hostilities in the village of Tiracol.

Besides the problems of the native subjects, the Viceroy had to tackle the problem of the army, and abuses and misuses by the Portuguese, both military and nobility. To begin with, Count of Rio Pardo reorganized and disciplined the army. The local sellers had complained that they were cheated of their produce by the *fidalgos* and the officers, who used to send their servants and subordinates to pick up goods in the market and pay very little or almost nothing. This caused great inconvenience to the poor, who unfortunately could not do much to overcome the problem. The Count of Rio Pardo was apprised of the situation and took the necessary measures to overcome it. An order was issued, and three police posts were set up in Pangim to see that no more such exploitation continued.[2] The Count of Rio Pardo also sent circulars to other municipalities to tackle this problem with rigour and allow the impoverished natives to live in peace[3].

During the tenure of his predecessor, influential army officers had been swiftly promoted to the detriment of their senior colleagues. The Count of Rio Pardo stopped this injustice and issued clear orders dated, 17th January 1817, to the authorities to revoke the out of turn promotions and promote deserving officers as per the existing law. Before the Count issued these orders, under other viceroys, the *casticos* were preferred over the *mesticos*, and from amongst the former, those who belonged to the nobility[4]. Natives were absolutely not considered for promotion[5].

---

[2] Antonio Bruto da Costa, *Goa sob a dominacao Portuguesa*, p.106

[3] The Count issued orders dated 7th January 1817, to the police and other authorities to take strict action against the exploiters. A copy of this letter was also sent to the Salcete and Bardes Municipalities.

[4] Portuguese colonial society was divided according to three different, though overlapping, criteria: "purity" of blood, rank, and marital status. The highest-ranking were those born in Portugal; casticos or Indiaticos were descended through those born in Asia of Portuguese parents; and those born in Asia of Portuguese and Indian, or Portuguese and African, parentage were mesticos and mulattoes respectively. Outside of this ranking, and beneath it, were the native Christians.

The Count, who was an upright man, took other measures that benefited the people. This approach did not stand him in good stead with the military and the noble *fidalgos,* who were upset by these measures. On the other hand, the people were extremely happy and the viceroy was considered as 'delicias da India Portuguesa'[6].

Such was the situation in the *Estado da India* when the revolution took place in Oporto. The disgruntled officers and nobility in Goa took this opportunity to promulgate the constitution without waiting for any official announcement, so as to get rid of the Count of Rio Pardo.

The news of the revolt at Oporto, which subsequently moved to the capital, Lisbon, took some time to travel to Goa. The news from Portugal reached Goa in mid-March of 1821 through some English newspapers and private letters from Bengal and Bombay, which mentioned the revolt in the city of Oporto, in August of 1820 to proclaim a new political constitution in Portugal. Subsequently, in May 1821, the news that King D. Joao VI had sanctioned the same constitution by his decree of 24th February 1821 at Rio de Janeiro reached the *Estado da India*[7].

It was decided in Lisbon that those who affirmed the constitution would be declared *benemeritos* (worthy). However, the decree declaring *benemeritos* to those who proclaimed the constitution overseas was passed only on 18th April 1821 and issued on 24th April of the same year. In the same decree, immediate elections of members of parliament were ordered and, as soon as they were elected, they had to present themselves at the Court in Lisbon. The expenditure of travel and stay in Lisbon was to be borne by the representing government from funds raised locally[8].

However, some of the officers and influential men of the *Estado da India* decided to act quickly and declare the revolution on the basis of the news they had received, without waiting for official orders. Some of them approached the Viceroy, asking him to promulgate the constitution. He decided not to take any action unless he was officially informed[9]. Since

---

[5] Bruto da Costa, op.cit, p.109

[6] M.V.de Abreu, *O Governo do Vice-rei Countdo Rio Pardo*, in Gabriel Saldanha, op.cit., p.239.

[7] M.V.de Abreu, *Relacao das alteracoes politicas de Goa, desde 16 de Setembro de 1821 ate 18 de Outubro de 1822*, p.1

[8] M.V. Abreu, op.cit., p. 2.

[9] Bruto da Costa, op.cit., p.111.

the Viceroy's decision was not to their satisfaction they decided to proceed and proclaim the constitution. The reason given by them was that the bases of the constitution were freedom to each citizen, personal security, and the right to property, which were not enjoyed under the absolute monarchy[10].

They claimed that monarchy could be despotic, and more so in the far-away colonies with their separate governors. They also claimed that in each colony there was a new arbitrary legislation, the military officers also followed arbitrary procedures, and the judiciary had absolute powers, which they exercised with utter disregard for the laws. To make matters worse, some judges in other courts also exercised judicial functions in the High Court[11]. It is important to mention that there were elements in the army, as well as the nobility, who were not happy with Viceroy the Count of Rio Pardo for having taken strict action against their behaviour, both in the service as well as in the public. These persons therefore grasped the opportunity to revolt and proclaim the constitution, and thereby eject the Viceroy from the governorship[12].

A number of officers and influential men joined together to lead the revolt. It was led by Lt. Colonel of Artillery and Lecturer of the Military Academy Joaquim Pereira Marinho[13]; Chief Physician and Official of Agriculture, Antonio Jose de Lima Leitao; and the High Court judge Manoel Duarte Leitao, also Judge of Orphans of the City and Bardes. The revolt was also supported by the High Court judge Goncalo de Magalhaes Teixeira Pinto, who was a judge for criminal matters and also an Intendant-general of police and judge of customs in the city of Goa; the High Court judge Joao Maria d'Abreu Castello Branco, attorney of the crown and revenue, Viscount of Fornos de Algodres and councillor of the supreme tribunal of justice; and the High Court judge Joao Carlos Leal, all Portuguese Europeans who were important people with prestige and authority in the country. They all collaborated to bring down the Viceroy, proclaim the constitution and install a provincial government. Almost all the colonial officials backed the move, except for the High Court judge

[10] M.V. Abreu, op.cit., p. 3.
[11] M.V. Abreu, op.cit.,p. 4.
[12] M.V. Abreu op.cit.,p. 1.
[13] Marinho was from Porto, and wished to bask in the glory of establishing the new system in Goa. He felt that the initiative of proclamation of the constitution was due to his home city.

Antonio Ribeiro de Carvalho and the chancellor Manoel Jose Gomes Loureiro, who was informed of the plot at the last moment[14].

To guarantee the success of the revolt, they enlisted the support of the Lt. Marshal-General of the Viceroy, Joaquim Manoel Correa da Silva e Gama (a Portuguese). He had close relationships with the officers who headed the artillery regiment, as well as the troops stationed in the islands of Goa. The revolt party persuaded these troops to acknowledge a liberal constitution. By then, the constitution had already been adopted and received with enthusiasm in almost all the colonies of the Portuguese monarchy[15].

The revolutionary heads spoke to other officers, and tried to win over to their cause the commander of the Gaspar Dias fort and all the forces stationed in Pangim quarters, Field Marshall Manoel Godinho de Mira. Negotiations were held successfully by the Chief Physician, Doctor Lima Leitao, and High Court judge Manoel Duarte Leitao. Others also behind the move included Bernardo Peres da Silva, physician of the military hospital, Francisco Antonio da Silva Pimenta, Innocencio Marano Mendes, Joaquim Manoel Correa Mendes, Manoel Camilo Severim d'Athaide, Bento Zeferino Gonsalves de Macedo, all military officers, and the lieutenant of artillery, Thomas Peres da Silva (son of Bernardo Peres da Silva).

The plan of attack:

The night between the 15th and the 16th of September was selected by the conspirators to take over the palace and oust the Viceroy. They had the support of in total 800 armed men from different divisions. The troops were secretly informed that they should gather opposite the residence of the Viceroy at midnight on the 15th of September.

From the Fort of Gaspar Dias came the second battalion of *sipoys* led by major Agostinho Jose Lopes Pereira; another 300 men of the Legion of Royal Volunteers of Ponda, which was posted in the old City of Goa. led

---

[14] M.V. Abreu, op.cit. ,p. 2.

[15] The following Juntas Provisionais were established in different overseas provinces. 1. In Mozambique, on 25th June 1821, presided over by D.Frei Barthalameo dos Martyres. 2. In Madeira, on 28th January1821, in Bahia on 10th February 1821, Para on 1st January1821, and on 17th April 1821 the provisional juntas in Pernambuco, S.Minguel and Cabo Verde were approved.

by captain Dionisio de Mello Sampaio; and four companies of guards (*granadeiros*) of the 1st and 2nd regiments of infantry, posted in Pangim. These were in fact part of the viceroy's guards. They were accompanied by all their officers except the captain of one company, captain Joao Pedro d'Aranha da Cotta Falcao, who did not participate in the conspiracy. The regiment of artillery, with two artillery pieces, was headed by Lieutenant Colonel Joaquim Pereira Marinho, who was posted in Ponda as punishment. Three days before the revolt, he feigned illness and was admitted to the military hospital in Panelim, so that he was closer to Pangim and could lead the regiment in the revolt[16].

At the agreed time, 2.30 a.m., the majority of the heads of the conspiracy, along with their men, encircled the government palace, and began shouting aloud in favour of the constitution of the Portuguese nation. Manoel Duarte Leitao, Joao Maria d'Abreu Castello Branco, and the chief physician Lima Leitao entered the palace, as representatives of the people and the troops, along with a group of 12 guards, led by Lieutenant Manoel Francisco Correa[17].

The lieutenant was ordered by Marshal Godinho to knock or break down the door if there was no response. They knocked down the door, got into the palace in darkness, and failed to find the Viceroy. Lieutenant Correa reported this to the chief, who ordered lights and asked him to ascertain the whereabouts of the Viceroy. This short interlude allowed the Viceroy to compose himself; he, in the meantime, dressed in his uniform of Lieutenant-General, and was found by Correa in the chamber, with the doors open, in the company of Lieutenant-Colonel Francisco Diogo Vellez, his subordinate. An officer from the revolutionaries brought the latter from his house to the palace[18].

The revolutionaries informed the Viceroy that they were representatives of the military and the people and that they wished to implement the constitution, and therefore his governance was over. However, the Viceroy refused to accept anything without any formal announcement from Portugal. He told the revolutionaries that in the present circumstances he had nothing to say, and was ready to move out from the vice-regal palace.

---

[16] M.V. Abreu, op.cit., p.5.
[17] M.V.Abreu, op.cit., p. 6.
[18] ibid.

The Viceroy was arrested, and governance was taken over by some of the main revolutionaries. The Viceroy was taken to the Cabo, where he was imprisoned and was not allowed visitors. A force of thirty guards accompanied the Viceroy. There were other arrests of persons close to the Count, including Lt.-Col. Luis Manoel Correa de Mello, who was placed under house arrest; Lt.-Col. Francisco Diogo Vellez, who was taken to Reis Magos; the lieutenant of cavalry of Bardes, who was sent to Aguada; and Manoel Ribeiro de Moraes, a protégé of the Count, who was forbidden to talk to or meet any person[19].

However, though the Count of Rio Pardo was a prisoner, he was given due respect and was in the Cabo until the 2nd of October, on which day he left for Bombay.

At this juncture it is be interesting to note that if the revolutionaries had waited for a formal letter from the kingdom informing them of the revolution and the proclamation of the constitution, the latter would have been promulgated without any military revolt or deposition of the Viceroy. In fact the people did not want to depose the Viceroy, which led to anarchy in the country. This is proved by what happened later, in February 1821, when the Count of Rio Pardo, who had been in Bombay, returned to Goa. He was received with all pomp and honours, and he also swore allegiance to the constitution. He left in March for Rio de Janeiro in the *Luconia*, in which his successor had come to Goa[20].

What happened after the Viceroy was deposed?

A provincial government was installed, namely the "Junta Provisional do Governo". The junta was composed of five members: Councillor Manoel Jose Gomes Loureiro, the marshals Manoel Godinho de Mira and Joaquim Manuel Correia da Silva e Gama, and High Court judges Goncalo de Magalhaes Teixeira Pinto and Manoel Duarte Leitao. However, the junta left out the Archbishop of Cranganor, D.Fr. Paulo de Aquino, who at the time was in Goa, and the chief physician Lima Leitao, who should also have been part of the junta. The two resented the exclusion and began plotting a coup against the junta. To this end Chief Physician Lima Leitao requested a confidential meeting with the Count of Rio Pardo at the Palacio do Cabo. He told the Count that the revolt had taken place without

[19] M.V.Abreu, op.cit., p. 7.
[20] Gabriel Saldanha, op. cit., p. 241.

the consent of the majority or the consent of native persons, and that those who had taken part in the revolt were traitors. He offered a counter-revolt and promised to hand over power to the Count. However, the Count refused such an offer, called Leitao duplicitous and without character, and asked the physician to leave[21].

The documents of the meeting for installation and swearing of the junta were drawn up at six a.m. on the 16th of September. On the installation of the junta, it was called "Junta Provisional do Governo do Estado da India". On the same day, they invited the members of the senate of the Municipality of Goa, members of the legislative, civil and ecclesiastical authorities and important individuals to swear allegiance to the constitution. They also swore allegiance to the constitution on the morning of the 16th of September. The document was signed by 1768 persons. The junta also issued two proclamations, one to the troops and another to the populace, wherein they proclaimed freedom from the tyranny of the Viceroys, which were signed by Manoel Jose Gomes Loureiro, Manoel Godinho de Mira, Joaquim Manoel Correa da Silva e Gama, Goncalo de Magalhaes Teixeira Pinto and Manoel Duarte Leitao[22].

The Provisional Junta formed the Guarda Nacional, a battalion of European military and their descendants, command of which was given to Lt.-Col. Joaquim Pereira Marinho, with a special salary of 60 xerafins. This force was well supplied and well paid in reis fortes, and they were posted at the quarters of the guards, near the palace[23]. The first step taken by the Junta was to declare amnesty for all prisoners except criminals[24]. To rejoice in the event and the proclamation of the constitution and to show public pleasure, the junta ordered the archbishop to sing the "Te Deum" in thanksgiving in the cathedral; it also asked the municipality of Goa to order illumination for three days[25].

On 1st October, the junta called a meeting with the representatives of the municipalities of Salsete, Bardes and Ilhas and the chiefs of the military, ecclesiastical and judiciary, to discuss and deliberate on different issues affecting the Estado. It was decided that if a successor to the Count of Rio Pardo was nominated with the simple title of captain-general or viceroy, or

[21] M.V.Abreu, op. cit., p 16.
[22] M.V.Abreu, op. cit., p 10.
[23] M.V.Abreu, op. cit., p 12.
[24] Bruto da Costa, op. cit., p.112.
[25] M.V.Abreu, op. cit., p. 16.

any other rank as done usually, he should not be recognized as governor. However, he would be offered the presidency of the Provisional Junta. It was also resolved at this meeting that the members of the parliament should be elected, and that the "gentios" should be excluded from representing the Estado[26].

The junta took the liberty of unilaterally promoting some military officers by bypassing others who were rightful candidates for promotions. This created unhappiness amongst others. On the next day the Junta declared *meritorious* not only those who had participated in the proclamation of the constitution, but all military men, on the basis that all had shown loyalty and fidelity to the cause. They also disbanded the Guarda Nacional, which was established soon after the revolution, and the salary continued in reis fortes only for the European soldiers[27]. This led to displeasure amongst the others troops and it also led to the instability of the junta.

The junta also proposed to reorganize the troops by deciding to disband some regiments. This decision of the junta was not well received by the legion of Bardes, which revolted. It moved out from its quarters in Colvale on October 23rd, under the command of Lt.-Col. Joaquim Jose Pinto de Gouveia, and went to Verem, on the other side of Pangim, where the legion took possession of the forts of Aguada and Reis Magos, and threatened to attack the capital[28].

The junta prepared to defend the city, but at the same time decided to find out the reason for the revolt, and once they came to know that it was because of the threat to disband the regiments, they sent an emissary, Brigadier Antonio de Melo Souto-Maior Teles, to Verem with a decree of pardon to the revolutionaries and also to inform them that the rumours about disbanding were untrue[29].

On 15th October, the Count of Rio Pardo left for Bombay in the *Pegazo*, after having spent sixteen days at the Cabo. In the meantime, the Provincial Junta sent its report on the incidents which took place when the constitution was promulgated. This report of the junta was undeniably a biased one, making it appear that the Viceroy had been the culprit, a

---

[26] Saldanha, op. cit., p. 242.
[27] Bruto da Costa, op. cit., p.112.
[28] Saldanha, op.cit., p. 242.
[29] Ibid.

person who opposed the constitution and one who was not ready to promulgate it[30].

On 25th October, the junta ordered the imprisonment of Chief Physician Lima Leitao, Lt.-Col. Marinho, and some army officers. It also appointed High Court Judge Antonio Monteiro da Rocha to proceed with a judicial inquiry in Bardes on the rebellions which had occurred in some of the regiments[31]. In October, the junta proceeded with its plans of reorganizing the army by dissolving both the legions of Ponda and Bardes. This led to the discharge of 1318 soldiers. The entire force now consisted of seven battalions of infantry and one regiment of artillery.

In the meantime, the judicial inquiry on infidelity imprisoned many, and discontent increased amongst all sectors of the population, even those who had joined in the formation of the Junta[32].

On 25th November D. Manoel da Camara arrived, who was appointed as governor and captain-general of India. The influential members of the party who were unhappy with the Provisional Junta met him to persuade him not to form part of the junta, and to pretend that he was unwell until they carried out another revolution to overthrow the Provisional Junta. This they managed to achieve a few days later, on 3rd December, by another revolt.

Second Junta Provisional do Governo

The Provisional Junta was deposed eight days after the new governor D. Manoel da Camara arrived in Goa. It is interesting to note that the main conspirators involved in this, Lt.-Col. Marinho and Chief Physician Lima Leitao, were in prison at the time. The former was in the Naroa fort, and the latter, in Aguada. In spite of this, they managed to enter into secret consultations between themselves, in which they were helped by a large number of military men as well as civilians. Another point of interest is that in this move, the populace were also involved[33].

---

[30] The letter, dated 15th October, 1821, was signed by the members of the junta, and sent to the Parliament in Portugal.
[31] Portaria, dated 24th October, 1821, ordered the inquiry.
[32] Saldanha, op. cit., p. 243.
[33] Saldanha, op. cit., p.244.

Lt.-Col. Marinho managed to escape from prison on the night of 2nd December, the day the conspirators had planned to execute the coup. On this night, some military regiments marched towards the capital under the command of Brigadier Antonio de Melo. At the head of the artillery was Lt.-Col. Marinho, who was their commander. They surrounded the houses of the three main members of the Governing Junta (Governativa), and waited until dawn of the following day, when a delegation, along with representatives of Salsete municipality, which had a representation signed by a large number of important people of the taluka, went to request D. Manoel da Camara to take over the direction of the new provisional junta, as per the Portuguese constitution, which was sworn to by all.

D. Manoel went to the Viceroy's palace accompanied by a number of military officers and almost all the important people of the Estado, and the assembly was formed. The Archbishop and other high-ranking staff, and representatives of the municipalities of Ilhas, Salcete and Bardes, were invited to the installation of the new government. They disbanded the junta elected on 16th September, and elected another one composed of D. Manoel as president, and the following members: D.Fr. Paulo de Aquino, Archbishop of Cranganor; Antonio Jose de Mello Souto-Maior Telles, Brigadier; Joao Carlos Leal, High Court judge; Antonio Jose de Lima Leitao, Chief Physician, who, having received orders of release, came from Aguada and signed the minutes of the election document[34].

Soon after the installation of the new junta, orders were issued to withdraw the military forces, which were placed around the houses of the deposed members of the Junta Provisional. The new junta also revoked the judicial inquiry started by High Court Judge Rocha, putting at liberty all the individuals who had been imprisoned as a result of it[35]. It also revoked the judicial inquiry carried out by the first junta and released all those who had been imprisoned because of this inquiry.

On 8th December, a larger meeting was called, which confirmed the election of the junta. There were 62 delegates. With this meeting, comments challenging the legitimacy of the new junta were put to an end[36]. The junta

---

[34] Bruto da Costa, op. cit., p. 118,

[35] Saldanha, op. cit., p.245.

[36] There were 62 persons, as representatives of various institutions. The distribution was as follows: 2 members for each of the Municipalities of Salcete, Bardes and Ilhas, 2 members of all military bodies except for 3 regiments of

also abolished the difference in salaries between European and native soldiers, claiming it to be unconstitutional. In the same way, it was decided to create a company of guards, one in each regiment, and that of bombardiers in the artillery. Antonio Monteiro da Rocha, the High Court judge who was presiding over the inquiry, refused in writing to accept the orders of the junta to abolish the inquiry, and also alleged that he did not recognize the new junta. This stand of the judge and some other rumours about the legality of the second junta led it to revalidate the election by calling another, larger, assembly[37].

The new junta decided to create a medium for disseminating news which could be read by the people in Goa and abroad, by printing a periodical, which became the official organ of the junta. It was named "Gazeta de Goa" and it was the first periodical published in Goa. A printing machine was brought from Bombay and set up on the ground floor of the palace. The editor of the paper was the chief physician, Dr. Lima Leitao. The first issue of the Gazeta was printed on 22nd December 1821[38].

Elections to the Portuguese Parliament

On 14th January 1822, the electors assembled under the presidency of Fr. Paulo Antonio Dias da Conceicao in the senate of the Camara de Goa to elect members to the Parliament as required under the constitution. There were 17 provincial electors. The following individuals were elected: Bernardo Peres da Silva, Constancio Roque da Costa and Dr. Antonio Jose de Lima Leitao[39]. The majority of the Europeans and their descendants voted for the bishop of Cochin, Fr. Thomaz de Noronha. They resented the election of natives, and nominated Noronha as special attorney, alleging that the whites did not have a representative. All the three went to Lisbon in 1823 in the *Luconia*, in which also traveled the Count of Rio Pardo and

recruits, and 2 each of the chapter of cathedral and of all the authorities and higher officers of the Government, and 6 important persons of each judicial division.

[37] M.V.Abreu, op. cit., p.64.

[38] The first printing press in Goa was set up in the Jesuit College of St.Paul at Old Goa in the year 1556. The first printed work was "Conclusoes Philosophicas". With the expulsion of the Jesuits from the Portuguese territories in 1571 by Marques de Pombal, printing activities also stopped.

[39] Bernardo Peres da Silva received 16 votes, Constancio Roque da Costa 15 and Lima Leitao 10. The first two were Goans and the last a European.

Lt.-Col. Marinho. Fr. Thomaz de Noronha also travelled on board, alleging weak health[40].

At this point, King D. Joao restored the monarchy and dissolved parliament. This action of the King led Bernardo Peres da Silva to protest against the dissolution of parliament, while Constancio Roque da Costa addressed some representations to the King on benefits to the country.

Meanwhile, in Goa, Captain Joaquim Mourao Garces Palha was elected to replace Dr. Lima Leitao in the Provisional Junta[41]. This election was carried out by a legislative body consisting only of officials. It did not take into consideration the votes of the people and neither did it pay heed to representations made by the Municipality of Bardes and of various proprietors of Goa. This led to unhappiness amongst many. In fact, the junta was apprehensive that if the popular representatives were allowed to vote, a native might win the election, as had happened at elections to the parliament[42].

Things did not go well with the second Provisional Junta, which did not keep to its promise to honour the constitution to which it had pledged all support, as well as taking some actions which went against the interests of the Taluka of Bardes. It provoked public opinion in such a way that the influential people of Bardes, encouraged by members and followers of the deposed first junta, began calling meetings in various villages to look into these issues.

The government was apprehensive and ordered High Court judge Joao Maria de Abreu Castelo Branco to open a judicial inquiry in Bardes. The accused were the Lt.-Col. Jose de Assa, commander of the troops of Bardes, who was a European and brother-in-law of Marshal Godinho; Fr. Pedro Antonio Ribeiro (from Pilerne and professor of philosophy of the college established by him in that parish); Fr. Joao Mariano Cardoso, hailing from Candolim and vicar of Pangim; Advocate Eusebio Mariano Goes, from Calangute; and various other persons. Besides this measure, the government disarmed the regiment of Bardes, which consisted of native officers and soldiers from this taluka, and also posted a strong force in Guirim[43].

---

[40] Bruto da Costa, op. cit., p.119.
[41] Saldanha, op. cit., p.246.
[42] Bruto da Costa, op. cit., p.119.
[43] Saldanha, op. cit., p.246.

Frei Manuel, Archbishop Primaz de Goa, had sent a letter to the junta regarding the harassment meted to the people of Bardez and was worried that it might be taken over by any other nation, that is, not the Portuguese[44].

The indictment and the guards sent to arrest the accused aggravated the discontent of the people of Bardes, and the accused were almost desperate, such that they attempted to storm the Colvale military barracks by surprise. On 9th May 1822 around 500 men, who were not properly armed, divided into two groups, one captained by Lt.-Col. Jose de Assa, and the other by Fr. Pedro Ribeiro, marched toward the barracks. They hoped to use the men stationed in the barracks to defeat the junta and constitute another. However, the plan did not succeed, and the Lt. Colonel and 112 men, including some priests, were arrested, though others managed to escape with Fr. Pedro Ribeiro, who hid in Malvane. The prisoners were put at the disposal of the judge of inquiry, who eventually prosecuted forty of them. Most of them were from leading families of Bardez, including eight priests. They remained prisoners for a year and eight months in different prisons, finally being confined in Aguada fort. These prisoners included Eusebio Mariano Goes, Jose Paulo Lobo, Antonio Filipe Rodrigues e Caetano Xavier Furtado. The parish priest of S. Matias, Antonio Jose de Sa, who was also sentenced, absconded[45]. As the conspirators included the brother in law of Marshal Godinho, member of the earlier junta and some priests, the troops thought that the movement was inspired by Marshal Godinho and Archbishop S. Galdino. As a consequence of this, on 16th May the entire force, headed by six artillery pieces, standing opposite the palace of the Governor, demanded that the junta expel from Goa the main persons responsible for the insurrection of Bardes within 24 hours. They alleged that the events since 3rd December were creating nuisance and unnecessarily tiring the troops, who had to be constantly on the alert and marching the roads. Besides, these events had created fear amongst the important families of the Estado[46].

The government acceded to these demands and asked the persons named by the troops, Marshal Correia, Lt.-Col. Luis Manoel Correia de Melo, Counsellor Loureiro, and the High Court Judges Magalhaes, Rocha and Abreu, to leave Goa. The other two named by the troops, Marshal Godinho and the Archbishop S. Galdino, were exempted from being

[44] The letter is dated 20th April, 1822.

[45] Saldanha, op. cit., p. 247.

[46] Saldanha, op. cit.,p.248.

expelled because of the efforts of the Archbishop of Cranganor. However, the latter was made to go to his residence at Sinquerim. Since most of the judges were expelled, they needed to be replaced. The following lawyers were appointed to the posts: Cipriano Silverio Rodrigiues Nunes, Joaquim Mariano Alvares and Andre Francisco de Braganca, magistrates of Ilhas, Salsete and Bardes respectively[47].

Those who were expelled protested. However, the government did not change its decision. In the meanwhile, the four members of the junta handed in their resignation, complaining of coercion. This request was repeated several times and each time the troops rejected it. This clearly showed that at this stage the troops were in command.

The result of the expulsion of the High Court judges and other functionaries in the Estado, instead of putting an end to the disorders, was on the contrary to lead to clashes between the military and the supporters of those exiled. These started with demonstrations and protests, as a result of which the editor of the "Gazeta de Goa" was killed, because he supported liberal doctrines and wrote a protest condemning the movement of 16th May, which was not welcome by the army. In retaliation, he was murdered in broad daylight on 15th July when going home from Pangim to Ribandar, while passing in front of the quarters of the company of the guards, which was situated a few meters away[48]. On 18th October 1822, in consequence of a decree of parliament and a royal document (provisao regia), the second junta was dissolved and D. Manoel da Camara (1822–25) began to govern the territory alone. However, in November 1823 he received the news that the monarchy had been reestablished in Portugal, and he then began to govern in the old manner, and with the title of Viceroy, until his death, which took place in the Cabo on 16th November 1825[49].

During his tenure the High Court judges who had been expelled and who resided in Malvane went to Lisbon, and the officers who had been deported, and Archbishop S. Galdino, returned to Goa. All political prisoners were set free, and an amnesty was granted to the revolutionaries by a decree of 5th June 1824[50].

---

[47] M.V.Abreu, op. cit., p.163.
[48] Saldanha, op. cit., p. 248.
[49] Saldanha, op. cit, p. 249.
[50] Saldanha, op. cit, p. 250.

After the death of D. Manoel da Camara, the government functioned, in succession, under Archbishop D. Fr. Manoel de S. Galdino, Admiral Candido Jose Mourao Garces Palha and High Court Judge Ouvidor Geral Antonio Ribeiro de Carvalho, up to 9th October 1827, on which date D. Manoel de Portugal e Castro became governor of Goa.

COLONIAL ADMINISTRATION IN GOA (1836–1961): THE GOVERNOR-GENERAL

MARIA PIA DE MENEZES RODRIGUES

Introduction

During Portuguese rule, Goa being part of the colony, i.e. the *Estado da India*, its administration depended on Portuguese policies, which were influenced by the political and constitutional changes taking place in Portugal.

The early nineteenth-century French invasions had a great impact on the constitutional movement in Portugal. After the revolution of 1820, constitutional rule was established in Portugal and a liberal regime was introduced. The first constitution was then proclaimed, in 1822. This marked the beginning of a new form of government based on a constitutional document. However, the constitutional monarchy in Portugal was marked by much unrest, with constant clashes between liberals and absolutists. The monarchy was finally overthrown in 1910 and a republican regime introduced. Though a new constitution was proclaimed in 1911, political instability continued. As a result, in 1926, a military revolt overthrew the democratic regime. Later, in 1928, Dr. Antonio Oliveira Salazar joined the Portuguese Cabinet as the Finance Minister, and in 1933 he took over power in Portugal as the Prime Minister. During his dictatorial regime, the constitution of 1933 was promulgated; this constitution defined the Portuguese state as a unitary and corporate republic. The Colonial Act of 1930, which emphasized the colonial nature of the Portuguese empire, was incorporated in this constitution with certain amendments. The post-Second World War period brought a change in world political climate, and after the independence of India from British rule in 1947, there was international pressure on colonial empires towards decolonization. The constitution could, therefore, no longer carry its incorporated Colonial Act. As a result, in 1951,

Portugal was forced to revise its constitution. Portuguese possessions were termed as Overseas Provinces which formed an integral part of the Portuguese state, and maintained solidarity among themselves and with Portugal.

During the era of the absolute monarchy up to 1820, many decisions and Government laws pertaining to Goa required the confirmation of the King in Portugal. The king used to play an effective role in the administration of the *Estado da India* through the central organs based in Portugal. However, after the introduction of the of the constitutional monarchy, only legislation and administration of important matters related to the Overseas Provinces were to be referred to the Government of Portugal, whereas the Governor-General, who was the representative of the central government in the province, was given powers over a number of other matters; nonetheless, overall control and supervision remained with the central government. The present paper will outline various decrees and regulations concerning colonial administration in Goa from 1836 to 1961.

Colonial Administration: The Governor General

During Portuguese rule prior to the nineteenth century, the powers of Viceroys or Governors were regulated by the regiments issued to them. Later, various organizational decrees were promulgated, which regulated governors' powers in the administration. Though, in the 20th century, various legislative acts mentioned the governments of the Overseas Provinces as autonomous bodies as regards administration and finance, overall control still remained with the Metropolitan Government, which had to superintend the government and administration of the Overseas Provinces. The Metropolitan Government enjoyed legislative as well as executive power over the Overseas Provinces. The powers of the Metropolitan Government and those of Overseas Governments were clearly specified in various decrees . At the provincial level the Governor was the highest authority; he was a representative of central government, under whose supervision and control he ran the provincial Government.

The Decree of 7th December 1836

This was the first decree which was promulgated concerning the administrative organization of the Overseas Provinces. For administrative purposes, the decree divided Portuguese African possessions into three separate governments (*Governos Geraes)* and the Asian possessions into a single government, *Governo Geral.*

To head the administration, each of the *Governo Geral* was to have a Governor-General, to whom all other authorities were subject. The Governor-General exercised administrative as well as military functions, but he had no power over judicial matters.[1] The administrative functions of the Governor-General were the same as those laid down in the Decree of 18th July 1835.[2] Below the Governor, there functioned a consultative body called the *Conselho do Governo* or Government Council. This body consisted of Heads of Departments from the judicial, military, fiscal and ecclesiastical sectors, with two or more councilors chosen by the Governor General from a list of four members elected by the respective *Junta de Provincia* or Provincial Board. The Government Council was presided over by the Governor-General or, in his absence, by the most senior member of the Council. Though the role of the Government Council was merely advisory, it was mandatory for the Governor General to consult the Government Council when deciding on important issues.[3] A *Boletim do Governo* or Government Bulletin was to be published under the supervision of the Governor General, wherein Government orders, decrees, statistical information and other official and non-official relevant matters of public utility were to be published.[4] It was compulsory for the Governor General to send yearly reports to the Government of Portugal. These reports had to include information on the execution of laws and orders promulgated by the Government indicating the hurdles faced in their implementation. Suggestions and proposals which, in the opinion of the Governor, were required for the welfare of the people, also had to be included.[5] In addition, the Governor General had to send a report of his consultations with the *Juntas Geraes*, along with the minutes of their sessions. The Governor General, as the president of the Government Council, had to study recent legislation and the best way of making it applicable to the province, and his conclusions had to be reported to the

[1] Decreto de 7 de Dezembro, 1836. In, *Collecção de Leis e outros documentos officiais publicados desde 1 de Janeiro ate 9 de Setembro de 1836* (Lisboa: Imprensa Nacional, 1837), pp.200–202.

[2] See *Collecção de Leis...desde 15 Agosto, 1834 ate 31 de Dezembro, 1835*, pp.203–204, Functions of the Governor Civil, Art.35 to 45.

[3] Op. cit., Decreto de 7 de Dezembro, 1836; see Art. 6–8, p.201.

[4] Ibid., art. 13, p.201.

[5] Ibid., art.14, p.201.

Government of Portugal.[6] The Governor was also empowered to invite experts to join in the discussion in the sessions of the Council.

It can thus be seen that every action of the Governor-General was to be reported to the Central Government. In addition, through the *Boletim do Governo* the public were kept informed about various measures taken by the Government. For the first time, provision was made for local participation, by inviting experts to participate in discussion.

The Decree of 1st December, 1869

Carta organica das Instituições administrativas nas Provincias Ultramarinas, 1869

This Decree divided the Portuguese possessions in Africa and Asia into six provinces, the *Estado da India* being one of them. Each province was to have a Governor or Governor-General with civil and military powers. Beneath the Governor there functioned a *Conselho do Governo* or Government Council and a *Junta Geral de Provincial* or General Provincial Board. An administrative tribunal, called the *Conselho de Provincia* or Provincial Council, was to adjudicate on administrative matters.[7]

The Governor-General was nominated by the king; in his absence he was deputised for by a Governing Council. He had the same privileges as an old captain. His tenure was of five years. He had civil and military powers. He could not interfere in judicial matters, except in cases where he was installed as a president of a tribunal by special law. In civil administration, he had all the powers granted to the Governors of *Ilhas Adjacentes* or Adjacent Islands. The following are some of the administrative functions which were part of the responsibilities of the Governor: to fill temporarily all posts the regular appointments for which were under the purview of the king; to make appointments for the posts whose yearly salary would not exceed 300 *reis*; to appoint administrators or *Chefes do Conselho* (Taluka Heads); to order the dissolution of any elected body; to order the

[6] Ibid., art.16, p.201

[7] *Carta organica das instituições administrativas nas provincias ultramarinas, 1869, anotada por J.A. Ismael Gracias.* (Nova-Goa: Imprensa Nacional, 1899),.art. 1–6, pp. 9–19.

syndicate of Government employees; to select members for the *Conselho de Provincia.*[8]

He was the President of the Government Council and the Board of Revenue, and also had a number of other powers. He was the Head of the Military Services of the Provinces. In cases of urgency, when it was not possible to wait for the decision of the Sovereign or Government of Portugal, he could act after consulting the Government Council. However, the Governor had no powers to act on matters pertaining to: increase in taxes; anticipation of collection of taxes; establishment of monopolies; acceptance of the cessation or exchange of any part of the territory belonging to the Nation; alteration of the judicial structure; or suspension of judges. Any extraordinary measure taken by him was to be reported to the Government of Portugal at the earliest opportunity, along with the minutes of the meeting of the Government Council. When the Governor felt it desirable to revoke, modify, or replace any legislative measure or provision of the Government of Portugal, he had to send his proposals to the Ministry of the Navy and Overseas.

The Governor-General presided over the Government Council, which was a kind of technical advisory body constituted of officers of the high rank including representatives from the Church and the judiciary. It was obligatory for the Governor to seek the opinion of the Council on all important and serious matters, especially those of a legislative character.[9] However, the Governor was not bound by the opinion of the Council, except in a few cases such as deciding on the urgency of legislative measures and contraction of loans, where an affirmative vote of the Council was essential.

The Governor General was the proper authority to execute the deliberations of the *Junta Geral de Provincia*, a body which assisted the Governor in the administration of the province. It was constituted by the following members: i. The Archbishop (or his representative) ii. The Secretary-General iii. The Procurator of the Crown and revenue. iv. The Director of Public works v. The Head of the Health Services. vi. one professor each from: *Escola Medica*/medical college, *Escola Matematica e Militar*/military college or lyceum and *Escola Normal*/educational college vii. one member elected by each of the municipalities of the *Estado da*

[8] Ibid., Functions of the Governor General, art. 7–19, pp. 20–63.
[9] Ibid., Functions of the Government Council, art. 26–32, pp. 67–76.

India. Functions of the *Junta* included voting on matters related to: public works, public health, establishment of primary educational institutions, imposition of taxes for execution and maintenance of works undertaken, and others.[10] The Governor-General or any member of the *Junta* could put forward proposals for approval. Though the *Junta* was empowered to make its own regulations, the Governor had to put forward such proposals to the Government in Portugal.

The Governor-General had a right of veto on the deliberations of the *Junta Geral de Provincia* when found to be illegal, unjust or inconvenient for execution. However, the Government in Portugal was to be informed of the exercise of the veto and all related documents submitted.

The Governor-General was also the President of the Provincial Council, which was an advisory and adjudicatory body for administrative matters. It was constituted by following members: the Secretary General, the Procurator of the Crown and Revenue or his delegate, and two members selected by the Governor-General from a list submitted by the *Junta Geral de Provincia.* The functions of the Provincial Council, were similar to those of an administrative tribunal, such as: adjudication of appeals against acts of administration; cognizance of cases concerning election to administrative bodies; approval of municipal budgets exceeding a certain financial limit; auditing of accounts of municipal corporations and other charitable institutions; judgment of appeals on taxation matters and stamp law; other taxes excluding customs; and some other functions.[11]

An important feature of this decree is that the Governor had a number of powers, including full powers regarding certain appointments, which earlier were held by the Government of Portugal. In addition, he presided over the Government Council, which was constituted of officers of high rank. The *Junta Geral de Provincia* also was presided over by him, however here the Governor enjoyed merely a veto, absolute power remaining with the Government of Portugal.

[10] Ibid. Functions of the Junta Geral de Provincia, art. 33–48, pp. 77–90.
[11] Ibid. Functions of the Provincial Council, art. 49–50, pp. 91–102.

Law no.277 dated 15th August, 1914

Lei organica da administração civil das Provincias Ultramarinas.

During the period 1910–1926, the political situation in Portugal was unstable and new ideologies were emerging, one of the outcomes of which was the law of 1914, which reorganized the civil administration of the colonies. It could be described as a piece of progressive legislation, as it envisaged a power-sharing structure between colonial governments and the Government of Portugal, as well as including principles of popular participation in the local government.[12] The legislation of 1914 provided *bases* or guidelines for the administration of the Overseas Provinces. The Governor, a nominee of the Government of Portugal, was the most powerful authority and was the nucleus of colonial government as indicated in the guidelines.[13]

Decree no.3266 dated 27th July, 1917

Carta organica do Estado da India,1917

This *Carta* was issued based on the model and principles set by the legislation of 1914. It had two hundred and ninety-six articles. As in earlier legislation, it reiterated the principle of the autonomy of the province under the supervision of Portugal. Further, the Government of Portugal was not to take any measure of a legislative or regulatory character on matters directly affecting the province without informing the provincial government, unless it would cause an irreparable loss.[14]

The Governor-General was the head of the administrative machinery of the Overseas province and was responsible to the Minister of Colonies. The functions of the Governor-General were divided under different heads as powers enjoyed by the Governor as a representative of the executive power in Portugal; powers of the Governor as a superior military official; powers of the Governor that were to be exercised with a consultative vote

---

[12] D'Souza, Carmo. *Legal system in Goa* (Calangute: Agnelo D'Souza, 1995), Vol. II, p. 163.

[13] Lei no. 277 dtd. 15th August, 1914.In, *Leis organicas da administracao civil e financeira da Provincias Ultramari nas.* (Nova Goa: Imprensa Nacional, 1914). For details of the powers of the Governor, see Bases 6–16, pp. 3–8.

[14] *Legislação...1917*, Apendice pp. 1–62. For Divisão terrtorial see art. 1–5 , pp. 1–2. *Das relacoes entre a Metropole e a Provincia* see art. 6–9, pp. 2–3.

of the Government Council; powers of the Governor that were to be exercised with the affirmative vote of the Government Council; powers exercised by the Governor with previous approval from Portugal in addition to the affirmative vote of the Government Council. Certain matters which were not under the purview of the Governor, even with the affirmative vote of the Government Council, were also clearly indicated in the *carta.*[15]

The Government Council was to be constituted by officials and non-official members. The Governor-General, Secretary-General, Procurator of the Republic and Directors or Heads of Public Works, Revenue, Navy, Military, Health, Agriculture and Customs were the official members. The non-official members included six members elected by general electoral circles and four members elected from selected fields such as industrialists, proprietors, major tax payers, and procurators of village communities. Thus persons with administrative experience, as well as local representatives from different occupations, were included in the Council.[16]

The Governor-General could veto the proposals of the Council; however the Government of Portugal had to be kept informed about such use of veto. Certain functions of the Council were deliberative, including budget and execution of projects. The Government Council could make representations to the Government of Portugal, on matters related to the province, provided they were approved by two-thirds of its members.

According to Dr. Carmo D' Souza, this *Carta* is more important for the trends it revealed than its actual implementation, and it represented the best advanced model drawn on the basis of the legislation of 1914.[17]

Amendments to the *Carta* were introduced in 1918 and 1919.[18]

---

[15] Ibid. For details see art. 70–95, pp. 18–27.
[16] Ibid. On the Conselho do Governo, see art. 98–125, pp. 28–34.
[17] D'Souza, Carmo, op. cit, p. 166.
[18] Decree no.4.627 dd. 1st July, 1918 and Decree no.5.779 dtd. 10th May, 1919.

Decree no.7008 of 9th October, 1920

Bases organicas de administração civil e financeira das colonias, 1920.

The Organic Bases of civil and financial Administration of Colonies, 1920, contained ninety-nine clauses or guidelines, which were termed *bases*, for colonial administration.

The first base stated that the colonies enjoyed financial autonomy and were in the process of decentralization under the supervision of Portugal. The extent of decentralization depended on the development of each colony and this was to be regulated by special laws in consonance with the constitutional law.[19]

The legislation made provision for a Governor-General of *Estado da India,* who was subject to the Minister of Colonies. He was the agent and representative of the Government of Portugal and was the highest authority in civil and military matters in the province. He was also the protector of the native population. The legislation also specified certain activities which were not under the purview of the Governor, such as alteration of basic laws on colonial administration, legislation in contravention of civil or political rights, suspension of judges and some others. Administrative decisions of the Governor could be annulled by the Colonial Council, on appeal made by the interested party[20].

An Executive Council was to be set up to give opinions to the Governor General, which was to be composed of administrative experts, namely five official members and one non-official member, to be presided over by the Governor-General.[21].

In addition it was stipulated there was to be a Legislative Council, composed of the members of the Executive Council and elected members. The Governor-General had powers to assent to certain matters approved by the Legislative Council, whereas some matters required the approval of

---

[19] Gracias, João Baptista Amancio, *Administração colonial ou decreto no.7008 de 9 de Outubro, 1920, anotado e indice remissivo de legislação sobre assuntos de Fazenda desde 1913 ate 1924* (Nova-Goa: Typ. Arthur Viegas, 1924), p. 7.
[20] Ibid. See Base 13–20, pp. 33–105.
[21] Ibid. Conselho Executivo, Base 21–24, pp. 105–113.

the executive powers in Portugal. Matters assented to by the Governor could also be revoked by the executive power in Portugal.[22]

This legislation was amended in 1923. [23]

Decree no.12421 of 2nd October, 1926

Bases organicas de administração colonial, 1926.

As per the provisions of this decree, the Executive Council and Legislative Council were replaced by Government Council, a body which had deliberative as well as consultative functions. During emergencies, the Governor had special powers which he could exercise with an affirmative vote of the Government Council and telegraphic authorization from the Minister of Colonies [24]

Decree 12499-A, dated 4th October, 1926

Carta organica do Estado da India 1926

This *carta* enunciated the principle of administrative and financial autonomy, under the supervisory role of Portugal. It guaranteed to nationals as well to aliens or foreigners liberty and security of the individual and his property in terms of laws in force. The Governor General had to perform functions under the heads of: i. an agent and representative of the Republic; ii. a representative of the executive power in Portugal; iii. an administrator of public revenue and other matters. The functions of the Governor which needed the support of a consultative vote or an affirmative vote of the Government Council were indicated and certain matters which were beyond the purview of the Governor were spelled out .[25]

The Governor-General headed the Government Council which was a body constituted of four government officials, five citizens nominated by the

---

[22] Ibid. Conselho Legislativo, Base 25–30, pp. 118–148.

[23] Law no. 1511 of 13th December 1923.

[24] *Legislação...1926*, pp. 250–261.

[25] Ibid., pp.309–340. Do Governador Geral-disposições prelimjnares , see art. 6 and 7, p. 310. Das condições de exercicio do cargo do Governador Geral, see art. 8–19, pp. 310–312. Da competencia do Governador Geral see art. 20–30 , pp. 312–319.

Governor-General, and five representatives elected by general electoral ballot. The functions of the Government Council were of consultative nature on some matters and deliberative on others. In addition, there was a third category of deliberative functions of the Government Council which had to be approved by the Minister of Colonies. In urgent situations, when the Government Council was not in session or when Governor did not agree with the vote of the Council, he was empowered to take the required measures, however a telegraphic authorization from the Minister of Colonies was to be obtained .[26]

Decree no.15241 of 24th March, 1928

Bases organicas da admnistração colonial,1928.

A set of principles and guidelines were proclaimed in this plan. As in earlier legislations, financial and administrative autonomy for colonies under the supervision of Government of Portugal was enunciated. It made provisions for basic administrative organization headed by the Governor-General, who was to be assisted by a Government Council having deliberative and consultative functions.[27]

Decree Law no. 23228 dated 15th November, 1933

Carta organica do Imperio Colonial Portugues, 1933.

This charter made provisions for colonial administration based on dictatorial policies propounded by the dictatorial regime of Dr. Oliveira Salazar. It stated that for administrative purposes the Portuguese colonial empire was to be divided into eight colonies, which each formed an integral part of the nation. Colonial administration was to be exercised through the National Assembly, central Government in Portugal and government in the colonies. In addition, there were consultative bodies in Portugal as well as in the colonies.[28]

---

[26] Ibid. Conselho do Governo-disposições preliminares; da composição do Conselho do Governo; exercicio e funções; atribuições do Conselho do Governo see art. 33–82, pp. 319–330..

[27] Ibid. 1928, pp. 103–116. Administração geral including Governor General see Base iv–vii, pp. 105–106. Funções legislativas, Base viii and ix, pp. 106–108. Funções executivas, Base x, pp. 108–109.

[28] *Legislacao...1933*, pp. 653–708.

Each colony was to be administered by a Governor under the supervision of the Minister of Colonies, in consultation with the Council of the Government, or its permanent section. The appointment of a Governor was made by the Council of Ministers under the proposal of the Minister of Colonies, and his tenure was of four years. Civil, commercial and criminal actions against the Governor were to be tried only by the *Comarca* or Court in Lisbon. At the end of each year, within six months, the Governor had to submit to the Minister of Colonies the annual report of his administration. As per the rules, the report had to be published by the order of the Minister of Colonies.[29]

In the executive domain, the Governor was the highest agent and representative of the Republican Government in the entire territory of the colony, and an authority superior to all in civil and military ranks. He was also the superior authority in the administration of the *Fazenda Publica* or Public Treasury and a protector of the natives. In all his functions he was responsible to the Minister of Colonies. The *portaria* or orders issued by him were to be preceded by a preamble, wherein the authority whose approval was sought or consulted, as per the provisions of the law, was to be indicated. As an agent and representative of the Republican Government, he had to represent the Republican Government in the colony, to uphold the rights of sovereignty of the Portuguese nation, and to promote the welfare of the colony in harmony with the principles of the Colonial Act and the *Carta Organica*. He had to execute and implement the laws and regulations in force. As a superior civil authority in the colony, it was part of the responsibilities of the Governor to assure citizens' individual rights and guarantees; to protect the liberty, plenitude of functions and independence of the judicial authorities; to provide for the appointment, promotions and confirmation in post of Government employees who were not under the Ministry of Colonies, as well other matters such as leave, disciplinary proceedings, contracts etc. The Governor had to visit the different parts of the colony and receive complaints and petitions and inquire about general needs. As the first military authority of the colony it was part of the responsibility of the Governor to superintend military operations wherein the military forces in the service of the colony were deployed, and also to take control of all matters related to the military personnel.

---

[29] Ibid., for Exercicios e funções do Governador see Art. 18–28, pp. 660–663.

As the superior administrator of the *Fazenda* or Public Treasury in the colony, it was one of the duties of the Governor to provide directions in the preparation of the colony's budget, and to order its execution, as well as to issue instructions to the Government Treasury to effect the payments of the expenditure incurred through the *Fazenda.* In *Estado da India*, the Governor had powers to undertake public works, with budgets of up to Rs. 17,500.

As a protector of the natives, it was part of the Governor's task to promote and improve the living conditions of the natives and to improve their aptitudes and natural faculties, their education, instruction and their security. Also, he had to propose to the Minister of Colonies any alterations felt to be desirable in the political, civil and criminal statutes as well other laws relating to the natives.

In addition, there were certain attributes which the Governor had to exercise with the consultative vote of the permanent section of the Government Council, such as: to issue regulations for the execution of laws, decrees and other diplomas in force; to issue regulations on political, civil and criminal statutes binding on the natives; distribution of funds; granting concessions on land, mines, industries, (exclusive) constructions and construction of roads and railways; construction of works of irrigation, drainage, sanitation, etc.; to regulate the watercourses and the use of hydraulic energy, fisheries and fishing rights; navigational services including coastal navigation and any system of land transport; the dissolution of administrative bodies and corporations in terms of law; to decide on projects of higher cost, related to public works, after obtaining the opinion of the Technical Council of Public Works.

The *Conselho Superior de Fazenda* had powers to nullify or alter administrative and managerial actions of the Governor.[30]

The Governor exercised his legislative functions under the supervision of the Minister of Colonies and as a rule according to the vote of the Government Council, which consisted of official and non-official members; these included three nominated and five elected members.[31]

---

[30] Ibid., Da função executiva do Governador , see Art. 30–41, pp. 663–669.

[31] Ibid., Competencia e composição do Conselho do Governo see Art.50–65, pp. 670–673.

It was the legislative responsibility of the Governor to publish legislative diplomas in the *Boletim Official,* preceded by the preamble referring to the vote of the Government Council or approval of the Minister of Colonies, according to the provisions made by the law. The following matters required approval from the Ministry of Colonies:
Concessions of administrative autonomy; establishment of superior penalties and correctional punishments; opening of special accounts; any measure which would bring decrease in the revenue. The Governor could propose to the Minister of Colonies any reform of a legislative nature which he found convenient.[32]

From the above *Carta,* it can be seen how important was the institution of the Governor and how sweeping were the powers which he had; however, sensitive issues and matters related to public works whose expenditure exceeded the given limit were to be referred to the Government of Portugal.

Law no.2066 dated 27th June, 1953

Lei organica do Ultramar Portugues, 1953

In 1951, in order to counter global pressure against Portuguese colonialism, Portugal declared its colonies to be provinces which were all integral parts of one Portuguese state.[33] This was made applicable to all colonies irrespective of their development and status of civilization. In order to effect the theory of one nation, with its Overseas Provinces extending over the continents, Portugal had to revise the principles and policies of its administrative organization, and the *Lei Organica do Ultramar Portugues* was therefore issued in 1953.[34]

This law provided the basis and guidelines for each province to have its own statute. It reinforced the rhetoric of one nation and referred to the Overseas Provinces as an integral part of the Portuguese state. As envisaged by the constitution, it promised decentralization of administration and financial autonomy to Overseas Provinces, depending on the stage of development of the province. Political administration was to be organized and specified in a special statute, adequate to the

---

[32] Ibid., Da função legislativa do Governador see Art. 42–49, pp. 669–670.
[33] Law no.2048 dtd. 11th June, 1951, in *Legislação...1951*, pp. 430–444.
[34] *Legislação.*, 1953,Pt. I, pp.516–560.

geographical and social conditions of the province. The law laid down that, if special circumstances prevailed in a province, it was permissible to establish an administrative regime similar to the one functioning in Madeira and the Azores. Central Government was the controlling authority on certain matters of importance. The National Assembly legislated on proposals of the Minister of the Overseas on matters within its purview. In addition, certain administrative and legislative functions were exercised by the Government of Portugal.[35]

At the provincial level, there had to be a Governor or Governor-General nominated by the Council of Ministers, politically responsible to the Government of Portugal and civilly and criminally responsible for his actions before the Court, generally in the judicial circle of Lisbon. The Governor could take over the full control of Government in the province in cases of emergency. The Governor enjoyed legislative competence in matters related exclusively to the Province and which did not pertain to the National Assembly, the Government of Portugal or the Minister of the Overseas.[36] The province of *Estado da India,* like those of Angola and Moçambique, had to have a Legislative Council to carry out provincial legislation. The Legislative Council was to be presided over by the Governor-General or his deputy, and it was his privilege to place matters before the Council. The Legislative Council had to have more elected members than nominated ones. It had to guarantee adequate representation to tax payers and administrative and corporate bodies, as well as representatives from the economic, cultural, spiritual and moral sectors [37] After giving his assent, the Governor had to publish legislation enacted by the Legislative Council within the time limit fixed by the law. In the case of disapproval, the matter had to be referred to the Overseas Minister, who after hearing the Overseas Council, would decide about the publication of the legislation and the required changes.

In provinces where there was a Legislative Council, as in *Estado da India,* there had to function a compact consultative body called the Government Council to advise the Governor.[38] Though, on declaration of provisional emergency, the Governor had to consult the Government Council, it was not mandatory for him to abide by their advice. However, when the decision of the Government Council was overruled on important or

[35] Ibid., Administração central see Bases vii–xvi, pp. 517–524.
[36] Ibid., Governador Geral see Bases xxiii–xxiv, pp. 526–527.
[37] Ibid., Conselho Legislativo, see Bases xxv–xxvii, pp. 527–529.
[38] Ibid., Conselho do Governo, see Bases xxviii–xxx, pp. 529–536

sensitive matters, the Overseas Minister had to be kept informed of the overruling along with the justification.

Decree no.40216 dated 1st July, 1955

***Estatuto do Estado da India*, 1955.**

On the basis of the law of 1953, the *Estatuto do Estado da India* was enacted in 1955[39]. It stated that the *Estado da India*, which was integrated into the political unit of the Portuguese nation, comprised the territories of Goa, along with the islands of Angediva, S. Jorge and Morcegos in the Malabar Coast and the territories of Daman, Nagar-Aveli and Diu.

The governing bodies of *Estado da India* comprised the Governor-General, the Legislative Council, and the Council of the Government. It was within the competence of these organs to take necessary legislative and executive measures in the interest of *Estado da India*[40].

The Governor-General was the highest agent and representative of the Portuguese nation, the superior authority among all to whom he served, civil as well as military, and also the administrator of the *Fazenda Publica* or public treasury[41].

The legislative competence of the Governor depended as a rule on a vote of the Legislative Council, which consisted of 23 members, of which eighteen were elected. They represented the tax payers, corporate associations, and economic, cultural, spiritual, moral and other interests, as well as the administrative bodies, and five were nominated. The Legislative Council was presided over by the Governor-General[42]. However, during the intervals of the ordinary sessions of the Legislative Council and when there was no extraordinary session, the Governor General could publish legislative diplomas with a favourable vote of the Government Council; however, this procedure had to be reflected in the preamble preceding the legislative diploma. In the case that the diploma was not signed it was presumed that the Governor did not agree to it. If it

[39] *Legislação*, 1955, Vol. II, pp. 3–25.
[40] Ibid., Disposições gerais see art. 1–6, pp. 4–5. Da administração provincial, normas gerais, see art. 12, p. 7.
[41] Ibid., Governador Geral, see art. 13–23, pp. 7–11.
[42] Ibid., Conselho Legislativo, see art. 24–43, pp. 11–17.

was found unconstitutional or illegal, it had to be referred to the *Conselho Ultramarino,* and the Governor-General had to abide by their opinion.

As regards executive competence, the Governor had to exercise all the superior powers conferred by the *Lei Organica do Ultramar*. He was assisted by the *Conselho do Governo* or Government Council in exercising these functions. The Council, which was constituted of high-ranking officers as well as official members and two nominated members from the Legislative Council, had to give their opinion in all matters related to the government and administration of *Estado da India*.[43] It was compulsory for the Governor to seek the opinion of the Government Council for the following actions: protective action as per the law on administrative bodies and *pessoas* colectivas or associations; distribution of funds to districts and other administrative divisions for public works; approval of statutes , rules and regulations of corporate organizations; issuing of *portarias* suspending rules and regulations; to introduce, alter or suppress taxes; to grant concessions on land, mines, construction and exploration of roads, and bridges; constructions related to irrigation, drainage and sanitation; to regulate entrance, transit, residence and departure of nationals and foreigners; to dissolve administrative bodies in terms of law; and all works exceeding the cost of one thousand *contos*. In some of these matters, a favourable vote of the Government Council was mandatory, including works exceeding a budget of two thousand *contos*. As regards suspension of rules and regulations, if protested by the Government Council then the matter was to be referred to the *Ministerio do Ultramar* or Ministry of Overseas.

The office work of the Governor-General was carried out in the *Repartição do Gabinete,* which functioned under his direct control. The Governor-General could delegate his executive functions, excluding financial administration, to the *Secretario Geral* or Secretary-General.

An Overview

From the foregoing information, it can be seen that the Governor-General of *Estado da India,* had twofold functions, the first one being that of a representative and agent of the Government in Portugal and the second that of the highest authority in the Province, in civil as well as military matters. He was the representative of the Government of Portugal, the

[43] Ibid., Conselho do Goveno, art. 44–49, pp. 17–18.

head of the executive power in the province and a military authority. He was also the administrator of the *Fazenda Publica* and a protector of the natives according to some legislations. In certain instances, the competence of the Governor depended on a consultative or deliberative vote of the Government or Legislative Council. The Governor exercised his powers under supervision of the Government in Portugal or the Minister of Colonies.

The nomination of the Governor was made by the central Government in Portugal, to whom he was directly responsible for his political activities. In cases of civil and criminal liability he was personally responsible for his actions and could be prosecuted before ordinary courts. However, generally, laws provided that such a prosecution in which the Governor was the defendant in a legal suit had to be filed in the courts of Lisbon.

The Governor enjoyed legislative powers and was mainly responsible for formulating legislative actions in the Province. However, matters of great importance or those of general interest of more than one overseas province were legislated on by the Government of Portugal or Parliament. There were matters, carefully specified in the various organizational decrees or laws, which required the Governor to consult the Government Council or Legislative Council. The legislative powers of the Governor were curtailed to a certain extent when the number of elected local representatives in the Legislative Council was increased, and Governor had to abide by their vote. Whenever the Governor did not abide by the Council's opinion on important matters, it was mandatory for the Governor to inform the Government of Portugal or the Minister of Overseas. In addition, there were certain matters which required an affirmative vote of the Government Council. Very important and sensitive matters required the approval of the Government of Portugal in addition to an affirmative vote of the Council. On declaration of emergency the Governor could assume entire responsibility and could take decisions without consulting other Governing bodies in the province; his only obligation was to keep the Minister of Overseas informed about it. The Governor also had the special privilege of publishing legislative diplomas in between the ordinary sessions of the Legislative Council, and when the Council was not in extraordinary session.

The administrative acts of the Governor could also be nullified or altered by the Overseas Council, through appeals by interested parties, on grounds such as incompetence, excess of power, violation of laws and other matters of similar nature. According to some legislation the Secretary of State or the Overseas Minister had the power to nullify or alter the administrative acts of the Governors.

GOAN *COMMUNIDADES*—
RURAL SOCIAL WELFARE INSTITUTIONS

REMY DIAS

Introduction

The fundamental function of the Goan *communidades* (village communities) as agricultural associations was to effectuate measures which were necessary for agricultural development. Better agricultural production meant higher profits for the *communidades*. However, during the Portuguese occupation of Goa, many *communidades* often had little or no distributable surplus at the end of the year. This was to a great extent due to the fact that the *communidades* were made to undertake various welfare activities for the benefit of the rural society which ultimately reduced the size of their distributable surplus.[1]

The Portuguese government conveniently shifted several welfare activities onto the shoulders of the *communidades*. The *communidades* had to contribute towards road construction; taking care of destitute women, widows and orphans; building culverts and erecting dykes and embankments; providing medical facilities for the people in times of epidemics;[2] building schools and providing for the salaries of school teachers;[3] repairing schools, churches and cemeteries, etc. The

---

[1] Joaquim Bernardino Catão da Costa, *O Triumpho da Verdade em Referencia a Varios Escriptos Publicados em Goa* (Nova Goa, 1857), pp. 7–39.

[2] Filippe Nery Xavier, *Bosquejo Historico das Communidades…*, ed. José Maria de Sá, Vol. II, (Bastora, 1907), pp. 155–156. From 1845, the *communidades* were obliged to cater to society during epidemics by defraying the costs of the physicians and their transport, and also providing those infected with medicines; Filippe Nery Xavier, *Collecção das Leis Peculiares das Communidades Agricolas,* Part I (Nova Goa, 1840), Doc. No. 300, p. 388.

[3] *Portaria Provincial do governo do Estado da India*, dated 17th August, 1841, which created the parish schools maintained by the *communidades*. This disposition was reaffirmed on 23rd September, 1841, 14th November, 1842 and 29th

communidades were made responsible for public works which were earlier carried out by municipalities and local boards.[4]

The execution of the above works was made the responsibility of the *communidades* by the colonial rulers, and expenses on them became their liability. No other institution elected by universal suffrage existed at the village level for promoting social welfare. The *gaunkars* were made to feel 'all-powerful' and the existence of the institution of *communidades* continued, perhaps, to make them shoulder these responsibilities. In this manner, the *gaunkars* (founder members of village communities) were made to channel their agricultural surpluses into rural development, thus relieving the burden of the State in this regard. The budget of the *Estado* did not earmark any significant funds for rural development.[5]

To better understand the everyday functioning of the rural society and economy, it is important to investigate the nature of the social edifice fabricated by the *communidade* system and the various welfare activities undertaken therein. These welfare activities might be divided into two broad categories. Firstly, those which were undertaken by *communidades* as agricultural institutions and were related to increasing agricultural production. Secondly, those intended to make life better for the residents and which were not related to the *communidades*' functioning as agricultural associations.[6] The Portuguese government insisted on making the *communidades* contribute towards welfare activities, despite the vehement protests of the *gaunkars* and without paying heed to the fact that the villages had ceased to be occupied only by the *gaunkars*. In fact, by the

---

January, 1843, but it was recognized by the authorities that it was not fair to make the *communidades* solely responsible for this. Therefore, the proceeds collected by way of '*Subsidio Litterario*' since 1773 were also to be concurrently utilized for this purpose. But the *communidades* were not relieved of the burden. J. A. Ismael Gracias, *O Imposto e o Regimen Tributario da India Portugueza* (Nova Goa, 1898), pp. 78–79.

[4] Rui Gomes Pereira, *Goa,* Vol II, *Gaunkari: the Old Village Associations* (Panaji, 1981), pp. 24–29; see also, Regimento de 1735, as reproduced in Filippe Nery Xavier (Jr.), *Collecção das Leis Peculiares das Communidades Agricolas das Aldeas dos Concelhos das Ilhas, Salsete e Bardez* (Nova Goa, 1878), Cap. 20 & 21, pp. xxv ff.; specifically, Doc. No. 542, pp. 165–169.

[5] J. A. Ismael Gracias, *O Imposto e o Regimen Tributario da India Portugueza,* pp. 51-90; also see, *Collecção do Legislação Novissima do Ultramar, 1866 e 1867,* Vol. VI, Lisboa: Imprensa Nacional, 1875, pp. 147-195, 223-273 and 555-559.

[6] Filippe Nery Xavier, *Bosquejo Historico das Communidades ...*, ed. José Maria de Sá, Vol. II, pp. 41–254, 276–411 and 419–485.

mid-nineteenth century *gaunkars* constituted a minority (though a dominant one) in most Goan villages and the *communidade* structure was also found to be significantly modified.[7]

Calls for the *Communidades'* Dissolution

From the mid-nineteenth century on, there were in fact repeated calls for the dissolution of the *communidades* in Goa. Writers such as Joaquim Bernardino Catão da Costa, Jeronimo Salvador Constantino Socrates da Costa, Felix Antonio Gracias and others called for the abolition of the *communidades* and the distribution of their assets among the shareholders in a manner which would have led to the consolidation of landed estates amongst enterprising capitalists, thereby bringing about economic revival in Goa.[8] Their argument was that a large part of the *communidades*' distributable surplus was diverted to non-agricultural activities, thus affecting adversely the agricultural development of Goa. *Communidades*' spending on various welfare activities obviously meant that shareholders (*joneiros*) received smaller dividends at the end of the financial year. This in a sense acted as a disincentive to invest, and obviously meant that less capital was invested in agricultural development.

The views of Catão da Costa were countered by Filippe Nery Xavier and J. H. da Cunha Rivara. Two important works by Xavier are *Bosquejo Historico das Communidades das Aldeas dos Concelhos das Ilhas, Salsete e Bardez* (1852), and *Defensa dos Direitos das Gão-carias, Gão-cares e dos seus Privilegios, Contra a Proposta da sua Dissolucção, e Divisão das suas Terras* (1856).[9] These works give in detail the contribution of the

7 Joaquim Bernardino Catão da Costa, *O Triumpho da Verdade,* pp. 7–39; Francisco de Rancon, "As Communidades Agricolas de Goa", in *Boletim do Instituto Vasco da Gama*, No. 12, pp. 26–76; Filippe Nery Xavier, *Defensa dos Direitos das Gaõ-carias, Gaõ-cares e dos Seus Privilegios, Contra a Proposta da Sua Dissolução* (Nova Goa, 1856), pp. 71–72.

8 Joaquim Bernardino Catão da Costa, "*Ao publico*", dated 11th May, 1856 and distributed with the *Boletim...* No. 43; also see, "*Ao Sr. Filipe Nery Xavier*", dated 17th July, 1856 and distributed with the *Boletim…* No. 57; and, "Appendix", article by the same author combating the dissenting vote given by Francisco Luis Gomes on the Projecto do Regimento das Communidades. The article is dated 21st of March, 1857 and was distributed with *Boletim...* No. 23; *O Triumpho da Verdade em Referencia a Varios Escriptos Publicados em Goa* (Nova Goa: Imprensa Nacional, 1857).

9 While the *Bosquejo* is the bible for the study of the Goan *communidades* the *Defensa* may be said to be its commentary. The contribution of the erudite scholar

communidades to the economy of Goa and pleaded for their preservation—taking into consideration their utility—to safeguard the interest of the Public Exchequer and maintain public tranquility. Similarly, J. H. da Cunha Rivara, in *Brados a Favor das Communidades* (1870), appealed for the preservation of the village communities in order to bring about the economic development of Goa by making them invest in infrastructure projects.[10]

During Portuguese rule, the *communidades* were so deeply involved in providing services that were of the nature of public welfare that even

---

Filipe Nery Xavier to Goan history is really noteworthy. Some of his works are as follows: (1) *Collecção de Bandos, e Outras Differentes Providencias Que Servem de Leis Regulamentares para o Governo Economico e Judicial das Provincias Denominadas das Novas Conquistas, Precedida da Noção da sua Conquista*, (3 vols.) published from 1840 to 1851. Volume one begins with the Edict of the Viceroy Conde da Ega dated 5th June, 1763 and terminates with the *Portaria Provincial* of 17th May, 1842. The second volume continues from there and terminates with the *Portaria Provincial* of 31st December, 1849. The third volume of this series is the repertoire of the earlier volumes. (2) *O Gabinete Litterario das Fontainhas*. This was a literary journal started on 18th January 1846, of which publication ended in December 1848. The work consisted of three journals published in 1846, 1847 and 1848. The author gives a lot of statistical and descriptive data regarding the villages of Goa and especially of the talukas of Salcete, Bardez and Ilhas. (3) *Esboço de um Diccionario Historico-Administrativo, Especialmente Applicado ao Estado da India Portugueza*. This work was published as the fourth volume of the *Gabinet Litterario* and published in 1850. The work, though of immense value in understanding the various terms then in use, remains incomplete to this day. (4) *Collecção das Leis Peculiares das Communidades Agricolas das Aldeas dos Concelhos das Ilhas, Salsete e Bardez*. This work consists of two parts. Part one, published in 1852, commences with the *Foral* of 1526, gives the various legislation passed by the Portuguese government at different times, and ends with the *Officio* of the chief secretary dated 17th July, 1855. The second part was published in 1855 but remains incomplete. The full work was published as the fifth volume of the *Gabinete Litterario*.

[10] The *Brados a Favor das Communidades,* is an anonymous work published in 1870, but its authorship has been attributed to Cunha Rivara. In it one can find much useful information on the organization and administration of the *Communidades*. The work was published in response to the critical articles which appeared in the daily paper *Ultramar*, wherein the editor, Antonio Anastasio Bruto da Costa, was highly critical of the proposal of governor José Fereira Pestana to ask the *communidades* to invest 10% of their distributable surplus in the government treasury for building roads and other infrastructure works.

scholars like Cunha Rivara[11] and Filipe Nery Xavier were led to think that social service and municipal functions were 'inherent and essential functions' of the *communidades*. Both these scholars were employed by the *Estado*, which perhaps might have compelled them to publish works which argued for the continuation of the *communidades* as welfare institutions.[12] The fortunes of the *Estado* had dwindled following the decline of trade from the 17th century onwards. Moreover, constant wars with its European rivals in the 17th century and skirmishes with the neighbouring Indian rulers depleted the financial resources of the *Estado*.[13] Because of this, the *Estado* was eager that its social welfare obligations be shifted on to the *communidades*. The works produced by the above-mentioned historians should be seen in the perspective of the government's attempts to make the *communidades* shoulder these burdens. Thus, "besides the functions which the *communidades* performed as agricultural associations", opines Cunha Rivara, "they are corporations of public order with an extensive municipal power and administrative, judicial and electoral jurisdiction. This is proved by the laws; it is referred to in history; and is seen with one's own eyes. The municipal nature of the *communidades* was so obvious, that the *communidade* was called *Camara* and based on the social composition of the *gauncarias* of Goa".[14] Cunha

---

[11] J. H. da Cunha Rivara, *Brados a Favor das Communidades das Aldeas do Estado da India* (Nova Goa, 1870), pp. 2–3. He writes in the following manner, justifying his views that the *communidades* were organizations with municipal functions. "… *Se contemplarmos as vicissitudes, por que tem passado as aldeas indianas desde o tempo da conquista até ao presente, acharemos que em nada se alterou a essencia da organisação municipaes das gancarias e communidades; e assim concluiremos esta parte do nosso trabalho repetindo o que dissemos no principio do nosso 1.° Brado: As Communidades das aldeas da India são verdadeiros municipios. Proval-no as leis, refere-o a historia, e vemo-lo por nosso alhos.*"

[12] Cunha Rivara was Chief Secretary to the Portuguese government; Filippe Nery Xavier worked as *Official-maior* for the Portuguese government.

[13] Filippe Nery Xavier, *Bosquejo Historico das Communidades* …, ed. José Maria de Sá, Vol. I (Bastora, 1903), Docs. No. 52, 60 and 63, pp. 287–292 and 311–316.

[14] J. H. da Cunha Rivara, *Brados a Favor das Communidade* …, pp. 4–6. Here it must be stressed that the municipality structure in Portuguese administrative system was conferred only on leading cities and not on rural areas. Here the *communidades* seem to have been equated with the municipality, probably because of the similarity in the functions carried out both by municipalities and *communidades* in welfare-related activities. In the 19th century, Cunha Rivara and others considered the public welfare activities of *communidades* as their principal municipal functions.

Rivara further argued that the alterations the *communidades* had undergone over the course of history neither infringed upon nor contradicted their municipal functions, as the laws provided ample proof of them and history clearly indicated these roles also.

Cunha Rivara also stated that the *communidades* of Goa were competent to tax the villagers to meet such expenses. This had been done in the past in many other instances for various other purposes. The *communidades* imposed and collected taxes for extraordinary expenses which were not covered in their budgetary provisions. For instance, they collected, through their agents, the *malkhorch* (for the expenses of the *Camara Geral*) and *Gramkhorch* (for unforeseen expenses of the village). As we will see later, the *communidades* introduced certain charges or taxes such as professional taxes and levies for the transit of merchandise in their respective areas.[15] However, at no point were the *communidades* allowed to impose taxes on the rural population to meet the cost of the various developmental activities undertaken by them.

Often the *communidades* were required to provide innumerable services to the *Estado* and society at large. The government (mis)used its tutelary authority to extract as much as possible in the way of resources from the *communidades* to create and maintain rural infrastructure and carry out various welfare activities.[16] The government considered it as an obligation of the *communidades*, among other things, to construct and to maintain, at its own cost, the rural infrastructure.[17] The *communidades* were forced by the government to give land, labor, capital and even entrepreneurship for the use of the state and society. In fact, land was leased freely, labour was demanded as free service by right, capital once invested hardly earned any interest, and the entrepreneurship offered brought little tangible return for the *communidade*.

The *Communidades* and Infrastructure Development

In Portuguese Goa, roads were originally built at the cost of the Public Exchequer. For instance, the royal road (*Estrada Real*) from north to south Goa, together with other vicinal roads in the New and Old Conquests,

---

[15] J. H. da Cunha Rivara, *Brados a Favor das Communidades…*, pp. 65–68.
[16] Ibid., p. 72.
[17] F.N. Xavier, *Collecção das Leis Peculiares das Communidades Agricolas*, Part. 2, Nova Goa, 1850, No. 22 § 15, p. 53.

were built by the Portuguese government. However, in the mid-nineteenth century the government reconsidered this in a manner that suited its interest. The colonial rulers ordered that construction of roads should be the task of the *communidades* and ordered them to set aside every year a substantial amount of their revenues (which otherwise would have had constituted the distributable surplus for the *gaunkars*) towards building a network of roads in rural Goa.

The *communidades* had always helped financially and otherwise in executing public works in their respective villages. The Portuguese government, however, considered this an obligation and ordered the setting aside of a substantial sum of money annually by the *communidades* for this purpose. The government sought to demonstrate that roads between villages were works entrusted to the *communidades* of the villages under the direct supervision of the government, as was evident from study of the Portuguese Administrative Codes of 1836 and 1842.[18] The *communidades* were also asked also to provide for annual repairs and maintenance of these roads.[19]

Many *communidades* seem to have promptly responded to the government request of contributing to public benefit from the 1840s onwards. For instance, many *communidades* of Bardez responded to the government request by building roads in their respective villages. In 1847, Major Jose da Costa Campos, the Inspector of Public Works, reported to the Governor-General regarding the progress of the road-making undertaken with little administrative experience on the part of the villagers in Bardez taluka, which was then under his administrative jurisdiction. He was grateful to villages like Anjuna for the goodwill and zeal displayed in initiating with all promptness work on major parts of the road within their village. It was evident that the *gaunkars* had done solid and lasting work in these villages.[20]

---

[18] Filippe Nery Xavier, *Collecção das Leis Peculiares das Communidades Agricolas,* Doc. Nos. 314 and 334, pp. 397–398 and 415–416.

[19] See Government Note no. 221, dispatched by Victor Anastacio Mourão Garcez Palha, *Secretaria do governo geral*, dated 4th May, 1848, to the Administrador do concelho das Ilhas, Sr. Jeronimo Francisco Ferreira, as quoted in J.H. da Cunha Rivara, *Brados a Favor das Communidades ...*, pp. 63–64.

[20] See the report of Major José da Costa Campos, dated 13th December, 1847, as quoted in J.H. da Cunha Rivara, *Brados a Favor das Communidades...*, pp. 61–62. The *communidades* of Mapuçá, Coluale, Tivim, Sirsaim, Assonorá, Nerul, Pilerne and Saligão were also similarly praised for contributing to and working to

However, the roads constructed in other *communidades*, such as those of Calangute, Parrá, Siolim, and Candolim of Bardez taluka, were poorly constructed and of very inferior quality. Likewise, some *communidades*, like those of Sirulá, Guirim, Asagão and Nagoá, were yet to make their contributions towards the regeneration of the taluka of Bardez. It was suggested that it would have helped everyone's cause if efforts had been made to coordinate the activities of all the individual *communidades*.[21]

There were many hardships and problems in executing the governmental orders. Firstly, the works were undertaken by the individual *communidades* in the absence of any common master-plan for the network of roads for Goa or for its different provinces. Many roads were badly made; some works were well executed but abandoned later on; and others were destroyed by natural or man-made factors. Similarly, many of the contractors were ignorant of the art and science of road-making and only interested in the margin of profit to be made from the execution of a project, rather than being genuinely interested in executing good-quality works. Thus, even after the *communidades* had contributed for decades a substantial amount of their revenues for road-making, in the end instead of having a good network of roads, there existed only small and fragmented stretches of passable roads in many of the villages.[22]

The public works were commissioned by tender by the *communidades* to the powerful *gaunkars*, who often carried out shoddy work. And if any outsider or *interessado* won the bid for execution of the work, then the *gaunkars* adopted delaying tactics in making payments to the *interessado* contractor who executed the work. These frauds and delays in payment led

---

construct the stretches of road within their precincts. However, the construction was not of adequate quality in many of the villages. Nonetheless, the government praised and was appreciative of the efforts made by the *communidades* of Saligão and Pilerne towards the road built, by spending a huge sum of money and with great difficulty, across the hill separating the two villages. Transport and communication between these neighbouring villages became much easier and less expensive thereafter. It was stated that the better execution of works in Saligão was as a result of noteworthy efforts made by the respected procurator of the *communidade* of Saligão, who took a personal interest in seeing to it that the work was executed with strict adherence to rules and regulations.

[21] This is evident from the report of Major José da Costa Campos, dated 13th December, 1847, as quoted in J.H. da Cunha Rivara, *Brados a Favor das Communidades…*, pp. 61–62.

[22] J. H. da Cunha Rivara, *Brados a Favor das Communidades…*, pp. 57–58.

to intolerable financial loss to the contractors, and the government was burdened with unnecessary petitions and requests by the affected parties.[23]

The *Estado* recognized the inconveniences being caused by the unplanned nature of road-building by the *communidades*, which were resulting in huge wasteful expenditure by the agricultural associations. The government dispatched a Decree dated 8th November, 1869, to put into effect measures for building roads in a proper manner.[24] This provided that the *Camara Geraes* of Ilhas, Salcete and Bardez were to make arrangements to set aside one-tenth of the distributable surplus of the respective village communities, the proceeds of which were to be utilised for building roads. The overall plan for road-building was based on three key points. Roads were henceforth to: (a) connect churches with churches, (b) connect churches with the neighbouring wharfs and other landing places, and (c) connect all these with the royal roads (*Estradas real*).[25] The *Junta da Fazenda* (Public Exchequer) was to extend whatever help was requested by the *communidades* in this regard.

In the subsequent years, the *communidades* were forced to contribute regularly a tenth of their annual surplus for laying the network of roads.

---

[23] Antonio Floriano de Noronha, *op. cit.*, pp. 15–18, 21–25 and 44–47.

[24] Filippe Nery Xavier (Jr.), *op. cit.*, Doc. No. 486, p. 111. The government *Portaria* N.° 227 on the *10.ª parted as rendas para obras de caminhos vicinaes*, states that, "*O governador geral do estado da India, determina o seguinte: Art. 1.° As camaras geraes de cada concelho das Ilhas, Salcete e Bardez, receitarão annualmente nos seus cofres a decimal parted as sobras das respectivas communidades, para que a mesma quantia seja exclusivamente applicada á construcção dos caminhos vicinaes do respective concelho. Art. 2.° O plano, pelo qual se hão de delinear e construer esses caminhos, sera baseado nestes tres principios: 1.° ligar igreja com igreja; 2.° ligar igrejas com os embarcadouros e passos dos rios, o 3.° ligar tudo com a Estrada real. Art 3.° De accordo com a junta da fazenda está assentado que o thezouro publico reforçará annualmente com a quantia, que fôr possivel, cada um dos cofres das camaras geraes, para o effeito pretendido da construcção dos caminhos vicinaes. Art. 4.° a inspecção das obras publicas, os administradores dos concelhos, e mais funccionarios, a que tocar, receberão ao seu tempo e successivamente as ordens convenientes para se levar a seu devido effeito a construcção dos referidos caminhos vicinaes. As authoridades, a quem competir, assim o tenham entendido e executam. Palacio do governo geral em Nova goa, 8 de novembro de 1869. O governador geral, José Ferreira Pestana.*"

[25] Filippe Nery Xavier (Jr.), *op. cit.*, Doc. No. 486, p. 111; see also J. H. da Cunha Rivara, *Brados a Favor das Communidades*, pp. 59–60; see, *Boletim…*, No. 15, 1870, pp. 160–69.

The government did, however, very little to ensure that the *communidades* or the concerned authorities rigorously followed the guidelines laid down for better utilization of the funds so collected. It is doubtful if the *Junta da Fazenda* at all contributed, financially or in any other possible manner, to this noble cause.[26]

The province of Salcete had the following royal and municipal roads constructed with the help of the *communidades* by the middle of the 19th century: (a) A road was made from the village Cortalim to Cuncolim. It started at the wharf called S. Lourenço in Cortalim, and passed through villages including Quelossim, Nagoá, Vernã, Margão, Navelim, Dramapur and Sarzorá and reached Cuncolim, covering a distance of approximately 30 km. Further, from Cuncolim one road went to Canacona and another proceeded via the village of Assolna to the military post of Cabo da Rama. (b) The second royal road was from the *Praça* of Mormugão to Cortalim passing through Dabolim, Vaddem, Chicalim and Sancoale, covering a distance of about 14.65 km. This route was eventually linked to the railway station at Dabolim by a link road. (c) A third road started from Margao and, passing through Dicarpalle, reached Ambora. The distance covered was approximately 9 km. Further, from Ambora the road extended via Curtorim, Mullem, and Cussumane and terminated in Quepem market. (d) The fourth major road was from Chicalim to Baradi. It passed through the villages of Assoy, Palle, Velção, Cansaulim, Utordá, Orlim, Carmoná, Cavellossim and Velim. Of this long route, by the end of the 19th century only a small fraction of about 3.18 km was constructed. (e) Another road, measuring about 3.85 km, connected Margao to Colva, passing via Mungul and a branch line proceeding to Betalbatim. (f) A road measuring 2.09 km connected Margao with Benaulim. (g) The route connecting Cansaulim to Loutulim and passing through Verna was partly constructed, by a road measuring 3.69 km, by the end of the 19th century. (h) Similarly, one route from Carmona to Macazana passed through the villages of Chinchinim, Sarzora, Mulem, Cavorim, Chandor and Guirdolim. A part of this route, measuring about 3.26 kms, was constructed by the end of the 19th century. (i) Macasana was similarly linked by a road passing through Sonsoró and Curtorim to Margão, with a branch road linking Sonsoró with Rachol. The total length of the road measured about 13.96 km. In this manner almost all the important villages of the province of Salcete were

[26] *Relotorio do Exmo. Sr. Governo Geral a Junta de Districto do anno de 1869,* in *Boletim ...,* No. 92, 1869.

linked by land routes by the beginning of the 20th century.[27] The roads in Salcete were built by the *communidades*, even when the province lacked adequate manpower resources.[28]

The *Communidades* had to donate or lease their land for the construction of roads in the villages under their jurisdiction. For instance, in 1879, the *communidades* of Margao and Raia had to lease prime agricultural land for the construction of a road connecting the two villages. The *communidades* were obliged by the government to give the necessary finances for the construction of roads. Moreover, as stated above, the *communidades* also had to lease their lands for the purpose. Many of the *communidades* had to contribute even when they were deeply in debt. For instance, during this period the *communidades* of Vaddem, Camorlim, Dicarpalle, Gandaulim, Loutolim, Margão, Mormugao, Nagoa, Raia and Sirlim had no distributable surplus for distribution among their members.[29] Yet they still had to contribute to meet the State demands, perhaps by acquiring loans. The following table gives an idea of the proportions in which they were made to contribute towards road-building in their respective provinces.

Thus evidently the *communidades* were made to contribute to constructing infrastructure networks at the village level. As mentioned earlier, this decreased the distributable surplus of many *communidades*. Moreover, the State, taking advantage of the mild nature of the people, also demanded free labour to execute various projects of public utility, especially road construction. This further adversely affected the farming sector.[30]

[27] Filippe Nery Xavier, *Bosquejo Historico das Communidades das Aldeas dos Concelhos das Ilhas, Salcete e Bardez* (Nova Goa, 1852), Part I, p. 28; see also Filippe Nery Xavier, *Bosquejo Historico das Communidades …*, ed. José Maria de Sá, Vol. II, pp. 267–268.

[28] Filippe Nery Xavier, *Bosquejo…*, Part I, p. 28; *Boletim…*, 1836, p. 279. This work gives a list of six principal routes that traversed the province of Salcete in the first half of the 19th century. It was the *communidades* which made major contributions to the construction and maintenance of these roads.

[29] *Boletim…*, No.30, dated 21st April, 1876, pp. 197–198

[30] Francisco Xavier Ernesto Fernandes, *India Portugueza Estudos Economico-Sociaes* (Bastora, 1905), pp. 39–40.

Contributions made by the *communidades* of Salcete for building the road from Rachol to Margao (1879):[31]

Communidades	Amount (*xerafins*)	*Communidades*	Amount (*xerafins*)
Aquem	34,000	Guirdolim	34,000
Betalbatim	36,000	Gandaulim	34,000
Cavorim	34,000	Loutolim	170,000
Clová	18,000	Margão	170,000 (besides the lease of land for the construction of the road.)
Curtorim	170,000	Mormugão	17,000
Camorlim	34,000	Nagoa	85,000
Chicolna	3,400	Quelossim	15,000
Chicalim	6,800	Raia	170,000 (besides the lease of land for the construction of the road.)
Dicarpalle	25,500	Sancoale	34,000
Doncolim	68,000	Seraulim	85,000
Dramapur	8,500	Sirlim	27,000
Davorlim	68,000	Telaulim	34,000
Dessua	10,200	Varca	170,000
Gonsua	17,000	Vaddem	3,400
Total		**1,751,800**	

Other Projects Executed by the *Communidades*

The various other projects which were undertaken by the Goan *communidades* included: making wastelands and marshy and swampy areas suitable for cultivation; similarly, undertaking measures to make agricultural fields suitable for two crops in a year; erecting embankments, sluice-gates and digging ponds, puddles and lakes, aqueducts, etc. Furthermore, the masonry, carpentry and furnishing works of all public edifices including parish churches and military quarters was also made the

[31] The data is collected from *Boleti …*, No. 83, dated 7th October, 1879, p. 661.

responsibility of the local *communidades*.[32] In the execution of these the *communidades* had to scrupulously follow certain guidelines. The *communidades* had to report to the government on the utility of projects proposed to be executed. The government then had the proposals examined by qualified engineers and other experts.[33]

The works undertaken and executed by the *communidades* were praiseworthy and helped lighten the burden of the Public Exchequer. All these projects were executed in accordance with the procedures laid down by the government to avoid embezzlement. The government had provided that the *gaunkars* could not participate in the bidding process for these projects with ulterior motives.[34] Once this was ensured, all the possible means that could have resulted in embezzlement of funds were avoided. This was to ensure that the earnings of the members by way of yearly *jonn* were not unduly affected.[35]

Whenever any *communidades* wished to undertake any of the works indicated above, the proposal had to be discussed at its general meeting. All the *gaunkars* of the *communidade*, and also the *interessados* (influential villagers other than *gaunkars*) had to compulsorily attend the meeting. The necessity and the utility of the proposed project(s) were discussed thoroughly. The specification of the project and all its other details were considered. The views of the twenty most influential *interessados* were also recorded. Similarly, the full project was divided into smaller portions or stages as was possible, so that the *communidade* was not burdened financially with the execution of the project in one financial year. The decision arrived at was signed by all those who were present and then this was brought to the notice of the *communidade's* procurator for further necessary action.[36] These steps had to be followed scrupulously in all cases, except in instances when dykes and embankments were ruptured. Such emergencies, conversely, had to be attended to immediately.[37]

---

[32] See *Regimento de 1735,* as copied in Filippe Nery Xavier (Jr.), *op. cit.*, Ch. 20, pp. xxiii-xxiv; see also ibid., Doc. No. 542, p. 165.
[33] Filippe Nery Xavier, *Defensa...*, Doc No. 3, pp. 5–6.
[34] Filippe Nery Xavier, *Collecção das Leis Peculiares das Communidades Agricolas,* Docs. No. 150 and 338, pp. 241 and 418–419.
[35] Filippe Nery Xavier, *Defensa...*, Doc Nos. 5 and 6, pp. 22–34.
[36] Filippe Nery Xavier (Jr.), *op. cit.*, p. 165.
[37] *Regimento de 1735,* as reproduced in Filippe Nery Xavier (Jr.), *op. cit.*, Ch. 21. p. xxiv.

The *communidades* also had to take measures for the reclamation of lands or making agricultural fields suitable for cultivating two crops in a year, so as to increase agricultural production. For this, certain formalities were followed while preparing the yearly budget.[38] All lands suitable for the cultivation of a second crop, whether it was *sorodio* or *vangana* (*rabi* or *kharif*), were to be developed at the cost of the *communidades*.[39] If there were any such lands in any of the villages, then the Administrator of *Communidades* proceeded to inspect them together with experts and assessors. This had to be preceded by the submission of a report to the Administrator finalized after the procurators, village secretary and assessors carrying out a stipulated annual survey within specified period.[40]

Thereafter, the money necessary to facilitate the work to make lands suitable for the cultivation of a second crop was kept aside from the annual budget of the *communidades*. *Communidades* which obtained the permission of the government for this purpose had to finish the work as fast as possible. To enable the concerned parties to finish the work on time, the full project was divided into phases for completion. Under any circumstances, the work related to making the land suitable for a second crop had to be completed before the start of farming activity related to the first crop.[41]

After finalizing the estimate for the proposed work, a tender was issued in the government bulletin and the bidding for the award of the work was held either in the session house of the *communidade* or at the office of the Administrator of *Communidades*.[42] The contractors who had to make lands suitable for the cultivation of a second crop had to unfailingly finish the work within the stipulated period. If, for any reason, a delay resulted in the fields being left fallow without cultivating even the first crop the

---

[38] Filippe Nery Xavier (Jr.), *op. cit.*, Doc. Nos. 533 and 542, pp. 155–158 and 166.
[39] Ibid., Doc. No. 542, p. 166; *Bando* of 8th August, 1782, §§1 and 4, as quoted in José Maria de Sá, *Projecto de Codigo das Communidades ou Digesto da Legislacão Peculiar das Mesmas Associacões*, Nova Goa, 1879, pp. 156-158; Filippe Nery Xavier, *Collecção das Leis Peculiares das Communidades Agricolas*, Doc. No. 92, pp. 171-172.
[40] Filippe Nery Xavier (Jr.), *op. cit.*, Doc. No. 542, pp. 166–167.
[41] See José Maria Sá, *Projecto de Codigo das Communidades,* pp. 161–162; also Filippe Nery Xavier (Jr.), *op. cit.*, Doc. No. 542, pp. 166–167.
[42] See Filippe Nery Xavier (Jr.), *op. cit.*, Doc. No. 542, p. 166–167; *Bando*, dated 8th August, 1872, as quoted in José Maria de Sá, *Projecto de Codigo das Communidades*, pp. 156–158.

contractor was imprisoned, besides paying a fine of 100 *xerafins* and reimbursing to the *communidade* the consequent loss of revenue.[43] This is significant, as the *communidades* were assured of their revenue; but this may not have been the case with the ordinary cultivator *gaunkars*. They suffered deprivation and loss as they were unable to cultivate the fields of their ancestors and had no means of protest.

However, in spite of clear guidelines which were set for the execution of work, the *communidades* often executed sub-standard projects. For instance, works related to the dykes and embankments were almost always poorly executed. There were constant ruptures to the embankments which were raised along the course of rivers and streams on inadequate foundations. The newly-raised dykes and embankments were also exposed to the attack of heavy currents of monsoons and tidal activity. The quality of stone used to lay the foundation was poor, as they were highly porous in nature and disintegrated due to the salinity of the river water. Sufficiently matured timber was also rarely utilized in the *manos* (dykes).[44]

Often these works were not executed properly and so were not durable. The reason was that the procurators nominated by the *communidades* for assisting the execution of these works conspired with the contractors to siphon off the construction materials. This went on year after year. This deplorable state of affairs could have been avoided only if the *communidades* had themselves undertaken the execution of the various projects, rather than giving contracts for them. The supply of construction material and other resources only could have been bid for by tender. The *communidades* could have appointed inspectors to judge the quality of the work. The inspectors could have been appointed, one from amongst the *gaunkars* and the other from the *interessados*.[45]

Public Health in Goa

Goa faced the constant outbreak of periodic epidemics. Outbreaks of contagious diseases were also frequent and epizootic attacks not less so. In fact, the constant outbreak of epidemics was given as the prime reason for

---

[43] See José Maria Sá, *Projecto de Codigo das Communidades*, p. 162.
[44] Filippe Nery Xavier, *Defensa...*, Doc. No. 7, pp. 36–37
[45] See Filippe Nery Xavier, *Defensa...*, Doc No. 7, pp. 34–39. For instance, the *Juiz das communidades* of the province of Salcete, João Pedro d'Abreu Tavares, stated that an embankment raised round Rumdem lake in Margao, around 1825, under his personal supervision, was sure to last for centuries to come.

the abandonment and depopulation of many Goan villages. For instance, the *Alvará* of 4th March 1788 listed the following villages as decadent and depopulated after the outbreak of epidemics there in 1783: Corlim, Carambolim, Azossim, Mandur, Gancim, Neurá o grande, Neurá o Pequeno, Goalim-Moula and Telaulim.[46] The case was similar in villages such as Chorão, Piedade. S. Mathias, Naroa, Gandaulim, Bambolim, Seridão, Chimbel, Panelim, Agaçaim and Ella, where there were epidemics in 1790. Likewise, many villages of Salcete had few inhabitants, especially those from Mormugão to Quelossim. [47] In the New Conquests region the situation was still worse; indeed constant epidemics, especially of malaria, were cited as the chief cause dissuading the residents of the Old Conquests from taking up residence in the New Conquests to exploit the natural resources abundantly available there.[48]

In 1845, the government determined that the expenses of the medical profession, including the dispensary, had to be maintained by the *communidades* in times of epidemic. The *communidades* were made to contribute in times of epidemics for the care and treatment of non-privileged sections of the rural inhabitants. The *communidades* were also made solely responsible for defraying the cost of rural sanitation.[49] Previously, by the *Portarias* of 10th March, 1845, and 25th April, 1845, the *Junta de Saude Publica* (Public Health Department) had been made responsible for taking measures to contain the outbreak of disease. [50] However, from 1849 onwards this responsibility was handed over to the *communidades*.[51]

---

[46] F.N. Xavier, *Collecção das Leis Peculiares das Communidades Agricolas*, Part. II, p. 184.

[47] *Boletim...*, dated 3rd October, 1865, No., p. 496.

[48] Jaime Rangel (ed.), *Oitava Congresso Provincial da India Portuguêsa*, Vol. I (Nova Goa, 1929), pp. 39–77.

[49] Filippe Nery Xavier, *Collecção das Leis Peculiares das Communidades Agricolas,* Doc. No. 289, pp. 370–374.

[50] Joaquim Bernardino Catão da Costa, *O Triumpho da Verdade,* §103, p. 28.

[51] Filippe Nery Xavier, *Collecção das Leis Peculiares das Communidades Agricolas,* Doc. No. 289, pp. 370-374. The *Portaria* of 25th April, 1849, stipulated the following: "*...Art. 12.° As despezas do Facultativo, e da Botica portatil serão satisfeitas pelas respectivas, para cuja despeza ficam desde já authorisadas.*
Art. 21.° Os Facultativos, sendo da propria Aldea terão huma machila effective, e huma rupia de vencimento diario para tartar od doentes pobres. Os doentes, que tiverem meios, satisfarão a importancia dos medicamentos; e os abastados serão tambem obrigados a remunerar of Facultativos...

According to the *Portaria* dated 25th April, 1849, during the outbreak of epidemics the *communidades* were to spend daily a sum of 2 *xerafins*. Of these one *xerafin* was for the payment of the attending physician, and the other was towards defraying the cost of his transport. If the physician came from outside the limits of the particular village the *communidade* had to spend out 3 *xerafins*. However, if the attending physician came from outside the limits of a particular province then the daily contribution rose to 4 *xerafins* per day.[52] If we take the minimum, then a *communidade* ended up spending 2 *xerafins* per day, and this was exclusive of expenses on medications, which amount was also charged to the *communidades*.

Often the *communidades* incurred enormous expenses during the outbreak of epidemics by paying the physicians itself.[53] The minimum amount that each *communidade* had to spend in a year was about 750 *xerafins*. But many of the *communidades*, like those of Dambolim, Curca, Talaulim, of Ilhas, Adsulim, Canã, Velim, etc., of Salcete, and Arporá Corlim, Marra, etc., of Bardez, had net revenues far less than 750 *xerafins* a year.[54]

The *Portaria* of the government dated 25th April 1849 defined an epidemic as when there were four known cases of contagious diseases or 15 reported cases of fever in any particular village. In Goa throughout the 19th century, as also earlier, outbreaks of smallpox were frequent, especially when migrant Goans returned from British India. Similarly, in any season it was rare for many a village not to have less than 15 reported cases of fever.[55] Therefore at any given time Goa remained officially a perpetually epidemic region. Moreover, the medications prescribed by the attending physicians were said to have been barely effective. Under these circumstances, the people were forced to take herbal medicines whose efficacy was also doubtful in positively controlling the outbreak of epidemics. In the end, while the officiating physicians were remunerated and were on the pay rolls of the *communidades* it was the people dealing

---

Art. 22.° Se o Facultativo nemeado fôr de huma Aldêa a outra, terá amchila effective, e tres serafins de vencimento; e se fôr mandado para for a da Comarca, salvo sendo menos de tres legoas, terá além da machila effective, quarto xerafins de vencimento diario…"

[52] Filippe Nery Xavier, *Collecção das Leis Peculiares das Communidades Agricolas,* Doc. No 289, pp. 370–374.

[53] Filippe Nery Xavier (Jr.), *op. cit.*, Doc. No. 383, p. 9.

[54] Joaquim Bernardino Catão da Costa, *O Triumpho da Verdade*, §161, p. 39.

[55] Filippe Nery Xavier, *Collecção das Leis Peculiares das Communidades Agricolas,* Doc. No 289, pp. 370–374.

in herbal medicines who attended to the sick. In this manner many *communidades* spent their resources unjustly and with little or no tangible benefit to the people.[56]

Construction of Cemeteries

Ever since the arrival of the Portuguese in Goa, in 1510, some of the dead were buried in the graveyards of the churches.[57] This is evident from a field study of the old churches of the Old Conquests of Goa. This, however, often created health problems. For instance, in 1782, there was an epidemic in Margao, and within two years a thousand people died.[58] The cause was supposed to be the foul smell emanating from the graveyard of the church where the dead were buried. Parishioners of other villages may have also suffered due to similar cause. And thus from the late 18th century many parishes started constructing cemeteries.

The *communidades* were made to defray the cost of the construction of cemeteries in many parts of Goa. For instance, the *communidade* of Gancim contributed 1999:0:39 *xerafins* for the construction of a cemetery in 1819-20.[59] Similarly, the *communidade* of Nagoa constructed a cemetery in 1842. Earlier, in 1832, the *communidade* of Orlim in Salcete gave 1000 *xerafins* to purchase a cemetery for its parishioners.[60] Likewise, a sum of 2054:2:30 *xerafins* was set aside from the revenues of the village Jua in 1840 for the construction of a cemetery in that village.[61]

It was in fact the Municipal Councils that had to construct and maintain the cemeteries. In times of lack of resources, the Municipal Councils were entitled to tax the people.[62] But the responsibility of building cemeteries was conveniently handed over to the *communidades*.

---

[56] Joaquim Bernardino Catão da Costa, *O Triumpho da Verdade*, p. 38.
[57] *Boletim...*, No. 76, dated 3rd October, 1865, p. 496.
[58] Ibid.
[59] Historical Archives of Goa, Panaji (HAG), *Registo das Portarias do Governo*, Vol. 1406, fl. 79.
[60] HAG, *Registo das Portarias do Governo*, Vol. 2428, fl. 83.
[61] HAG, *Registo das Portarias do Governo*, Vol. 2438, fl. 32v.
[62] *Codigo Administrativo*, Art. 137, as quoted in Joaquim Bernardino Catão da Costa, *O Triumpho da Verdade*, §158, pp. 28–38.

Communidades and Maintenance of Prisoners

The *communidades* also had an obligation to make provision for the maintenance of poor captives and prisoners in Goa. Governor-General Viscount d'Ourem burdened the *communidades* by making them solely responsible for the maintenance of poor captives and prisoners. Later, realizing that this was too heavy an imposition on the meager resources of the *communidades*, the government asked the Municipal Councils to partly defray the cost of maintaining the poor prisoners and other captives. The *Portaria* of 9th March 1854 asked the Municipal Councils to take measures to collect revenue for this purpose from the *communidades* as well as from all the tenant-cultivators, dessais, and other title-holders (bhatkars) of the Old and the New Conquests.[63] It seems that the governmental authorities looked at the institution of *communidade* as a banker and were extracting resources from their treasury.

Communidades and Construction of Rest Houses

The indirect process of extracting surpluses from the *communidades* was also clearly visible in the cases where the *communidades* were compelled to contribute both land and money for the construction of rest houses for travelers and pilgrims. In the second half of the 19th century, the *communidades* were made to give away lands on lease for this purpose.[64] The *communidades* were asked to give lands to facilitate the construction of public hostels for the benefit of travelers and pilgrims. Such types of obligation that were thrust on the *communidades* eventually led to the weakening of these agricultural institutions financially. The *communidades* may have lost much of their prime land to the government to help the latter provide rest houses for pilgrims and travelers.[65]

Conclusion

Thus, the *communidades* had responsibilities which were not intrinsic to their function as agricultural associations. In principle the construction and

[63] Joaquim Bernardino Catão da Costa, *O Triumpho da Verdade*, §136, p. 34.

[64] Joaquim Bernardino Catão da Costa, *O Triumpho da Verdade*, §146 and 147, p. 36.

[65] Ibid., §181, pp. 43–46. Herein is copied verbatim the reply given by João Francisco Piedade da Cruz, *Escrivão da Communidade de* Loutolim, regarding the deteriorated state of the lands leased out to individual capitalists. The lands leased for a specific purpose were rarely utilized appropriately.

conservation of the vicinal ways and public roads, bridges, aqueducts, culverts, etc., were within the competency and jurisdiction of the Municipal Council. Taking this into consideration, the government made the *communidades* to pay the *dizimos* at the rate of 10% from 1851 onwards.[66]

Similarly, the *communidades* had to defray the cost of sustaining medical personnel which included physicians, surgeons, nurses, etc., including their salary. Public health charges, like paying the salaries of teachers imparting instruction to village children, had to be met by the Municipal Councils.[67] Yet in Goa the burden was borne by the *communidades*.

In 1817, the total revenue of the *communidades* of Ilhas was 1,55,402 *xerafins*. From this, after providing for the servicing of debt (payment of interest), the divine cult, and paying other expenses, what remained to be distributed as surplus among the *gaunkars*, *cuntocares, interessados*, orphans and widows was only 42,855 *xerafins*, an amount that was far less than a third of their revenue.[68] This was the position in 1817; the obligations of the *communidades* increased tremendously thereafter throughout the nineteenth century. At the beginning of the 20th century the *communidades* were increasingly losing the identity of agricultural associations with production-oriented activities, and were acquiring a different character, that of welfare associations. The members, who found that the *communidades* were paying them less and less every year, began

---

66 Filippe Nery Xavier, *Collecção das Leis Peculiares das Communidades Agricolas*, Doc. No. 333, pp. 412–415.

67 Codigo Administrativo, Art. 120, nos. 4—49, Art. 123, nos. 3, 11 and 12, and, Art. 133, nos. 5, 6 and 11, as quoted in Joaquim Bernardino Catão da Costa, *O Triumpho da Verdade*, §157, pp. 38 ff.

68 Filippe Nery Xavier, *Bosquejo Historico das Communidades…*, ed. José Maria de Sá, Vol. I, Doc. No. 84, pp. 358–363: "*… Devem as communidades das aldeas das Ilhas de Goa 425279 xerafins; o presente rendimento annuo dellas é 155402 xerafins; se gasta em juros de dividas 20975; dão em pagamento dos foros e meios foros á real fazenda 17302 3/5 xerafins; despende com a camara geral para congrua, ordenados dos representantes e mais despeza 9556 ¼; paga ao senado da camara de meio por cento 999; despenderem as communidades em service da conservação de suas propriedades, contribuições, freguezias e seus officiaes 44407 1/5 xerafins, ficaram algumas communidades alcançadas em 2246 xerafins; separou-se a terça parte, da qual a metade foi recolhida no thesouro region e a outra metade existe em respectivos cofres até ultima decisão do governo sobre se tambem deve hir ao thesouro geral dos gancares, cuntocares e interessados, orfãos e viuvas 42855 xerafins …*"

looking beyond the boundaries of Goa for better pastures. Many started to emigrate for better conditions to British India and elsewhere.

Thus, the *Estado da India* devised a strategy to extract surplus indirectly from the *communidades* and the individual *gaunkars* by devolving many of its welfare functions directly to the *communidades*. With the decline of maritime trade, the Portuguese authorities looked more and more to rural surpluses to lessening the burden of administration. However, this resulted in the radical shrinking of the distributable surpluses of the *communidades*, impoverishing in turn the *gaunkars*. The result was that the *communidades* started gradually losing their prime position as dominant agricultural associations in rural Goa, and the *guankars* were compelled by circumstances to emigrate from Goa in order to earn a viable living.

APPENDIX I

CIVIL LAW STUDIES: A REPORT OF THE 2008 LECTURE SERIES

The 2008 lecture series on the Civil Law system was a major contribution to the achievements of V. M. Salgaocar College of Law and a landmark in the legal history of Goa. Its effects on the legal field in Goa are expected to be tremendous, which will bear fruit in the near future. Its consequences will be seen when the participants of the course take up legal practice in Goa or proceed with their further studies in India or abroad. It is hoped that many of the participants will make original contribution to Indo-Portuguese / Indo-European Studies.

The Lecture Series was a result of the MOU signed between V. M. Salgaocar College and the Faculty of Law, University of Lisbon. Eminent Professors from the faculty of Lisbon, including Doutor Fausto Quadros, Prof. Doutor Jose de Oliveria Ascencao, Prof. Doutor Dario Vincente Moura, Prof. Luis Menezes Leitao Leitao, Prof. Doutor Jorge Duarte Pinheirao and Prof. Doutor Loureiro Bastos delivered lectures on various topics related to European Jurisprudence , European Law, the Portuguese Civil Code and International Law of the Sea. The topics were scheduled considering the future requirements of Goan students.

It was a proud moment for the college and the staff to see that some of the participants gave ample proof of their abilities and capabilities by being able to comprehend and analyze Civil Law traditions. They also carried out a comparative study of the topics on Civil Law traditions with regards to the prevailing Common Law system in Goa. Their discussion and questioning was admired by some of the visiting faculty. Some of them produced detailed summaries of the day's presentation.

The Lectures were an intellectual treat to the participants, giving them new perspectives in the legal field. Doutor Faustos Quadros took the audience through the historical evolution of the European Union and the intricacies of the European Constitution. He also discussed the enforcement of European Law by Member States and the remedies available. At the concluding lecture he adroitly raised the issue of a Constitution for Europe, the current situation and the future intentions.

In his contribution, Doutor Dario expounded the intricacies of the major legal traditions of the world, explaining clearly the comparison between the Common Law and the Civil Law system. Doutor Ascencao, Doutor Pinheiro and Prof. Luis Menezes Leitao did justice to the two major Civil Codes of Portugal, the one of 1867 and that of 1966. The participants were given a total grasp of the meaning of a Civil Code. Some of the participants enjoyed comparing the various provisions of the Civil Code with their own Tort Law and Indian Contract Act. They were also given insight into the differences between the Code of 1867 and the Civil Code of 1966. New trends in Family Law worldwide as regards marriage, adoption, parental control, protection of children etc. captured the imagination of the participants as possible areas for their future research. Lastly Prof. Bastos took the class through the International Law of the Seas, navigating clearly through internal waters, straights, Archipelagic States, High Seas and International Sea Beds, all the time respecting the Marine Environment. His maps and charts put the concepts in concrete terms. The lecturers were stimulating as they opened successive new viewpoints of interest.

In continuation of the last year's experience, another series of lectures has been scheduled for January–February 2009.

APPENDIX II

A COMPARATIVE STUDY OF THE PORTUGUESE CONSTITUTION AND THE INDIAN CONSTITUTION

CARMO D'SOUZA

This chart is intended to provoke comparative research on the Indian and Portuguese Constitutions. It is to be noted that the chart is based on the book published in 2000.[1] It is hoped that the chart may also motivate comparative researches between Indian Constitution and Constitutions of other Continental countries.

---

[1] (See for details Carmo D'Souza, *The Indian and Portuguese Constitutions :A Comparative Study,* Vol. I)

Indian Constitution	Portuguese Constitution
Teaching of Constitutional Law *Text Books* Text books tailored to Case Law approach. Less use of views of authoritative texts by legal experts. Doctrines discussed follow from case law. *Research Point: (For Comparative Study)* *Teaching of Constitutional Law in India and Portugal is an excellent area for comparative research.* *To identify authoritative texts used in text books on Indian Constitution* *To identify authoritative texts in books on Portuguese Constitution.* *To identify case law in text books on Indian Constitution,* *To identify case law in text books on Portuguese Constitution.* *To analyze some case laws in Indian Constitution and check if similar concepts may figure as authoritative texts in Portuguese Constitution and vice versa.* *Research Issue:* *Whether there is convergence on some points i.e. arriving at same conclusion using two different methods.*	**Teaching of Constitutional Law** *Text Books* Oscillates between professional and academic orientation. Recourse to theory and dogmatic method. Frequent reference to constitutional theory. Text books refer to material developed by constitutional experts. Case law not used with same emphasis and style as in India. Today case law is developing in Portugal with the setting up of Constitutional Court.

Identifying Articles of Constitution Students identify articles with their contents e.g. Art. 21 with life and liberty When Amendments are introduced numbers of other articles don't change. If need be amendments are added, for example: Art. 243A, 243B, 243Z, 243ZA,…243G	**Identifying Articles of Constitution** Article numbering changed at revisions.
Constitutional Developments Government of India Act, 1858 Indian Councils Act, 1861 &1892 Morley-Minto Reforms and Indian Council Act, 1901 Government of India Act, 1915 Government of India Act, 1935 Indian Independence Act, 1947 Constitution of 1950	***Constitutional Historical Developments*** Development in France, Spain etc. Constitution of 1822 Constitutional Charter of 1826 The Constitution of 1838 Constitution of 1911 Constitution of 1933 Alterations to Constitution of 1951 Alterations to Constitution of 1959 Constitution of 1976
Remarks *Earlier developments in pre-Independence India were not exactly heading towards a constitutional document.* *Portugal has rich experience of constitutions.* *Constitutional movements can also be studied from political events in Portugal as well as Goa.* *Interesting to research into constitutional movement in then Estado da India and whether there are reflections in British India or French Pondicherry and vice versa.* *Study of how dictatorial Constitution of 1933 came about in Portugal will be enlightening*	

Study of events in Goa for and against the Constitution of 1933 will bring new material to light. *Alteration of 1951, floating the concept of the overseas provinces—A Constitutional device, real or illusory, pragmatic or not* *What were the reactions in the then Estado da India? Reactions in Colonies to the Constitution of 1933 in light of the Colonial Act of 1930?* *What were the reactions of the Estado da India to the Constitution of 1933 in the light of amendments in the fifties?* *Reflection of constitutionalism in Portugal (1822–1961)and in Goa as seen in newspaper articles, books, political events etc. in Goa.*	
Constitutional Theory Constitutional theories are expressed especially via the case law. *Remarks* *Do Indian Law Schools need a bigger curriculum of constitutional theory?* *Is there a need for dogmatic method/ doctrinal approach?* *Does abstract method adopted in Portugal hinder proper development of law?* *What are the advantages and disadvantages of abstract constitutional theories?* *What could be the result of substantial case law development if it took place for instance on Portuguese Constitution of 1933?* *Is case law a rudder that safeguards constitutional developments?* *Is reference to other constitutional theories in Europe including European*	**Constitutional Theory** Constitutional theories are sometimes derived from abstract ideas, at times influenced by other foreign schools of law.

constitutionalism aiding the development law in Portugal? *How foreign influences come in through the process of case law in India.*	
Constitutional Framework Part I: The Union and its Territories Part II: Citizenship Part III: Fundamental Rights Part IV: Directive Principles of State Policy Part IV A: Fundamental Duties Part V: The Union Part VI: The States Part VII: The States in Part B of the First Schedule (Repealed) Part VIII: The Union Territories Part IX: The Panchayats Part IX A: The Municipalities Part X: The Scheduled Tribes and Tribal Areas Part XI: Relations between Union and States Part XII: Finance, Property, Contracts and Suits. Part XIII: Trade, Commerce and Intercourse within the territory of India Part XIV: Services under the Union and States Part XIV A: Tribunals Part XV: Elections Part XVI: Special Provisions to certain classes Part XVII: Official Language Part XVIII: Emergency Provisions Part. XIX: Miscellaneous Part XX: Amendment of Constitution Part XXI: Temporary, Transitional and Special Provisions. Part XXII: Short Title, Commencement, Authoritative text in Hindi and Repeals. *The Twenty Two Parts are followed by Twelve Schedules*	**Constitutional Framework** Fundamental Principles (Art. 1-11) Part I: Fundamental Rights and Duties Part II: Economic Organization Part III: Organization of Political Power. Part. IV: Guarantees and Revision of the Constitution. Final and Transitional Provisions (Arts. 290–299)
Remarks *Comparative study on the division of the*	

two Constitutions would give insights into their divergent structures. *A study can be made on various parts of Indian Constitution introduced later through Amendments which did not figure in the original Indian Constitution* *A Comparative study can be made why the two Constitutions differ in their framework.*	
Quasi-Federal Model India has a Quasi-Federal model. It is a Union of States. *Remarks* *Interesting to compare Portuguese unitary model with India's Union of States.* *In India relation between Union and States is interesting for a Portuguese scholar.* *Division of powers between Centre and State is unique, not exactly following American model.* *The Indian model has characteristics of federalism as well as few characteristics of unitary constitutions with some powers to the centre. It is termed as Union of States with strong centre or quasi-federal structure. It is interesting to study the difference on models in relation to history, geography etc. of the two nations*	**Unitary Model** Portugal has a Unitary model. It has autonomous Regions of the Azores and Madeira.
Schedules Indian Constitution has several schedules *Remarks* *Use of Schedules in the Indian Constitution and the nature and purposes of various Schedules will provide rich experience to Portuguese scholar.*	**Absence of Schedules**

It is interesting to compare the various material in the schedules and how such material has been dealt in Portuguese Constitution, e.g. Schedule I of Indian Constitution mentions the territory Bharat and Art. 5 of the Portuguese Constitution outlines the territory that comprises Portugal.	
Fundamental Rights Part III of the Indian Constitution refers to Fundamental Rights. Part IV A refers to Fundamental Duties—Not in original Constitution . Added later. *Remarks:* *Interesting to do a comparative study of the Fundamental Rights and Duties under the two Constitutions.* *Interesting to find if they cover the same area.* *Some Fundamental Rights in Portugal may figure as Directive Principles in India.* *Directive Principles in India have an interesting case law development by which they have been enforced by reading together with Part III of Indian Constitution. This is an interesting development for Portuguese constitutionalists.* *Some Fundamental Rights in Portugal which are expressly conferred have entered the Indian Constitutional arena via case law* *Right to strike as Fundamental Right in Portugal is interesting for Indian scholars*	**Fundamental Rights** Part I of the Portuguese Constitution has Fundamental Rights as well as Fundamental Duties.
Directive Principles Part IV of Indian Constitution contains Directive Principles. *Remarks* *Interesting for Portuguese scholars to*	

research into the influences on Directive Principles, their nature, their enforceability in India.	
Preamble WE THE PEOPLE OF INDIA *(Power flows from People)* SOVEREIGN SOCIALIST SECULAR DEMOCRATIC REPUBLIC Secure JUSTICE.. LIBERTY EQUALITY FRATERNITY *Remarks* *Interesting to research into historical references in the preambles of both the constitutions.* *Research into their values is another interesting area for comparative study.* *Influences that shaped Preamble of Indian Constitution and the Portuguese Constitution interesting for historical analysis.* *Constituent Assembly debates in India on the Preamble are interesting for Portuguese Scholar.* *Role of the Preamble in interpretation of Indian Constitution enunciated by court decisions is interesting and provides material for interpretation of Indian Constitution.* *Reference to liberation from colonialism in Portuguese Constitution is interesting for historico-legal analysis.* *How the end of colonialism was made realistic is worth researching.*	**Preamble** Historical reference to armed forces movement that overthrew the Fascist regime. Reference to liberation from dictatorship, oppression and colonialism represented a revolutionary change and historic new beginning for Portuguese society. Revolution restoring fundamental rights and freedoms.

Amendment of Constitution Amendment of Indian Constitution contemplated in the Constitution itself. To date there have been several amendments to the Indian Constitution. Parliament has power to amend the constitution though it cannot amend the basic structure, a theory developed by courts. Interesting case law followed on amendment of Indian Constitution, which are interesting for Portuguese scholars. *Remarks* *Amendment of Indian Constitution can be studied over a period as S.C. moved from one interpretation to another to arrive at the present position.* *Case law on amendment is very fascinating for Portuguese scholars.* *The Basic Feature Doctrine as expounded by the S.C. is thought-provoking for comparative constitutional scholars.* *Limits in matter of revision in Portuguese Constitution can aid comparative research.* *Articles from original Constitution have even been amended in India.*	**Revision of Constitution** Periodic revision contemplated / also Government may assume special powers with special large majority. Limits in matter of Revision. There have been seven revisions of the Portuguese Constitution. Present is the Seventh Revision (2005) Portuguese Parliament sits on a Revision process.
President In India, Cabinet System exists. President is titular head, exercises hardly any powers independently. To exercise powers on advice of Prime Minister and not as a rule on his discretion. Lot of Case law developed on this area.	**President** Not conventional Presidential type nor conventional Parliamentary type. Described as semi-presidential with essential characteristics of parliamentary regime. Has important constituent powers,

	not merely formal or nominal. President represents the Fourth Power i.e Regulating Power.
Indirectly elected. *Remarks* *Interesting to compare the parliamentary system in India with the semi-presidential and semi-parliamentary system in Portugal. Historical circumstances of adopting the divergent models enhances the value of comparative study in this area. Development of the role of President in India both through historical events and case law is interesting for a Portuguese Scholar. Powers of the President in Portugal are interesting. Obligatory interval between presidential and parliamentary elections interesting.*	Directly elected.
Parliament House of the People, Council of States *Remarks* *Interesting to research into the nature of two houses, the influences on such a system, how it is specially relevant to the Indian Constitution , which has to protect the interest of the States in the Indian Union too.*	**Parliament** Assembly of the Republic
The Executive The Council of Ministers—headed by Prime Minister *Remarks* *The Government in Portugal is responsible for its actions both to the President and the Assembly of the Republic.*	**The Government**

Judiciary & Tribunals The Union Judiciary (Supreme Court)	**Judiciary & Tribunals** The Supreme Court of Justice
High Courts in the States	Courts of Law of First and Second Instance
Subordinate Courts etc.	
Tribunals	The Supreme Administrative Court and other Administrative Courts and fiscal courts
	The Court of Audit
Supreme Court and High Courts decide on constitutional cases	The Constitutional Court
Remarks *Development of Constitutional Court in Portugal interesting for Indian scholars. The style of judgment from Portuguese Constitutional Court and Indian Supreme Courts and High Courts on constitutional cases is interesting area for comparative research.*	
The States Governor of State State Legislature Council of Ministers and Chief Minister. *Remarks* *Part VI of the Constitution deals with States. So there are provisions for the Governor, Council of Ministers, the Advocate General at the State level. Part VIII provides for Union territories. Part XI provides for relations between Union and the States.* *All these are important aspects of comparative study.*	**Autonomous Regions (Azores and Madeira)**

Relation Between Union and the States. *Interesting area for research .* *Legislative and Administrative relations* *Use of Lists: Union, State and Concurrent Lists in Schedule VII is interesting .*	
The Union Territories *Remarks* *The Union territories can be studied from historical angle.* *The additions of Goa, Daman and Diu to the Union territories list brought about changes in nature of powers of Union Terriotries—This is interesting area for Portuguese scholars too.*	
Amendment of the Constitution Number of Amendments from inception. *Remarks* *Pressures that bring Amendments.* *History of Amendments interesting.* *Amendments declared unconstitutional, and to what extent.* *Case Laws on Amendments and doctrines propounded like Basic*	**Revision of Constitution** Periodic Revisions Need for revision in view of European Union. Historical facts that influenced revision processes.

Structure **Emergency Provisions** Part XVIII deals with Emergency Provisions. Also includes Financial Emergency and what is termed as Presidential Rule in State. *Remarks* *Presidential Rule has interesting case law development as well as history which provides insights to a Portuguese scholar.* **Scheduled Areas and Tribes** Part X of the Indian Constitution. ***Union and State Government in India.*** ***Official Language***	**Declaration of State of Siege or Emergency**
Constitutionality *Remarks* *Whether Review of Constitutionality in Portugal differs from the concept of unconstitutionality found among common law countries.* *Discussion on Review of Constitutionality: positive unconstitutionality, constitutionality by omission, preventive review of*	**Review of Constitutionality in Portugal**

constitutionality, unconstitutionality of original or revised constitutional norm etc. are interesting to Indian scholars. Whether the establishment of Constitutional court in Portugal has modified its earlier theory of strict separation of powers. Whether the Review of Constitutionality has brought about a change to the approach of case–law i.e. the theory of Precedent. Unconstitutionality of legislation in India is a very interesting area for comparative research with Review of Constitutionality in Portugal. • Books : *Legal System in Goa, Boletim Official, Diario de Governo, Carta Constitucional da Monarquia Portuguesa* (1880)	

CONTRIBUTORS

Maria Alexandra de Sousa Aragão

Maria Alexandra de Sousa Aragão was born in 1967, in the city of Guarda (Portugal). She is married, has two children and lives in Coimbra (Portugal). She is Professor at the Faculty of Law of the University of Coimbra (https://woc.uc.pt/fduc/person/ppgeral.do?idpessoa=130), where she teaches European law, European governance, environmental law, environmental jurisprudence, waste law and nature conservation. In the Faculty she is member of the Scientific Council and coordinator of the International Relations Office for the Public Administration degree. In the Centre for planning law, urban law and environmental law she is Vice Director of the Review on Planning law, urban law and environmental law (http://www.fd.uc.pt/cedoua/revista.html) and also member of the Scientific Council and of the teaching and research staff. At the international level she is: a) Jean Monnet professor and member of the European Community Studies Association; b) Portuguese representative at the Observatoire juridique du Réseau Natura 2000 (http://www.cidce.org/), and; c) Full member of the Avosetta group of experts in European Environmental Law (http://www.avosetta.org/). Her main publications are in Portuguese but she also published in English (Europa Law Publishing, Amsterdam) and French (Pulim, Limoges, and Bruillant, Brussels).

Anthony D'Souza

M.A., LL.M., Ph.D. (Law). Hon. Director of Ismilda Research Consultancy. Edited *Towards a World Constitution* by Carmo D'Souza (2003). Co-edited with Dr. Carmo D'Souza "World Constitutionalism" (Cambridge Scholars Publishing, 2007). Also co-edited present book.

B. S. Patil

B.Sc., LL.M. Graduated in Law and obtained LL.M. in 1999 from Karnataka University, Dharwad. Has been teaching law since 1999, then in V. M. Salgaocar College since 2001. Registered for a PhD on the topic 'Right to Education and Employment of Disabled Persons'. Chairman of the Legal Aid Society for two years, involved with organization of various Human Rights activities in the college campus, including conducting seminars, certificate courses, national-level Moot Court competitions, etc.

Visiting Lecturer for the LL.M. program on Human Rights and ADR certificate program at Shivaji University, Kolhapur. Has been empanelled as a resource person in The Karnataka Institute for Law and Parliamentary Reform (KILPAR), Bangalore. Current area of research interest is Alternative Dispute Resolution Systems including the Arbitration and Conciliation Act, 1996, labour laws and human rights in general and rights of disabled persons in particular. Articles include :'The Right to Education of Disabled Persons in the State of Goa', *Lexpressions* 2006; 'The Development of International Standards on Rights of Disabled Person', serial publication for a special issue on Disability Rights . Paper presentations include :'The Right to be Normal', National Seminar on Human Rights, organized by V.M.Salgaocar College of Law in association with UGC, New Delhi, 2008 ;'A Critical Appreciation of the Power of the Chief Justice to Appoint Arbitrators', National Seminar on ADRS, among others.

Carmo D'Souza
M.Sc., B.Ed, LL.M., Ph.D.(Law), Reader in Law at V.M. Salgaocar College of Law, Goa. Published books in Law and Fiction. Books on law include *The Legal System in Goa* (Vols. I & II) (1994–95), *The Indian and Portuguese Constitutions: A Comparative Study* (Vol. I) (2001), *Towards a World Constitution* (2003) and *Concepts in Law* (2004). Co-edited with Dr. Anthony D'Souza *World Constitutionalism* (Cambridge Scholars Publishing, 2007). Co-edited the present book. Hon. Director of Ismilda Research Consultancy.

Chidananda Reddy S.Patil
B.Sc., LL.M., Ph.D.; graduated from University of Mysore, Mysore in 1983. LL.B. 1986 from Karnatak University. Master's Degree in Law from University of Mysore, in 1988, specialising in Constitutional Law. First class and first rank at LL.M., for which awarded two gold medals and a cash prize by the University of Mysore. In addition, the Government of Karnataka has awarded him a cash prize for securing first rank in LL.M. Doctorate in Law from the Karnatak University, Dharwad. Has taught law for 19 years and published more than 50 articles in various law journals and magazines. One of the experts asked to submit a research paper to the Committee on Reforms of Criminal Justice System appointed by the Union of India, of which the Hon. Dr. Justice V. S. Malimath was the Chairperson. Has drafted legislations for the Government of Karnataka including the Karnataka State Human Rights Courts Rules, 2006. Has a deep interest in legal aid and legal literacy programmes.

Dário Moura Vicente

Born in Lisbon, Portugal, in 1962. Graduate in Law (1985), Master in Law (1990) and Doctor in Law (2000). Professor of the Faculty of Law of the University of Lisbon, where he has taught Private International Law, Comparative Law, International Commercial Law, Civil Law (General Theory), Civil Procedure Law, Copyright Law, Industrial Property Law and Information Society Law. Member of the Portuguese Bar since 1987. Legal Adviser of the Minister of the Presidency and National Defence of the Government of Portugal (1990/1994). Vice-President of the Directive Council of the Faculty of Law of the University of Lisbon (2002/2004). Chairman of the Institute for Juridical Cooperation of the same Faculty (since 2006).

Fausto de Quadros

Professor of Administrative Law, European Law and Public International Law at the Faculty of Law of the University of Lisbon. Master's Degree in Law 1966, LL.M. Public Law and Economic Law 1968, Ph.D. 1985, Professor of Law 1986, Full Professor ("*Catedrático*") since 1998. Jean Monnet Chair in European Constitutional and Administrative Law, Jean Monnet Centre of Excellence of the Lisbon University, both administered by the European Commission, Brussels. Has held visiting professorships at universities in France (Robert Schumann University, Strasbourg), Germany (including the Academy of Administrative Sciences, Speyer), and the United States. Regularly advises governments and corporations on matters of European Law, Public Law and International Law. Advised Austria and Poland on the preparation of their respective accessions to the European Union. Has acted as consultant for the OECD in relation to public administration reform of a number of member states. He has participated in numerous international conferences and symposiums, principally on European Law and Administrative Law. He has been involved in the writing of some of the most relevant laws on the implementation and consolidation of democracy in Portugal since 1974. Has given evidence at hearings of the Portuguese Parliament in all revisions of the Portuguese Constitution since 1974. Has been invited to Parliamentary Committee hearings of the Legal Affairs and Constitutional Affairs Committees of the European Parliament. He is invited regularly to arbitrate in proceedings, both in Portugal and abroad. Was *ad hoc* arbitrator of "Mercosul" ("Mercado Comum do Sul") by appointment of the Brazilian Government. Member of the Portuguese Bar since 1974, practicing lawyer for the European Court of Human Rights and the European Court of Justice since 1986. Member of a number of scientific associations in European and Latin American countries. Official representative of the Portuguese Government on the High Council of the European University Institute, in Florence, Italy, and the Consulting Committee of the Academy of European Law, in Trier, Germany. He has innumerable publications to his credit in several languages. Some recent publications include: *Global Law, Plural Constitutionalism and Global Administrative Law* (London: Sweet and Maxwell, 2008, forthcoming). *Droit de l'Union européenne* (*European Union Law*) (Brussels: Bruylant, 2008). "L'effet de la supranationalité dans la séparation horizontale des pouvoirs", in H. Bauer and A. D'Atena, eds., *The impact of supranationality on the separation of powers*, SIPE 2, Trilingual Edition (Brussels: Bruylant, 2007) among others .

Gandaman Shaber Ali

MA., LL.M.,(NLSIU) M.L., (SKU) . LL.M., from National Law School of India University, Bangalore. Started carrier as part time lecturer in 1992 at Sri Vijayanagar College of Law, Anantapur, A.P. subsequently became full time faculty in the year 1994 till 1997. Presently Senior Faculty at V. M. Salgaocar College of Law, Miramar, Panaji from 1997 . Recognized as PG Faculty to teach LL.M., by the Goa University in 2000. He published 16 articles in various national law journals and magazines like All India Reporter (AIR), Legal News and Views, Consumer Confrontation , Radical Humanist, Journal of Islamic Law Review (JILR) , Lexepressions etc. He organized various programmes on behalf of UGC, HRD Ministry GOI, CPR, CII and DIPP (GOI), like seminars, certificate courses, workshops, training programmes, debates, inter university law related programmes etc. Invited as guest faculty and resource person for various PG Courses, seminars, workshops, UGC sponsored Refresher Courses, symposium, certificate courses, etc. Attended, actively participated and presented research papers in various National and State level seminars, workshops, training programmes, symposiums, and conferences

Kim Rocha Couto

B.A. History & Psychology, Goa University, Goa. (First Class First in Goa). LL.B. Goa University, Goa (Top of Goa University in all three years of LL.B. securing First class First.) LL.M. (Criminal Law& Administrative Law) University of Pune. LL.M. (Human Rights) Goa University. (.First Class First. Recipient of three Gold Medals for highest mark in an LL.M. Examination, securing highest marks in Jurisprudence and Constitutional Law.) She specialized in Criminal Law and Human

Rights. Full-time Lecturer at V.M. Salgaocar College of Law since 1998. Has taught courses on Law of Torts, Jurisprudence, Interpretation of Statutes and Criminology. Her current area of research interest is Human Rights . Some of her publications include: "The Reproductive rights of Woman: Violation with Impunity", *Indian Journal of Human Rights and the Law*, Serials Publications, New Delhi, 1 (2004); "Bending the Rules of Interpretation" *Lexpressions*, V. M. Salgaocar College of Law, 2006. She provided reading material with analysis of case law for a ready reference book on *Land Laws* for students (2005–2006). She wrote a chapter on "Protection of Women Domestic Violence Act, 2005" for a book on *Women and Law* for students, 2009.

Jatin Naik
Student of five years (Hons) course at V. M. Salgaocar College of Law.

Jorge Duarte Pinheiro
Graduate in Law (1989), Master in Law (1995) and Doctor in Law (2004), from the Faculty of Law of the University of Lisbon. Practiced law in Lisbon 1989–1992 and held various other positions. Lecturer ("Assistente") of the Faculty of Law of the University of Lisbon, 1992–2004. Professor of the Faculty of Law of the University of Lisbon (since 2004), where he has taught Family Law, Succession Law and Child Law for graduate and postgraduate courses. Supervisor of postgraduate theses since 2004 at the Faculty of Law of the University of Lisbon. Member of Doctoral and Master's juries since 2004, Portugal (Faculty of Law of the University of Lisbon, Faculty of Law of the University of Coimbra, Faculty of Human Sciences of the Portuguese Catholic University and School of Law of the University of Minho). Member of Conselho Superior da Magistratura, organ that supervises Portuguese Judiciary, 2004–2005.
Member of the Jury for Admission to Magistrature, Centro de Estudos Judiciários, Portugal, 2005 and 2007. Main publications: *Legado em substituição da legítima* (1996), thesis on Successions Law (includes study of legitimary or mandatory succession in Portuguese, Spanish, French, Italian and German Law); *O núcleo intangível da comunhão conjugal* (2004), thesis on Family Law (includes study of legal consequences of marriage in Portuguese, Spanish, French, Italian, German, English and US Law); *Direito da Família e das Sucessões* (2005–2008), lessons of Family and Successions Law.

Luís Menezes Leitão

Professor Luís Menezes Leitão is Chair Professor of Contract and Tort Law, Labour Law and Insolvency Law at the Law Faculty of the University of Lisbon and also works as Lawyer and Arbitrator. He is also Vice-Chairman of the Institute of Consumer Law and the Institute of Labour Law at the Law Faculty of the University of Lisbon. He was the former Dean of the Law Faculty of the University of Lisbon, and former Vice-President of the Lisbon Section of the Portuguese Bar Association as well as former Member of the Pedagogic Council of the Portuguese Judges Formation Institution. He is author of more than 50 titles published about Contract Law, Tort Law, Labour Law, Tax Law, Insolvency Law, and Internet Law, and member of various scientific Academies in Portugal, Italy and Germany.

M. Pinheiro

B. Sc., M. A., B. Ed., LL.M., Ph. D. (Law). Principal of V. M. Salgaocar College of Law and Chief Coordinator and H.O.D. LL.M. Programme. Member of the Board of Studies for graduate and postgraduate courses in several universities in India. Member of the Task Force of the National Human Rights Commission to review all Human Rights curricula. Member and Executive Chairman, South Asian Forum for Clinical Law Teachers. Member, expert committee of U.G.C. for grant/renewal of autonomy to colleges. Member, Ordinances and Statutes vetting committee, Goa University. Education Consultant and managing committee member, Don Bosco Institution in Mumbai and Konkan provinces. Member, Legal Cell, Archdiocesan Board of Education. Member, Global Alliance on Justice Education. Editor-in-Chief, *Lexpressions,* a biannual Law journal. Member of the executive council of Goa University. Member of the academic council of Goa University.

Manuel Porto

Professor (former Dean) of the Law School of the University of Coimbra. Proficient in Portuguese, English, French, Spanish and German (understands Italian) .Graduate in Law (Law School of the University of Coimbra), M. Phil in Economics (University of Oxford), Ph. D. in Economics (Law School of the University of Coimbra). Full Professorship (Law School of the University of Coimbra). Professor of the University of Coimbra, also with teaching duties in other schools (Instituto Bissaya Barreto, Universidade Católica and Universidades Lusíada: coordinator of the Law degree). Director of the Course in European Studies (Coimbra). President of the European Community Studies Association (ECSA—

World). Chairman of the Regional Planning Commission of the Central region of Portugal (1976–89). Member of the Commission for the Portuguese Tax Reform (1987–8). Member of the City Council of Coimbra (1979–96; President since 2000). Chairman of the National Council of the Plan (1986–9). Member of the European Parliament (1989–1999), where he was Quaestor; Vice-Chairman of the Budgets Committee; Member of different Committees, such as the Committee for Economic and Monetary Affaires and Industrial Policy, the Committee for External Economic Relations, and the Committee for Transports and Tourism; member of different inter-Parliamentary Delegations, such as the Delegation for Relations with China and with Central Asia. Dean of the Law School of the University of Coimbra (2000–2005). Chairman of the National Council for Education (2001–2006). Member of the Commission for the 1988–9 of the National taxes Reform of the Commission for the Reform of Local Taxation (2007). Earlier participation in projects for the World Bank (project on trade liberalization and adjustment policies); OECD (projects on employment and tax problems); Council of Europe (project on emigration problems); European Commission (project on intra-industry trade). His main fields of research are International Trade, European Integration, Taxation and Regional Development and Physical Planning. He had published more than 100 works including the most recent ones : The English and Chinese editions of *Theory of Integration and EU Policies* (2004); *O Orçamento da União Europeia. As Perspetivas Financeiras para 2007-201* (Coimbra: Almedina, 2006); "State Aid in Portugal" (with João Nogueira de Almeida), in Paul Nemitz, ed., *Effective Application of EU State Aid Procedures: The Role of National Law and Practice*, (Holland: Kluwer, 2008), pp. 343–54 ; "The New Map of the World", in *Temas de Integração*, 2nd semester 2007, pp. 9–35; "O Fundo Monetário Internacional (FMI)" and "O Grupo Banco Mundial" (with Victor Calvete), in João Mota de Campos (cooord.), *Organizações Internacionais*, (Curitiba: Juruá Editora, 2008), pp.351–418; *O Ordenamento do Território num Mundo de Exigência Crescente* (Almedina, 2008); "A União Europeia: Um Projecto Europeu e Mundial", in Jorge Miranda and Marco António Meneses da Silva (coord.), *Tratado Luso-Brasileiro de Dignidade Humana*, (São Paulo: Quartier Latin), pp. 501–5. He is Commander of the Order of Infante D. Henrique (Portugal); Commander of the Rio Branco (Brazil). e.mail: mporto@fd.uc.pt

Maria de Lourdes Bravo da Costa Rodrigues.
B.Sc.(Hons), M.A., B.Lib Sc., M.Lib.Sc. Books: 1. *Goan Tasty Morsels*; 2. *Feasts, Festivals and Observances*; 3. *Remembering Goa*; 4. *100 Years of the Goa Chamber of Commerce and Industry*; 5. *Lifestyle in Goa (1910-1926.* Participated in Local, National and International Seminars including Vasco da Gama and India held in Paris in 1998, Urbanisation of Portuguese Cities held in Coimbra, Portugal in 2000 and conference organised by Lusotopie in Goa in 2000. Has been member of Expert Committees of the Goa Government and the Goa College of Hotel Management and Catering Technology. Papers presented were published in the proceedings. Regular columnist in local newspapers and magazines. Presently working as Librarian in the State Central Library and specializes in Goan history.

Maria Pia de Menezes Rodrigues
After completing fifth year of *Liceu (Segundo ciclo*) graduated in Science at the University of Bombay and then took post-graduate degrees in History and Library Science at the same University. Participated in a number of a seminars and conferences, at local, national and international levels, and presented papers in the field of Indo-Portuguese history and library science. Retired as Curator, Central Library, Panaji, Goa, after serving the said institution for a period of over three decades, initially as a Librarian and then as Head of the institution.

Mrunmayi M. Vaidya
B.S.L, LL.B, LL.M. Completed five-year Law course at the ILS Law College, Pune in 2001 and received post-graduate degree from the Dept. of Law, University of Pune in 2003. Diploma in Consumer Protection laws from the Institute of Advance Legal Studies, Pune. Joined the V. M. Salgaocar College of Law in the year 2004. Areas of research interest are Personal Law and the Rights of the Child. She published articles : "Position of Women under the Hindu Personal Law", *Lexpression* 2006, Compiled text material for text book on *The Land Laws of Goa.* Presented a paper on 'Human Rights: Inhuman Violations' at the conference organized by the Centre for Indo-European Studies at Goa University, January 2004.

Ojasvita Srivastava
Student of fourth year, LLB (Honours) at V. M. Salgaocar College of Law at Goa. She won 'Commendable' and 'Highly Commendable' titles at the Commonwealth Essay Writing Competition in the years 2001 and 2002.

She won the Best Advocate Award at the S. D. M. Law College National Level Moot Court Competition held at Mangalore in October, 2006. She was a semi- finalist out of 27 national and international teams at the D. M. Harish International Law Moot Court Competition at the Government Law College in Mumbai in February, 2007 and was also awarded the IInd Best Memorial Award there. She was also a semi- finalist out of 60 national teams at the International Henry Dunant Moot Court Competition in Humanitarian Law organized by the ICRC at New Delhi in September 2007. She bagged the Best Speaker award at the Student Parliament Competition organized by the Goa State legislature in the year 2006 and also the Best Speaker award by the Ministry of Parliamentary Affairs, New Delhi for her performance at the 16th National Youth Parliament Competition in the year 2003.

Paulo de Sousa Mendes
Graduate in Law (1981), Master in Law (1987) and Doctor in Law (2006). Professor of the Faculty of Law of the University of Lisbon. Has taught Criminal Law, Criminal Procedural Law, Criminology and Evidence Law. Professor at the Military Academy. Has taught Criminal Procedural Law. Vice-President of the Institute for Juridical Cooperation of the Faculty of Law. Member of the Board of Directors of the Portuguese Institute of Penal Law and Criminal Sciences (*Instituto de Direito Penal e Ciências Criminais*). Former Member of the Supervision Committee for the Portuguese Intelligence Services (*Conselho de Fiscalização dos Serviços de Informação da República Portuguesa*), 1998–1999. Former Member of the Portuguese Committee for the Reformation of the Penal Code and the Penal Procedural Code (*Conselho da Unidade de Missão para a Reforma Penal*), 2005–2007. Former Jurist of the Portuguese Securities Exchange Commission (*Comissão do Mercado de Valores Mobiliários*), 1998–2006. He has published in several European languages. Some recent publications include: "Kausalität als heuristisches Kriterium: dargestellt am Beispiel von Kursmanipulation am Finanzmarkt" (co-author António João Miranda, translation by André Hoelzer) in *Gerechtigkeitswissenschaft-Kolloquium aus Anlass des 70. Geburtstages von Lothar Philipps*, ed. Bernd Schünemann, Marie-Theres Tinnefeld and Roland Wittmann (Berlin: Berliner Wissenschaft-Verlag, 2005), pp. 329–367; "Positivistische Zurechnung" (translation by André Hoelzer) in *Sammelband IRIS 2005 / Effizienz von e-Lösungen in Staat und Gesellschaft: Aktuelle Fragen der Rechtsinformatik*, ed. Erich Schweighofer, Doris Liebwald, Silvia Augeneder and Thomas Menzel (Stuttgart: Richard Boorberg, 2005), pp. 567–575. "Estatuto de arguido e posição processual da vítima", *Revista*

Portuguesa de Ciência Criminal 17 no. 4 (October–December 2007) (Coimbra: Coimbra Editora), pp. 601–612 among others.

Ranjana Ferrao
B.Sc., LL.M. Lecturer in V. M. Salgaocar College.
Published article "Secularism in India, the U.S.A. and the United Kingdom" in *World Constitutionalism*, ed. Anthony D'Souza and Carmo D' Souza (Cambridge Scholars Publishing, 2007).

Remy Dias
Reader in History, Govt. College of Arts, Science & Commerce, Quepem – Goa, carried out doctoral research studies at the Goa University on the topic, "*Socio-Economic History of Goa with Special Reference to the Communidade System: 1750-1910*". Dr. Dias was awarded the Fundação Oriente Long Term Scholarship in 2002, to visit Portugal for working on the topic: "*Portuguese and the Communidade System of Goa*", under the guidance of Prof. (Dr.) Teotonio R. de Souza, Lisbon. Publications include: Dr. Remy Dias (ed), *Changing Scenario of our Higher Education – Enhancement and Sustenance of Quality Assurance*, Govt. College – Quepem, 2006 and Remy Dias & Pius Malekandathil (eds.), Goa in the 20th Century – Its History & Culture, Panaji: Instituto Menezes Bragança, 2008, besides other research papers on Goan History presented and published at National and International Levels.

Sairam Bhat
Assistant Professor of Law, National Law School of India University, Bangalore. He did his B.Com from Mahajan First Grade College, Mysore in 1994, LL.B from J.S.S Law College, Mysore in 1997, LL.M, and Ph. D from the Department of Law, University of Mysore. Before joining NLSIU, he served as Coordinator, LL.M, at Govind Ramnath Kare College of Law, Margao, Goa.[2004-2006]. He was Assistant Professor at HNLU, Raipur, [2003-04] and Research Officer, CEERA, NLSIU [2000-03]. He was awarded the 'Young India Environmental Law Fellowship' and served as Adjunct Faculty at Golden Gate University, California, USA, during the Fall, 2003. He has presented papers at the National University of Singapore [Jan 2004] and at the International Water Law Conference in Berlin, Germany [June 2006]. He was the Editor of Kare Law Journal in 2005 and 2006. His areas of interest include Contracts, Environmental Law and IPR. Published article "Environmental Sovereignty: Dilution of National Boundaries. A Case for World Constitution" in

Anthony D'Souza and Carmo D'Souza, eds. *World Constitutionalism,* Cambridge Scholars Publishing, 2007.

Shurpali Shruti Arvind

B.A., LL.B. (Hons.), LL.M. Presently Lecturer at K.L.E. Society's G.K. Law College, Hubli, Karnataka, India.

Vishwanath. M

B.A.L.LL.B., LL.M., currently Lecturer, University College of Law, Karnataka University, Dharwad, India. Formerly Lecturer at V.M. Salgaocar College of Law, Miramar, Panaji, Goa. Prior to joining V.M. Salgaocar College of Law, Lecturer at K.L.E's Law College, Bangalore. Specialises in Criminal Law; has published many articles in national journals in the field of Environmental Law, Human Rights and Criminal Law. He published article "Looking Beyond National Boundaries in the Era of Globalisation" in Anthony D'Souza and Carmo D'Souza, eds. *World Constitutionalism,* Cambridge Scholars Publishing, 2007.
e-mail: vishwanathucld@gmail.com